COSUMER BEHAVIORAL ECONOMIC PSYCHOLOGY

JOHN LOK

Copyright © John Lok
All Rights Reserved.

ISBN 979-888591485-7

This book has been published with all efforts taken to make the material error-free after the consent of the author. However, the author and the publisher do not assume and hereby disclaim any liability to any party for any loss, damage, or disruption caused by errors or omissions, whether such errors or omissions result from negligence, accident, or any other cause.

While every effort has been made to avoid any mistake or omission, this publication is being sold on the condition and understanding that neither the author nor the publishers or printers would be liable in any manner to any person by reason of any mistake or omission in this publication or for any action taken or omitted to be taken or advice rendered or accepted on the basis of this work. For any defect in printing or binding the publishers will be liable only to replace the defective copy by another copy of this work then available.

Contents

Preface

This book is concerned how to apply behavioral economy method to predict consumer behavior. Also I shall compare to explain what advantages and disadvantages between any one of my solvable suggestions and the any one of the company's choice of solvable method to these any one sample industry consumer behavioral economic challenges to aim to let any reader to judge whether how to choose the solvable method is better.

This book can provide sample industries to let students to learn how to behavioral economy method to predict consumer behaviors. This book divides part one and part two. Part one explains what behavioral economy function and mean is and how applying this method to predict consumer behavior. Part two explains what psychological method mean and function and how appling this method to predict consumer behavior.

In Behavioral economics part , it can provide more realistic psychological foundations. This book is intended to explain why consumer behaviors and economy has close relationship and apply economic concept to explain how the consumer chooses to do whose consumption of decision.

In part one, it shall indicate how the process of behaviour economic field develops, then I shall show what methods are used to measure behavioural economy. Next, I shall indicate what the main two categories of behavioural economy are as well as I shall explain what risky and uncertain outcomes of individual behavior economic theories are as well as what behavioral game theory is. Finally, I shall explain how policy makers or decision makers can apply behavioral economy concept to do whose policy decision as well as I shall also indicate why behavioral economy and psychology which has close relationship to influence consumption of decision.

In this part, I shall indicate underground train and Disney entertainment theme park and University and unground train transportation and environmental protection businessmen etc. enterprises to explain how which can apply psychological methods to predict which client's preferable behavioral choice to achieve economic benefits more easily. Thus, if company or individual businessman can predict labour psychology or client psychologic consumption behavior. Then, which can have more confidence to attract more clients or reduce labour turnover. This book is suitable to any economists or policy makers or individual consumption makers or students or businessmen who have interest to learn how to apply behavioural economy methods to judge to do the most reasonable or the most right economic activities to achieve economic benefit in everyday life.

I shall introduce the different kinds of behavioral consumption of prediction methods include: the standard economic model of behavioral consumption of prediction method, online psychological advertising of prediction method, brand image attention of behavioral consumption of prediction method, store atmosphere environment influence prediction method, knowledge of the factors prediction method, constructive consumer choice processes influence prediction method, survey research prediction method ,consumer neuroscientific research prediction method etc. different psychological research of consumption methods.

I shall explain why analysis of demographic trends is only important for industrial and business-to-business marketing and why it can't concentrate on consumer individual consumption marketing both as well as to explain why in an individual firm, which must understand not only the customer's minds, but also the minds of the customers'and to explain how to apply demographic analysis to predict consumer behavior factors include: changing structure of markets , geographic factors, economic resources and global markets. I shall explain why market analysis requires information about consumers with needs, ability to buy, willingness to pay and authority to pay, changing structure of consumer markets, such as how many consumers will there be? e.g. birthrate, national increase, fertility rate, total fertility rate, population momentum etc. information.

I shall give insurance and travel both industries to explain how to apply behavioral economy theories to solve consumer behavior prediction as well as I shall indicate some methods to explain how manufacturers or service providers can attempt to solve some challenges encountering when who attempt to predict consumer behaviors. Finally, I shall indicate what the methods are the most effective to attempt to predict consumer behaviors.

In part two, I shall explain what psychological method means and how to apply psychological method to predict consumer behavior. Consumer behavior is comparatively a new field of study. It led every manufacturer's attention from product to consumer and specially focused on consumer behavior. The evaluation of marketing concept from selling concept to consumer oriented marketing has resulted in buyer behavior becoming an independent discipline. The growth of consumerism and consumer legislation emphasizes the importance that is given to the consumer. Thus, consumer behavior is a study of how individuals make decision to spend their available resources (time, money and efforts) or consumption related aspects (what who buy? when why buy? how who buy? etc.) Hence, marketers need to obtain an depth knowledge to know to use what psychological method(s) is(are) the suitable to predict consumers buying behavior to raise customer numbers easily . Finally, this knowledge acted as a tool to the marketers to forecast the future buying behavior of customers to reduce any new products of investment risk before who decide to manufacture to sell to the market.

Consumer behavior is the study of individuals or organizations and the processes consumers use to research, select , use and dispose of products or services, experience or ideas to satisfy needs and its impact on the consumers and society. The term " customer" is specific in terms of brand , company or shop. It refers to person who customarily or regularly purchases particular brands or purchases from particular company's products or purchases from particular shops. Whereas, the " consumer" is a person who generally engages in the activities, search, select, use and dispose of products, services , experiences or ideas. Thus, consumption behavior concerns to predict how the consumer activities to be done to influence who chooses to buy the product or consume service among of all competitive and similar products or services provision to the market. However, consumer purchase decision and nature of motive which have close relationship. For example, in the psychological view point, when the consumer desires for saving money, who will decide to purchase when the price falls down; when the consumer feels fear, who will feel purchasing insurance policy need; when the consumer feels health need, who will choose to buy health foods to eat or/and to join to be membership in health clubs; when the consumer has possession need, who will decide to buy antiques for appreciating whose future values for saving. Thus, businessmen ought need to predict what the nature of motive will be whose target customer group, then who can persuade whose target customer group to choose to buy whose products or consume whose service more easily.

How to explain consumer behavior? Consumer behavior is said to be an applied discipline as some decisions are significantly affected by their behavior or expected action. The two significantly perspective that are micro and societal perspectives. The micro perspectives involve understanding consumer for the purpose of helping a firm or organization to achieve its objectives. Whereas, the societal or macro perspective applies knowledge of consumers to aggregate-level faced by mass or society as a whole. The behavior of consumer has significant influence on the quality of the standard of living.

Consumers can divide either organization buyer or individual buyer. First, organizational buyers are more geographically concentrated than consumer markets, who are fewer in number , but who are bulk buyers compared to individual buyers, whose markets are either vertical or horizontal. (vertical structures who cater only one or two industries, whereas, in horizontal structure , the buyer base is too broad. Organizational demand is derived from consumer demand. The nature of demand is influential and inelastic. Organizational buying lot of formalities have proposals , quotations, procedures are to be followed unlike consumer buying, e.g. decision process is much complex with high financial risk, technical aspects, multiple influencing factors etc. Also, it requires more extensive negotiation over larger time period than consumer buyer. Second, in psychological view point, individual consumer whose personal and/or product and/or situational factors can influence consumer decision making? self-concept, needs, and values are the three psychological factors that influence individual consumer how who chooses to buy one product or consume one service. For example, the more number of consumers share a certain self image, certain value and needs. They tend to use products and services the reflect whose life style. They get highly involved in purchasing products like designer wear, imported cars, health care products etc. On the product factor aspect, e.g. the consumer involvement grows as the level of perceived risk in the purchase of a product on or service increase. It is likely that consumers will feel more involved in the purchase of their house than in the purchase of tooth paste. It is a much riskier purchase. Beside, product differentiation can also affect consumer have to choose from increases. This may be due to the fact that consumers feel variety which means greater risk. On the situational factor aspect, the product is brought or used can generate emotional involvement. For example, buying a pair of socks for yourself is far less involved than buying a gift for a close friend. Social pressure can significantly increase involvement. One is likely to be more self conscious about the products and brand one looks at when shopping with friends than when shopping alone. So, individual consumer shopping decision will be influenced by whos friends, when whose friends give ideas to influence whose buying choice decision easily.

Models of consumer involvement have two level: First, low involvement products are those, which are at low risk, perhaps by important of being inexpensive and repeatedly used by consumers. Marketers may try to sell the product without changing the attitudes of consumers. For example, writing pen with the " uninterrupted flow" and tooth paste with " mouth wash" positioning attracts new consumers. Some buying decisions are taken will let of thinking or great feelings. Some are made through force of habit and others are made consciously, that attributes consumer choice to information (learn) , attitude (feel) and behavior (do) issues. Second, high involvement products are purchases in first requires more information, both because of the importance of the product to the consumer and thinking issues related to the purchases. Major purchases , such as cars, houses and other expensive and infrequently buying items. The purchases decisions in high involvement product involve less of information than feeling. Typical purchases tied to self-esteem, jewelry, apparel, cosmetics and accessories. The strategy model is feel-learn-do. To encourage purchases much approach customers with emotion and appeal. Otherwise, the purchase in low involvement product is primarily by the need to satisfy personal tastes, many of which are influenced by self-image products like newspaper, soft drinks, liquor etc. Marketers can promote these low involvement products through reference groups and other social factors . Because low involvement product involves less in thinking and more of habitual buying. Products like stationery, groceries , food etc. The role of information is to differentiate any point of difference from competitors. Brand loyalty may result simply from the habit. It suggests marketers induce trial through various sales promotion techniques.

How can marketing information influence consumer behavior? Consumer attention to advertisement or any marketing communication depends on four levels of consumer involvement: pre-attention, focal attention, comprehension and elaboration. Each calls for different level of message processing. Pre-attention demands only limited message processing, the consumer only identifies the product. Focal attention involves basic information as product name on use. In comprehension level, the message is analyzed, through elaboration, the content of the message is integrated with other information that helps to build attitude towards the product. It is suggested that marketers make advertisement with can induce elaboration. In general, steps in consumption decision making process include: first step, consumer feels need recognition. Second step, who will search any information concerns to the product. Third step, who will evaluate of alternatives. Fourth step, who will make purchase decision. Finally, who will do post purchase behavior to judge whether the product's price is reasonable or unreasonable to decide whether to consume the product again in the future. Thus, advertisement can be one factor to influence consumer choice.

In my this book, the main important aim, I give examples to explain how to apply psychological and behavioral economic both view point related methods to predict consumer individual behavior to let businessmen learn how to choose the reasonable or right methods to attract consumers to choose to buy whose products or consume whose services to win competitors more easily. I shall indicate clear reasons to explain why I agree behavioral economy method and psychological method can be used to predict consumer behavior in nowadays society.

Prologue

Explanation what are of Preferences over risky to behavioral consumption and utility function concept to company profit intention or government tax income intention

How can behavioral game theory apply to company income intention?
● Can predict consumer behavior with web search?
● Can firm's conduct and behavior factor influence consumer consumption ?

How to apply behavioral economic principles to assist policy makers or decision makers to make more reasonable decision.

Have behavioral economy and psychology methods close relationship.
How can consumer debt management psychological factors influence consumption behavior?
Can price change influence consumer behavior?
How can constructive consumer choice processes influence consumption behavior?
How can economical environment factor predict consumers consumption?
How can auctions or online experimentation respond to predict consumer behavior and sale forecast accuracy?

Chapter Three
Behavioral economy method of organization consumer behavior predicton
3.1 Apply knowledge management method to predict Walt Disney entertainment theme park behavioral consumption p.57-77
Disney market research method
Brand image attention of behavioral consumption of prediction method
Can scientific research method predict Disney visitors behavior ?
Can intentions Disney visitor behavior be predicted by survey research ?
Can food consumption for trust cooperation influence family or friend Disney client group ?

3.2 University campus choice and teaching method choice psychological prediction

 University campus location factor

 The resource based theory of university location competitive advantage

 The factor of student demand for alternative modes of course delivery

 Whether online and hybrid courses will influence to university students to choose the university to study.

 3.3 How to predict passenger individual consumption choice for airline industry

 How can airline gas or oil price influence passenger individual airline choice?

What is the relationship of oil price and terrorism to airline industry to influence ticket price increasing?

How can demand be caused by e-service transaction channel to predict passenger individual consumption choice for airline industry?

Can advertising influence travel consumption behavior?

 How can airline atmosphere environment influence traveller travel choice behavior?

 How can airline counter servicer knowledge influence traveller consumption behavior?

 In -store consumer digital signage behavior how can influence consumer behavior

3.4 How does MTR (Mass Train Railway) need to consider route design location of choice?

Introduction

Why MTR underground train transportation needs to know passenger behaviour

Why route choice can influence passenger behavioural choice

 Why trip time reliability and crowding factors can influence MTR passenger choice.

How to apply online psychological advertising method to predict passenger behavioral consumption?

Does habit strength moderate the intention behavior to consumption?

3.5 Why environment protection product businessmen need to concern what the degree of quality of life to their potential buyers

 (i) How environmental risk factor can influence different groups

 (ii) How Afria country environmental pollution influences

(iii) How human adult consumption and environmental quality influences future environment for human survival probability of life expectancy.

(iv) Why social and physical environmental factors have close relationship to influence economic growth

(v) How environmental factor can influence any country's house price.

(vi) How environmental pollution can influence social welfare

(vii) What is consumer neuroscientific research method to predict consumer behavior?

Whether design factor can predict consumer behavior for environment protection product

(i) Why environmental pollution and human right abuses has close relationship to influence quality of life and economic growth?

(ii) What is space and environmental technology?

(iii) Why does environment protective product need survey to enquire design questions?

(iv) Can implicit design questionnaire (survey) or /and interview methods can test consumer behavior for measuring consumer response to environment protection product?

Chapter Four

The Standard Economic Model Of Behavioral Consumption Of Prediction Method

How to apply online psychological
advertising method to predict behavioral
consumption? p.78-90

How can store atmosphere environment influence
consumer individual shopping behavior?

How can constructive consumer choice processes influence consumption behavior?

What is consumer neuroscientific research method to predict consumer behavior?

Can food consumption for trust cooperation influence food consumption choice?

Does habit strength moderate the intention behavior to consumption?

How can economical environment factor predict consumers consumption?

Can firm's conduct and behavior factor influence consumer consumption ?

Can scientific research be predicted consumer behavior by experts?

Can implicit design questionnaire (survey) or /and interview methods test product preference for measuring consumer response?

Reference

Behavioral economic method predicts stable basic income consumer individual spending behavior

Can apply behavioral economic method to predict that the consequences of a stable basic income consumer's consumption behavior? It may be significantly different than the ones are predicted by the standard economic model if more realistic assumptions of human consumption behavioral prediction success.

Behavioral economic method assumes that consumer will compare whether whose benefits are more than costs after they buy the product or consume the service. I assume the consumer is only the who have stable basic income source consumer target. This stable basic income target consumers who will evaluate or feel they will earn more benefits than costs to every product in their consumption process, after they will make final decision to choose to buy the product to use or consume the service. Otherwise, if they feel they won't earn more benefits after they buy the product or consume the service in the consumption process. Then, they won't choose to buy the product to use or consume the service. In behavioral economic view point, it indicates their consumption behaviors are depend on comparing the product or the service whether it can satisfy their desire benefits and their desire benefits to the product or service must be more than their consumption cost.

There are four points to apply behavioral economic method to predict each stable basic income individual income spending. They include: motivation, conspicuous consumption, social preferences and crowding theory.

Each stable basic income consumer individual spending amount will be different and it is represent that every high stable basic income consumer must decide to consume any high cost services or buy high cost products to use. Although some economic teachers assume general high income people will accept to spend more expenditures for enjoyment or buy high cost of products to satisfy basic high level necessary expenditures. But, applying behavioral economic analysis, it is not absolute true, some low income people also accept to spend more to buy high cost of products or increasing spending expenditures for enjoyment for their basic necessary expenditures.

The field of behavioral economic can be fined as a combination of economics and psychology that tries to capture human behavior in a more realistic. Understanding each consumer individual consumption behavior, we need to know how who does each decision to influence each consumption choice. Consequently, analysis reaches the conclusion. Every high or low level stable basic income consumer individual behavioral consumption that the microeconomic consequences of a stable basic income of individal consumer target consumption group could be efficiency enhancing, but at the same time incentives about positional concerns could lead to wasteful and inefficient spending to the stable low basic income consumer target group.

● How to apply behavioral economic method to contribute to the stable basic income target consumer group's consumption prediction?

What is basic income mean? A basic income is an income paid by a political community to all its members on an individual basis, without means test or work requirement. How to apply behavioral economic method to contribute to the basic income consumption prediction?

I assume high income tax is charged to one high income tax payee , it will influence the high income tax payee individual consumption desires to be fallen, also extrinsic incentives will effort and intrinsic motivation and how the labor market change these variables under and big changes predicting, how income security changes social consumption preferences, e.g. how a big change affects the overall level of status -seeking behavior and this effect with income inequality to influence consumer individual consumption attitude or habit.

How can behavioral economic methods predict consumer's consumption decision, in special the stable basic income consumer target group? In any consumption decisions are involving risk and uncertainty, the standard economic model usually assumes that decisions are based on final condition, regardless of the changes are caused by the results of a consumer's decision.

An alterative mode of how consumers make decision and judgement under risk and uncertainty. This situation is often occurred in consumption market.

In behavioral economic view point, it explains how consumer's consumption, however, which excludes the stable basic income earn factor can influence the stable basic income earn target consumer group decides to make final consumption decision to compare to the non-stable basic income earn target consumer group. The reasons include as below:

(1) Consumers evaluate decisions over gains and losses with repect to some natural reference point, when they feel need to consume, which is assumed to be judgement about a sequence of outcomes are based on changes in wealth, rather than whether how much absolute basic income earn to influence whose consumption desires.

(2) Thus, behavioral economic theory assumes the consumer is the low level of income group in society, but when who feels that he is still gains more than losses when who decides to buy the expensive product or consumes the expensive service. Then, the low level of income consumer who will accept to buy the expensive product or consume the service easily. Due to whose gains feeling is more than losses feeling, when who buys the product or consumes the service.

(3) Behavioral economic theory also assumes the taxpayer will pay high income tax in this year. The, even the high income taxpayer can earn high basic income, but due to whom needs to pay high income tax in this year. Then, he/she will reduce much spending, even he/she reduces spending on cheap products or cheap service consumption for enjoyment. This is the taxpayer's economic decision to influence whose consumption behavior, due to the high income tax expenditure factor influences whose consumption behavior to change to be reduced spending expenditures in this year.

● How to apply behavioral economic method to predict labor market changing behavior?

Instead of applying behavioral economic method to predict every consumer individual consumption effort. Behavioral economic method can be also be applied to predict every country's labor market changing behavior. Particularly, how salary clerical workers or low wage labor workers should move from one type of job to another based on these factors. They include as below:

Their intrinsic motivation and how their levels of effort would change after this movement, investigates the effects of income security on social perferences in labor market changing behavior, and how cooperation in social contribution is affected when income security is guaranteed, how to predict the role of positional externalities on conspicuous consumption and how would change the incentive to influence consumption. So, it seems that general labor market job changing behaviors will not influenced by external economic environment better or worse changing factor, or salary changing factor etc. different environmental condition changing factors influence to employees' job changing. Generally, employee's job changing behavior is more influenced to persuade who changes job by himself/herself intrinsic motivation negative emotion influence mainly.

How to apply motivation crowding theory to predict labor productivity? One of the main challenges of economic theory is to find what are the optimal incentives that increase productivity of labors. The standing point is usually extrinsic incentive be it is form of monetary compensations for high effort or fine for low effort.

It is a kind method of reward or punishment to increase or decrease number of productivity to every labor. But it can only raise short term number of productivity in possible and it can not guarantee high quality of productivity. So if one employer wants a labor to do more of an activity or with a higher quality, consider paying the labor for working hard on punishing whom if for providing a low level effort.

This idea is that people do not like to work, and therefore they used some sort of compensation for doing a specific activity, and that the more they are paid the harder, they will work. So, payment better compensation is only beneficial to encourage labors to do one specific task or activity in short term. This method can not be suitable to rise long term beneficial productivity and high level quality of production or excellent performance in long term and it can only keep in short term raising productivity and high level quality of production or excellent perofrmance benefits.

Consider paying the labor for working hard on punishing whom if for providing a low level effort. This idea is that people do not like to work, and therefore they used some sort of compensation for doing a specific activity, and that the more they are paid the harder they will work. So, payment better compensation is only beneficial to encourage labors to do one specific task or activity in short term. This method can not be suitable to raise long them beneficial productivity and high quality of products.

However, economists would argue that, is a labor has high intrinsic motivative to perform a task, who will provide a high level of effort without compensation by himself/herself but an even higher level of effort of whom is compensated. If a labor does not have any intrinsic motivation to perform a task or an activity, who will provide no effort or a low effort of whom. There is no compensation, but who will increase this level of effort of an extrinsic incentive is implemented.

Hence, in behavioral economic view point, the labor individual high level effort is a main psychological factor to influence whose productivity to be raised or the qualities of products to be raised, when the products are manufactured by the high level effort labor. It means that high compensation is not the good method to encourage labor productivity or raise quality. Otherwise, how to influence the one low level of effort of labor to change to be one high level of effort labor. It is the best psychological method to influence the labor to raise productivity and quality and service performance to any products or services in manufacturing process or service process for any organizations in long term beneficial possible.

● How can apply behavioral economy method raises basic stable income consumer consumption desire

Economists aim to develop models of human behavior and interactions in consumption markets. But consumers behave in complex ways, such as how to predict consumers to make rational decisions in consumption processes. Moreover, self-consumption control and motivation can vary significantly across different individual consumer.

In order to build useful consumption prediction models, economists make simplifying assumptions, aims to predict how to raise stable basic income consumer target group consumption more success. However, behavioral economy method is one kind of accurate consumption prediction method. It can be applied to predict economic decison-making to every consumer consumption choice more accurate raising whose consumption desire?

I shall indicate how to apply different behavioral economy methods to raise stable basic stable income target consumer group consumption desire in these different consumption situation (consumption environment) aspects as below:

1. Stable basic stable income consumer group consumption great or small amount desire

The consumption of products and services is a fundamental part of consumer's welfare. Basically, every one who has stable basic stable income, who will like to consume any products and services. Even, consumption great or small amount desire won't be depended on whether the person whose income is more or less. It means low income level of people will still like to consume great amount to buy expensive products or consume expensive services, because consumption is human's part of life and basic needs.

This stable basic income people will like to consume, because they have stable income source when they do not worry about unemployment occurrence to cause them have no enough money to support their lifes. Otherwise, non-stable basic stable income people won't like to consume because they feel they have no stable basic income source to support their lifes and they will worry about unemployment occurrence any time. Hence, stable basic income people will have more consumption desire to compare non-stable basic stable income people in any countries usually. Behavioral economic method indicates they feel their economic benefits will be loss if they planned to buy any products or consume any services easily. So, they prefer to save money in bank more than consumption.

● Demand systems and micro-economic

Why stable basic income people will like to consume? Because who have more demand, a demand system shows the level of consumer demand for different products and services: e.g. one basic stable income person may refer to the demand for clothes, another the demand for food etc.

How the demand for that particular product varies with the prices and demographic factor will influence who to accept consumption. Such as stable basic income people who will not consider to decide to buy the cloth to wear or the food to eat if who feel the cloth or food price is even more expensive to compare other kind of cloth or food.

Otherwise, non-stable basic income people who will consider to decide to buy the cloth to wear or the food to eat if they feel that they still have enough cloths to wear or enough food to eat at homes , even these food or cloth price are less expensive to compare others. Because they feel they lack stable income effort to support them to consume. Hence, basic stable income factor can influence the consumer's consumption decision.

2. Life-cycle advertisement method can influence consumer individual consumption behaviors to be increased

Consumer behavior makes strong assumptions about the informational and computational bases of consumer behavior. Generally, consumer behavior is reasonably characterized as the maximization of expected lifetime utility subject to budget constraint and conditional on the available information.

Generally, consumers prefer to buy any discounted products or it is reasonable that consumers accept to buy many attractions to persuade them to buy any kinds of bargain discount products. Hence, low bargain discount product is one good behavioral economic principle to encourage or persuade or attract any consumers to increase consumption.

What is behavioral life-cycle model? This model explains consumer behavior can be persuaded to buy any discounted products by advertisement, e.g. television, radio, newspapers, magazine etc. promotion channels. Because frequent advertisement promotion method can let any consumers often remember the product's brand, discounted price, style, colour and image from advertisement content.

So, advertisement can be one part of consumer behavioral life-cycle. For example, when the television audiences often watch TV. Hence, when the brand of product advertisement often makes fun image and discounted message to let TV audiences to remember this brand of product, when they are watching TV. Then, it has possible to persuade any potential consumers to choose to buy this brand of any products or consume this brand of any services, due to its advertisement of discounted sale message is very attractive to every one to let this advertisement audience's attention to remember this brand of products or services are selling or serving in market at this moment. So, it is advertisement image behavior influences audiences to buy the brand's any products attractively and persuasively.

3. Raising electricity consumption from electricity user individual habit

For electricity use market case example, how to analyze people's behavior in consuming electricity using a behavioral economic framework ? Electricity consumption is modeled by the means of consumer's individual useful habit, electricity price, consumer satisfaction level, willingness to invest in new technologies, social interactions, and marketing strategies by the power utility. Because electricity is necessary to every home or electric vehicle users needs or businessmens' office etc. different needs every day. Power companies supply electricity to a region's homes and industries.

However, electricity needs modernization of power system companies expect to increase price. Due to competitive factor, such as other fuel resource choices, outdated kind of energy electricity supply, and renewable fuel energy source competition.

Hence, applying behavioral economic concept, I assume electricity consumers will compare to electricity and other kinds of energy choices to weigh up the costs and benefits of all alternatives, aiming to maximize their benefits, before making a decision to choose to use electricity for their house electricity demand or electric vehicle or shop or factory manufacturing etc. function of different aspects of electricity users.

For example, electricity business clients, they aim to reduce cost, such as energy expenditure, when they use any energy to manufacture their products in factories. If they feel electricity is expensive price to compare other kinds of energy power supply. When, they feel that they can not earn much beneficial advantages to use electricity to produce their products. Otherwise, if they feel other any kinds of energy supply can replace electricity to give more benefits to compare electricity energy. Then, many business electricity users will change to use other kinds of energies to consume to replace electricity power.

However, electricity can have competitive ability in electric vehicles market, if many drivers feel environment protection is more important to compare vehicles will be popular to be drived, due to many drivers don't want air pollution. They will like gas vehicles. Hence, the main attribute from the consumer side is one their habit electricity consumption behaviors, satisfaction level, energy efficient interaction with the power utility.

Consequently how to predict electricity consumer's demand. The important factor is how to let electricity users to feel power companies are changing a reasonable level to compare other similar energy supply products. When electricity users feel electricity which can bring more benefits to compare other kinds of energy products. Then, in energy supply market, if the demanding number of electricity consumers can increase more than other kinds of energy demanding number. Then, it is right time to raise electricity price to charge electricity consumers. Hence, how to persuade electricity consumers to feel that they can have more benefits to compare other kinds of energy products. It is the main successful factor to electricity power supply companies.

1.1 Consumer confidence is as a predictor of consumption spending

Behavioral economists believe it has link between confidence and economic decisions to cause consumers to choose spending, if the consumer has confidence to believe the product is worth to use, then who will accept to buy the product to use.

Concentrated on the conceptualization of confidence and its role in mode in theories of consumption. It also concerns on whether the confidence indicators contain any information beyond economic fundamentals. The concern is whether confidence can be explained by current and past value of variables, such as income, unemployment, inflation or consumption or in other way.

Whether confidence measures have any statistical significance in predicting economic outcomes once information from the above variables is used. Economic variable factor will also influence consumer confidence to decide consumption spending, e.g. real consumption expenditures (income, wealth or interest rate).

Finally, it will identify under which circumstances confidence indicates can be a good predictor of household consumption. Hence, survey is one good measurement method to predict whether how much every household has confidence to spend to consume the brand of products to use. Why is survey a good confidence consumption measurement prediction to every household in every country?

The reasons include survey can gather every household consumption habit historicial data to evaluate whether every survey person has how much confidence to consume the brand of products. Which in most cases correspond to periods where there are large changes in household survey indicators, liking during financial crises or geopolitical tensions to measure or predict whether the country's future good or bad economic condition factor will influence every household consumption desire in the year.

This modelling approach assumes that there is a certain (inknown) in confidence index changes beyond which confidence starts impacting consumption behaviors. So, sample household surveys can show the contribution of confidence in explaining consumption expenditures increases when household survey indicators feature large changes. So that confidence indicators can have some increasing predictive power during the survey investigation period in the year.

Other view point, surveys have been concerned on whether the confidence indicators contain any information beyond economic fundaments. The conern is whether confidence can be explained by current and past values of variables, such as income, unemployment, inflation or consumption or the other way. Whether confidence measures have any statistical significance in predicting economic outcomes once information from different external variable factors to influence the survey household group.

● What is confidence in consumption survey ?

   Confidence in consumption. For example, to measure whether how much degree of strong fluctations in the economy, such as recessions and recoveries will influence the country's household confident consumption in the year.

The surveys consumers' questions usually concern on major expenditures and changes in the respondant's financial situation, focus on job availability and current business conditions etc. questions. It is then possible that about consumer confidence depending on the relative performance of the variables that may be more relevant balances, with respect to the factors that determine unemployment and other labor market related issues. It aims to investigate whether those any one of variable factors will influence consumers general loss confident consumption desire in this year.

● What is a confidence indicator ?

A confidence indicator is considered as an explanatory variable for consumption together with standard variables used on predicting consumption expenditure. However, the natural real personal consumption expenditure is unexpected and unpredicted easily.

In conclusion, consumption expenditure depends the consumer individual confidence. If the consumer has much confidence to feel this year economic change will be better and he/she is easily to find job, then he/she will accept consumption easily in this year. It seems financial wealth and unemployment etc. economic factors will influence every household consumption desire. So, survey is one kind of good psychological consumption predicton method to predict consumption spending for any country in the year. I recommend manufacturers may choose to apply survey method to attempt to enquire sample survey people to gather data to predict whether what degree of consumption desire to them and find solution methods to solve low degree of consumption desire challenge.

   1.2 How to apply behavioral economy methods to influence employee individual psychology to achieve raise productivity of long term incentive intention?

● Increasing salary is short term incentive productivity method

Behavioral economy assumes labors will choose to do beneficial behaviors to themselves when they feel their work behaviors can earn more benefits to themselves more than their employers in the organizations. Otherwise, if they feel their work behaviors can earn more benefits to their employers more than themselves. Then, they won't choose to do their work behaviors, e.g. rasing productivities or work hard. Due to they feel work hard or raise productivities behaviors that only give more benefits to their employers more themselves.

Whether does cheap product price incenitve consumption desire to influence effective consumption behavior? Whether is monetary increasing salary payment incentive labors might be willing to work on task? I feel raising labours' productivities is similar to raise incentive consumption, which both have similar point, such as increasing salary payment or cheap product price is the main factor to influence incentive consumption or raising productivities. Hence, it seems monetary factor is not the main effort to encourage labors to work hard.

In labor's behavioral economic view point, for example, if a employer pays a employee more doing a task, who might be less willing to work on it, who might be less productive given whose efforts and who may enjoy the task less. If you want your employees to save more for retirement. You may want to give them fewer investment options. If you want them to engage more in a task, you might want offer them an additional alternative, instead of increasing salary to that task. Thus, increasing salary is not the onl method to encourage productivities of incentives.

● How to improve the design of incentive structures to encourage productivities in any organizations?

Any monetary incentive can only encourage productivities in short term. It can not only encourage productivities in long term in any organizations. It is similar to cheap or discount product price can only attractive consumers to buy the product in short term, it can not attract consumers to choose to buy the product in long term, it prefers to have more options to encourage labors to incentive productivities, e.g. investing good beneficial retirement plans. Suggesting that employees do not have free disposal of their investment options. These standard inventives seem irrelevant raising salary monetary factor, they can be quite effective in inducing labors to take particular actions to incentive productivities in long term. Due to when they can hard work, then they have more beneficial retirement plans or investing plans for their retirement. It means when they can achieve the most effective or efficient productivities to the employer for long term. It will give better retirement benefits and investment benefits to the better or even the best performance of employees. Otherwise, the worst performance employees won't earn good retirement benefits and investment benefits, when their employers feel their perform very poor in the organizatons in long term.

Hence, increasing salary level method is not one successful long term incentive method to persuade every employee to raise productivities or encourage excellent performance optional method. Increasing salary level is only similar to reduce product price and it is only short term encouragement to consumption or productivities method.

In conclusion, extrinsic monetary factor can not incentive labor's raising productivities more than every employee themselves intrinsic motivation to raise productivities as excellent performance in any organizations. Thus, organizations need to let employees to feel that they can give long term economic benefits to encourage their intrinsic motivation effort to be raised their productivities or performance more effective or efficient in order to achieve long term both win-win economic benefits to employees and employers both.

● Building employees and managers kindly co-operational relationship method

If you are an economist, your employer has no without any financial incentive to encourage your economic research tasks in your organizaton. It is equally difficult to vertify that such activity will contribute to your growth of human capital and increased productivity in research or teaching. The standard model, which explains employee's effort only through the way (determined by productivity), is therefore incomplete. In particular, it doesn't consider that incentives to work do not have to be monetary in other words, that there are other things besides the disutility of labor (Kamenica, 2012) and section 1.3 have.

Why will short term wage increasing method only influence short term labor supply to raise productivies? The effect of reference rasing wage can be most easily identified on short term labor supply to raise productivities. For US, New York city taxi drivers case, they have to decide every day for low long they are going to offer their services, given the day-to-day variable ability of demand they face (peaking during bad weather and/or when big conferences and public events are taking place in the city).

In the standard model, houes worked should grow with any growth in demand for New York taxi drivers' services. (one day's earning will have only a negligible income effect in the longer run). And yet actual cabbies work less on a demand heavy day. One of possible explanations suggests that New York city taxi drivers expect a certain income, they have set themselves a specific target income, who expect to achieve every day. During low demand for their taxi services, then they work longer hours to reach the target, when during peak demand, theit referential income is achieved quickly and they only work short hours. Elasticity of hours worked with respect to their earnings is therefore negative (Lamerer, Babcock, Loewenstein, & Thaler, 1997).

However, taxi driver is either one self employment business or one taxi company employment driving service occupation. It is similar to other kinds of service jobs in societies. Servicing employees, such as waiters, salepeople, securities, customer services, bus drivers etc. different kinds of service occupations. They are not similar to manufacturing occupation to be applied how many amount of piece of products production to evaluate their productivitie efforts. Thus these any one of service job nature is depended on their service performance to clients to feel their service performances are excellent to compare general service performance effort of service employees.

Considerably, respectly, I assume that if these service employees' managers can build kindly working environment, e.g. manager individual attitude and behavior can let their employees to feel happy to work together in their teams. Then, the managers' kindly as enthusiatic behaviors or attitudes will let every employee more positive encouragement of service attitude to serve their clients in their teams. Then, the client complaining number will be possible reduced, even none of any complains. Hence, building kindly relationship between managers and employees will raise excellent service performance to any orgnization's service nature employees.

● Can bonus method encourage service performance to be raised ?

In service job nature of bonus method can also raise employees' overall productivities or service performance. For example, when employees got a provisional bonus before the start of the workweek, but were warned that they would lose it on payday,unless they achieve the productivities or excellent service performance norm, they worked more productivites or let many clients to satisfy their service performance. Hence, managers can achieve bonus plan to compensate any excellent productivity or excellent services to them. Then, they can let clients to feel their service performance more satisfactory than employees of a control group who were merely given the standard promise to receive a bonus upon achieving the norm.

The effort was relatively small, however, productivity grew 1%. Interestingly, the effect of a loss was stronger when eholw teams were rewarded this way, social pressure came to bear on the less productivity team members. When the team members won't earn any bonus. So, long-term productivity gains were achieved through bonuses paid by excellent performance compensation method to compare to low service performance employees receiving no bonuses at all.

● Economic views of human motivation nature

There are only two main types of economic actors and by making simplifying assumptions about how these types of actors behave and interact. The two basic sets of actors in this mdel are firms, which are assumed in this model are firms, which are assumed to maximize their profits from producing and selling products and services, households, which are assumed to maximize their utility (or satisfaction) from consuming products and services.

It seems any employees will choose to do behaviors to achieve to earn much benefits from their organizations. The models of economic behaviors that consider consider employees' choice of goals, the actions they take to achieve these goals and the limitatons and influences that affect their choices and actions.

For university students choose which universities to study case, suppose that any college enrollment students are deciding which courses to study. Thus, it implies that if the university can provid many different kinds of suitable or right courses to any college enrollment students to choose to study. It means that if the university can provide many different kinds of courses to enrollment students to choose to study. Then, it will have much chance to attract enrollment students to choose this university to study. It's competition can be raised by many courses choice factor. but, in fact, it is not absolute right, although the university can provide many courses to provide to enrollment students to choose to study. But, it is not guarantee to represent it must attract many students to enroll this university to study.

For example, suppose that college enrollment students are deciding which courses to choose to study. Although, it has right course to prepare to these enrollment students to choose to study. But, they see a summary of evaluations from hundreds of other students indicating that a certain course is very good in this university. Then, suppose that they match a video interview of just one student to give a negative review of this university of the course. Even when students were told in advance that such a negative review was worse to this university of the course. They tended to be more influenced by the negative review than the summary of hundreds of evaluations, even although such behavior seems irratonal. Hence, although many right courses choice has much chance to attract students to enroll this university to study. But, if its bad educational quality from this course from negative review factor, which will influence the enrollment students number to be reduced.

It implies that students will compare this university's the cource educatonal quality whether is better or worse to compare other universities' similar course educational quality, even this university's this course fee whether is reasonable in educational market. This is cost and beneficial comparison behavioral economy principle to all enrollment students before they decide to choose which universities.

Hence, this case implies that universities how to train teachers' teaching skills to let students to feel that they can learn new knowledge from their teaching staffs absolutely. It means how to raise education training skills to raise teachers' teaching performance. It is very important factor to influence the university's teaching development success. So, many courses choice is not important factor to attract many students to enroll the university. Otherwise, although the university can not provide many courses to let students to enroll, but it's teachers can provide excellent teaching service to teach whose students. This is important factor to attract many students to choose to enroll this university to study.

1.3 Under-level productive efficiency and low- consumption desire behavioral economic influences

In behavioral economic influence view point, I feel that under-level productive efficiency is the represent low production number to the manufacturer as well as low-consumption desire is not represent less consumers demands or customers lose confidence to the product.

On the one hand, I shall apply behavioral economic method to analyze why inder productive efficiency is not represent low production number influence. Otherwise, I feel under-productive efficiency will have possible to increase production number after the manufacturer can review what factor(s) to influence under-productive efficiency.

I shall give reasons to explain as below:

As Jim, P. & Brendan. M. (2013) indicated who had ever been experiencing failure to do their businesses. Although, they had lost a million dollars, but they felt that they can be tought to learn undiscovered knowledge to know how to do their businesses successful by their wrong judgement and decision learning experience. They explained that " in ll risk taking, speculation, business ventures, entrepreneurial activities, it is the loss side on which you must focus first. This is even true for gambling, the gambler determines how much he's willing to bet, and loss, before the game is played. He doesn't wait for the game to end and then let the croupier or dealer assign his wager for him. How do you determine the downside, and how do you control or minimize it? With objective decision making and a plan that has as its starting point the stop-loss parameters"

Hence, it explains any business will have under-level productive efficiencies and low consumption desire business risk. However, to any any one entrepreneur, who needs to know it is one game between the himself/ herself and whose clients. They also need to know with objective decision making and a plan that has as its starting point.

Hence, I assume that if the entrepreneur has wrong decision to cause under-level productive efficiency, it is possible that, due to there is no enough employee number to manufacture the product or many employees are not skillful to manufacture all product in normal time or many employees are lazy etc. different factors to cause under-level productcivies. However, when they discover their productivities are very low to compare similar competitors their employees' productivities and efficiencies. Then, they can attempt to find what factor(s) to cause low productivities and loe efficiencies. it is possible that any one among of these factors case. They include many employees' lazy to influence low productivities or there is no enough employee number or many employees are not skillful to manufacture their products in production process.

Hence, wrong decision or plan is not represent failure. Otherwise, it can give chance to let the entrepreneur to lern whether what the factor(s) is (are) to cause low productivities and low efficiencies in whose product manufacturing process. As I feel that under-level productive efficiency is not represent low production number. Because I assume that if one worker lacks enough skills and manufacturing experiences to manufacture the product, but who can spend less time to manufacture the product and whose spending manufacturing time is same to the another owning enough skillful worker's time to do the product. Hence, I believe that the product quality from the low-skillful worker's manufacturing skill, it's quality will be worse to compare to the product quality from the high skillful worker's manufacturing skill. Hence, if the low skillful worker needs to spend much time to produce the product, but the product quality can be same to the high skillful worker's product quality. It means that it is sure because the low skillful worker has no excellent skill to compare to the high skillful worker to produce the product. Hence, his manufacturing spending time must be longer than the high skillful worker's time. It implies that the low skillful worker spends less time to raies high production number, but his product must be poor quality to sell. Then, his fast and efficient manufacturing speed that is not achieve economic beneficial to the organization's manufacturing process, e.g. less electricity spends to manufacture the product. Otherwise, the low skillful worker's fast and efficient manufacturing speed of behavior will raise the organization's cost in manufacturing process because consumers would not like to choose to buy any low quality product when they can choose which similar products to compare which one has the best quality and cheap price to buy.

Hence, efficient production is not the main factor to influence the business's success. Otherwise, good quality of the product factor is more important to compare it to influence the business's success.

On the other hand, I shall apply behavioral economic theory to analyze why low-consumption desire is not represent consumer demand lose to the business. As Jim. P. & Brendan. M. (20130 also identified " rather than looking for success to follow, who explained the formula for failure to avoid. As an Wang, founder of Wang laboratories said " it is my belief that there are no secret to success." The formula for failure is not lack of knowledge, brains, skills or hard work and it's not lack of luck, it's personalizing losses, especially of preceded by a string of wins or profits. It's refusing to acknowledge and accept the reality of a loss when it starts to occur because to so so would reflect negatively on you."

Thus, as whose feeling to explain why low-consumption desire is not represent less consumers demands or customers lose confidence to the product. The reasons include the causes of low-consumption desire are possible due to worse economic environment factor influences consumption desire to be reduced. It is not due to whether the product price is too high or quality is worse to compare others. Hence, as Jim & Brendan indicated the formula for business failure is not lack of knowledge, brains, skills or hard work and it's not lack of luck. It's not lack of luck. It's personalizing losses, means its reflecting to knowledge and accept the reality of a loss when it starts to occur. As it is applied to explain why low-consumption desire is not represent less consumers demands or customers lose confidence to the product. It's possible that external economic environment changing worse factor to cause the business personalizing losses, it is not reflect who lacks knowledge, skill, hard work factors to cause failure. Hence, ho to predict when and how and why economic environment changes worse will be important factor to predict when and how and why consumption behavioral changes to cause business's success.

Reference

Camerer, C.F. Babrocks, Loewenstein, G., & Thaler, R. (1997). Labor supply of New York city candrivers: One day of a time. The Quacterly Jounrnal of economics, 112 (2), 407-441. doi: 10.1162/003355399555244.

How do you view the outlook for consumer confidence in your key markets next year? Source from :

http://www.Just-food.com Confidence survey, Nov.

2015

Jim. P. & Brendan. M. (2013) . What I learned losing a million dollars, p.160. Colimbia University, Columbia business school press, New York, US.

Kamenica, E. (2012). Behavioral economics and psychology of incentives. Annual review of economics, 4 (1), 427-452. doi: 10.1146/ annurev- economics-080511-110909.

Maselli, 2012 Technology driven job polarization in

EU , 2000-2010. % change in labor supply

skilled/upgrade (ISCED) and labor demand for

skills/tasks (ISOD).

Behavioral economy is consisted from psychology and standard economic model. Standard economic model is the way most economists think about consumer welfare and consumer choice in microeconomic environment. I shall apply behavioral economic model to explain underground train and Disney entertainment theme park and University and unground train transportation and environmental protection businessmen etc. enterprises which rationality in the standard economic model relies heavily on the assumption that consumers are rational. In this case of consumer individual behavior consumption process, I assume that consumers are fully aware of all the options who have, who can always and consistently to rank their options in accordance will whose preferences and always choose the option who like best.

Thus, these assumptions of the standard economy model of consumer include such as: consumers have known preferences and consumers choose the best option available. The advantages of the standard model, from there three assumptions, such as a logically consistent theory of consumer behavior can be biult, that theory can be used to make predictions about consumer behavior and those predictions can be compared with reality. These models often correspond to actual consumer behavior. But behavioral economy model can give evidence from psychology to show that consumer often are irrational and also who are predictably irrational. Clearly, psychology has shown that the rationality assumptions of standard economics are wrong. For example, if irrational consumers were irrational in randomways, who would cancel each other out, leaving the overall outcome determined by the behavior of rational consumers. In that case, economic theories that ignored irrational between would work just fine. But psychology has shown that consumers are irratonal in similar and predictable ways, therefore, irratonality doesn't cancel out and can't be ignored. Moreover, the fact that consumers are predictably irrational means that whose predictably irrational behavior can be relatively easily inserted into economic theories to make economic predictions more accurate. In fact, consumers often are unable to make use of what who know about their available options and their preferences to figure out the best available option, and even when who know what is best for them, evidence shows tht who often make bad choices anyway. Unfortunately for economic view point, there's plenty of reliable evidence of predictably unselfish behavior to consumers. It is true, that the free market competitiion will encourage consumers to make the best option.

In summary, standard economic theories assume that consumers are rational and self interested. However, behavioral economic theories assumes that psychology shows who are not rational usually. I shall indicate how consumer's psychological decision to choose their behavioral consumption in actual life environment for
underground train and Disney entertainment theme park and University and unground train transportation and environmental protection businessmen etc. enterprises. Some consumption of these enterprises

evidences also show that consumer individual irrationality , these enterprises have predictable features in these enterprises consumption suitation. I shall use these enterprises to explain why behavioral economy can make economic predictions more accurate by using these enterprises' consumption evidences on their predictabl irrational behavior to these enterprises. Although, these global enterprises' market competition is serious, consumers may be expected to learn to reduce irrational behavior over time, these processes may not work well and may take. You can read these underground train and Disney entertainment theme park and University and unground train transportation and environmental protection businessmen etc. enterprises to make judgement why behavioral economic model is more accurate to predict consumer behavior to compare standard economic model.

In behavioral economy view point, if the manufacturer expect to advertise whose products to achieve the maximum sale numbers. So, the manufacturer must expect to pay the most reasonable advertisement cost to achieve the maximum sale numbers. How can marketing of advertisement information influence consumer has positive attitude to influence many consumers choose to buy the manufactuer's consumption behavior? Consumer attention to advertisement or any marketing communication depends on four levels of consumer involvement: pre-attention, focal attention, comprehension and elaboration. Each calls for different level of message processing. Pre-attention demands only limited message processing, the consumer only identifies the product. Focal attention involves basic information as product name on use. In comprehension level, the message is analyzed, through elaboration, the content of the message is integrated with other information that helps to build attitude towards the product. It is suggested that marketers make advertisement with can induce elaboration. In general, steps in consumption decision making process include: first step, consumer feels need recognition. Second step, who will search any information concerns to the product. Third step, who will evaluate of alternatives. Fourth step, who will make purchase decision. Finally, who will do post purchase behavior to judge whether the product's price is reasonable or unreasonable to decide whether to consume the product again in the future. Thus, advertisement can be one factor to influence consumer choice in behavioral economy view point.

Behavioral economics studies all human environment behavior: all types of consumer spending and saving behaviors, entreprepreneurship and all work related behavior including job choice and investments in human capital, all types of business behavior ranging from decisions on prices, output, investment, finance and preferences and reactions to economic policies and programs by consumers as well as businessmen. In addition, the analysis could be focused on the micro or the macro level. So, insights from behavioral economics would naturally be incorporated into the discriplines of economics as well as psychology. Thus, behavioral economy focuses on the rationality of the process of decision making when economics was mainly focused with the rationality of the outcomes.

Economics is used equailibrium conditions to define the apprpriate outcomes, but psychology's main focus is on how consumers learn and adapt to a constantly changing environment. Economic theory indicates cnsumers learn from whose mistakes, so that their behavior will change to the rational and optimum outcomes in equibilrium . However, consumption was not a passive, variable completely is determined by the rational calculation of economic factors. So, it explains that how behavioral economy theory can be applied to predict consumer behavior.

In general, human economic activities include production, distribution, consumption and resource maintenance. Economic actors can be individuals, small groups (such as a family, or a group of roommales) or large organizations, such as a government or a multi-national corporation. Economics is about how these actors behave and interact as who engage in economic activities. In conclusion, I agree that every consumer's realistic behavior is in economic theories that deal with judgemetn under uncertainty.

Psychological method predicts consumer behavior characteristics

Consumer behavior is comparatively a new field of study. It led every manufacturer's attention from product to consumer and specially focused on consumer behavior. The evaluation of marketing concept from selling concept to consumer oriented marketing has resulted in buyer behavior becoming an independent discipline. The growth of consumerism and consumer legislation emphasizes the importance that is given to the consumer. Thus, consumer behavior is a study of how individuals make decision to spend their available resources (time, money and efforts) or consumption related aspects (what who buy? when why buy? how who buy? etc.) Hence, marketers need to obtain an depth knowledge to know to use what psychological method(s) is(are) the suitable to predict consumers buying behavior to raise customer numbers easily . Finally, this knowledge acted as a tool to the marketers to forecast the future buying behavior of customers to reduce any new products of investment risk before who decide to manufacture to sell to the market.

Consumer behavior is the study of individuals or organizations and the processes consumers use to research, select , use and dispose of products or services, experience or ideas to satisfy needs and its impact on the consumers and society. The term " customer" is specific in terms of brand , company or shop. It refers to person who customarily or regularly purchases particular brands or purchases from particular company's products or purchases from particular shops. Whereas, the " consumer" is a person who generally engages in the activities, search, select, use and dispose of products, services , experiences or ideas. Thus, consumption behavior concerns to predict how the consumer activities to be done to influence who chooses to buy the product or consume service among of all competitive and similar products or services provision to the market. However, consumer purchase decision and nature of motive which have close relationship. For example, in the psychological view point, when the consumer desires for saving money, who will decide to purchase when the price falls down; when the consumer feels fear, who will feel purchasing insurance policy need; when the consumer feels health need, who will choose to buy health foods to eat or/and to join to be membership in health clubs; when the consumer has possession need, who will decide to buy antiques for appreciating whose future values for saving. Thus, businessmen ought need to predict what the nature of motive will be whose target customer group, then who can persuade whose target customer group to choose to buy whose products or consume whose service more easily.

How to explain consumer behavior? Consumer behavior is said to be an applied discipline as some decisions are significantly affected by their behavior or expected action. The two significantly perspective that are micro and societal perspectives. The micro perspectives involve understanding consumer for the purpose of helping a firm or organization to achieve its objectives. Whereas, the societal or macro perspective applies knowledge of consumers to aggregate-level faced by mass or society as a whole. The behavior of consumer has significant influence on the quality of the standard of living.

Consumers can divide either organization buyer or individual buyer. First, organizational buyers are more geographically concentrated than consumer markets, who are fewer in number , but who are bulk buyers compared to individual buyers, whose markets are either vertical or horizontal. (vertical structures who cater only one or two industries, whereas, in horizontal structure , the buyer base is too broad. Organizational demand is derived from consumer demand. The nature of demand is influential and inelastic. Organizational buying lot of formalities have proposals , quotations, procedures are to be followed unlike consumer buying, e.g. decision process is much complex with high financial risk, technical aspects, multiple influencing factors etc. Also, it requires more extensive negotiation over larger time period than consumer buyer. Second, in psychological view point, individual consumer whose personal and/or product and/or situational factors can influence consumer decision making? self-concept, needs, and values are the three psychological factors that influence individual consumer how who chooses to buy one product or consume one service. For example, the more number of consumers share a certain self image, certain value and needs. They tend to use products and services the reflect whose life style. They get highly involved in purchasing products like designer wear, imported cars, health care products etc. On the product factor aspect, e.g. the consumer involvement grows as the level of perceived risk in the purchase of a product on or service increase. It is likely that consumers will feel more involved in the purchase of their house than in the purchase of tooth paste. It is a much riskier purchase. Beside, product differentiation can also affect consumer have to choose from increases. This may be due to the fact that consumers feel variety which means greater risk. On the situational factor aspect, the product is brought or used can generate emotional involvement. For example, buying a pair of socks for yourself is far less involved than buying a gift for a close friend. Social pressure can significantly increase involvement. One is likely to be more self conscious about the products and brand one looks at when shopping with friends than when shopping alone. So, individual consumer shopping decision will be influenced by whos friends, when whose friends give ideas to influence whose buying choice decision easily.

Models of consumer involvement have two level: First, low involvement products are those, which are at low risk, perhaps by important of being inexpensive and repeatedly used by consumers. Marketers may try to sell the product without changing the attitudes of consumers. For example, writing pen with the " uninterrupted flow" and tooth paste with " mouth wash" positioning attracts new consumers. Some buying decisions are taken will let of thinking or great feelings. Some are made through force of habit and others are made consciously, that attributes consumer choice to information (learn) , attitude (feel) and behavior (do) issues. Second, high involvement products are purchases in first requires more information, both because of the importance of the product to the consumer and thinking issues related to the purchases. Major purchases , such as cars, houses and other expensive and infrequently buying items. The purchases decisions in high involvement product involve less of information than feeling. Typical purchases tied to self-esteem, jewelry, apparel, cosmetics and accessories. The strategy model is feel-learn-do. To encourage purchases much approach customers with emotion and appeal. Otherwise, the purchase in low involvement product is primarily by the need to satisfy personal tastes, many of which are influenced by self-image products like newspaper, soft drinks, liquor etc. Marketers can promote these low involvement products through reference groups and other social factors . Because low involvement product involves less in thinking and more of habitual buying. Products like stationery, groceries , food etc. The role of information is to differentiate any point of difference from competitors. Brand loyalty may result simply from the habit. It suggests marketers induce trial through various sales promotion techniques.

At the core of behavioral economics is used psychology of economics analysis to improve economics on its own terms generating theoretical insights, making better prediction of field consumption of behavioral phenomena, and suggesting better policy to any company or government decision makers. It rejects economic theories based on utility maximization, equilibrium and efficiency. It is useful because it provides economists with a theoretical framework that can be applied to almost any form of economic (and even non-economic) behavior to predict behavioral consumption more easily to businessmen. So, behavioral economy is different to general economy concept, it applies psychological methods to attempt to predict consumption behavior.

Simpifying much assumption that are not central to the economic theory to apply to psychological behavior. Other assumption simply acknowledge human limits on computational power and self-interest. These assumptions can be considered procedurally rational because human needs to solve problems that are often so complex that who can't be solved exactly by even modern computer technology. So, if businessmen apply psychological method to predict behavioral consumption to earn the more benefits or profit, it is more reasonable to compare to apply computer methods to predict consumption behavior.

Theories in behavioral economics should be judged by reality, generality and tractability concepts to apply why we (consumers) do our behavior (consumption of choices) from psychological analysis. We share the positivist view that the ultimate test of a theory is the accuracy of its predictions. But we also believe that better predictions are likely to result from theories with more realistic assumptions. In psychology, such as connectionist models that capture some of the essential features of neural functioning, which are based on utility maximization, yet are reaching the point where they are able to predict many judgemental and behavioral phenomena. Contrary to the positivistic view, however, businessmen ought believe that predictions of consumers' feelings (e.g., of subjective well-being) should be an important goal to earn more profit more easily.

Most of the ideas in behavioral economics are not new. When economics first became identified as a distinct field of study, psychology didn't exist as a discipline to apply to economy subject. For example, "invisible hand" and "the wealth of Nations" which belong to theory to moral sentiments, which laid out psychological principles of individual behavior that are arguably as profound as whose economic observations. Another example, such as a simple model of social utility means that one (consumer) or person's utility was affected by another person's , such as whose family or friends' influence why to choose to buy this product or use this service in consumption market.

Nowadays, economists hoped their discipline could be like a natural science to apply psychological methods to predict behavioral consumption to assist businessmen to earn more economic benefit or to reduce cost or profit to win whose competitors. But psychology was not very scientific. However, later economists are very much appealed to psychological insights to attempt to assist businessmen how to predict consumers how who will prefer to choose to consume to buy this product or use this service.

Throughout the second half of the century, many criticisms of the positivistic perspective took place in both economics and psychology. The economists of the time had less disagreement with psychology than they realized. They assume without foundation that behavior always aims at the goal of maximum pleasure and minimum pain; but behavior is not goal-oriented. Also the economists of the time believed false conclusions are drawn from false psychological assumptions to predict consumer individual behavioral consumption wrongly.

The importance of psychological measures and bounds on rationality. These commentators attracted attention, but did not alter the fundamental direction of economics. One development was the rapid acceptance by economists of the expected utility and discounted utility models which are making decision under uncertainty and choice, respectively. Whereas the assumptions and implications of utility analysis are rather flexible, and the expected utility and discounted utility models have numerous precise and testable implications. So, it seems economy and psychology can have close relationship to be connect to be applied to predict consumer individual consumption of behavior to assist any enterprises can earn more profit or more economic benefit more easily in global competitive consumption market nowadays.

In behavioral economy view, economists began to accept counter examples that could be not be permanently ignored, developments in psychology identified promising directions for new theory to be applied how to assist businessmen to predict behavioral consumption to earn economic benefits or profits. Beginning around 1960 year, psychology became to be dominated by the brain as an information-processing device replacing the behaviorist conception of the brain as a stimulus-response machine. The information-processing permitted a fresh study of neglected topics like memory, problem solving and decision making. These new topics were more obviously relevant to the conception of utility maximization than behaviorism had appeared to be to apply how to predict behavioral consumption in traditional psychological method.

However, behavioral economy and psychological consumption prediction method, psychologists began to use economic models as a benchmark against which to constrast their psychological models. Early research in behavioral consumption methds have followed these steps. First, identify assumption or models that are used by economists, who expected utility and discounted utility. Second, the assumption or model is a rule out alternative explanations (such as subjects' confusion or transactions costs). And third, the assumption or model creates alternative theories that generalize existing models. The final is to construct economic models of behavior using the behavioral assumptions to test them from the third step. This final step of economic models of behavior has only been taken more recently to be applied to predict why the consumer prefers to choose to do this behavioral consumption of decision finally.

In behavioral economy method, what is the standard economic model? It is the standard economic model, the way most economists think about consumer welfare and consumer choice. What is the rationality in the standard economic model? The standard economic model relies heavily on the assumption that consumers are rational. Standard economic model assumes that consumers are fully aware of all the options who have, who can always and consistently , rank whose options in accordance with their preferences, and always choose the option, who like the best option. Thus, what the assumptions of the standard economic model of consumer are? The assumptions include consumers act with full information, consumers have known preferences, consumers choose the best option available. In behavioral economic view point, It concerns consumers will compare cost to make decision to choose to buy which kind of product which can satisfy whose needs among of similar products of comparision.

The standard economic model of consumer behavioral prediction method advantages includes: A logically consistent theory of consumer behavior can be built, that theory can be used to make predictions about consumer behavior and those predictions can be compared with reality and those models often correspond to actual behavior of consumption reasons. What is the inconvenient truth? It includes clear evidence from psychology has shown that the rationality assumptions of standard economic model are wrong. Evidence from psychology has shown that consumers often are irrational and also who are predictably irrational. So these are wrong view point to influence how economists judge what cause consumption of behavior. Thus, it beings this question? What is mean of predictably irrational? It means that of irrational consumers were irrational in random ways, who would cancel each other out, leaving the overall outcomes determined by the behavioral consumption of rational consumers. As that case, behavioral economic theories that ignored irrational behavioral consumption would work just fine. But, psychology has shown that consumers are irrational in similar and predictable ways. Therefore, irrationality doesn't cancel out and can't be ignored to judge why the behavioral consumption has been caused.

How can behavioral economists judge each behavioral consumption cause? Economists will see evidence that consumers often are unable to make use of what consumers know about whose available options and whose preferences to figure out the best available option. However, although economic theory doesn't always assume self- interested behavior to any consumers, as a practical matter, most applications of economic theory assume that consumers act according to self- interest to decide every behavioral consumption of choice. For insurance industry is one good behavioral economy market example, insurance market competition can make rational consumption. Such as competitive market in auto vehicle accident insurance will charge very high rates to some insurance buyers who might to drive a fast speed, but unsafe motorbike, this one might argue will protect the driving insurance buyers from taking stupid risk. So learning can make rational consumers. Even if consumers are predictably irrational, who can learn from their families and other consumer' or friends behavioral mistakes, therefore, over time irrational consumers will learn to be rational to make the most irrational consumption. As a result, there are few opportunities to learn from consumer individual mistakes of any consumption of decision. Finally, if there are many potential; bad choices and one good consumption of choice, it might take a lot of costly experimentation to figure out the right consumption of choice. Thus, the standard economic model of behavioral consumption of prediction method, which is standard economic theories assume that consumers are rational, strong-willed , and self-interested, but evidence from psychology shows that who are not and that evidence also shows that consumer individual irrationality has predictable features. So, it seems behavioral economic model can make economic predictions more accurate by using the evidence on consumer individual predictable irrational behavioral prediction in any kind of the similar products in competitive market nowadays.

CHAPTER TWO

How to apply psychological method to predict consumption of behaviors

The methods how to predict to cause the (consumer's) person's consumption of behavior are the same as those in other areas of behavioral economic and psychological methods. In fact, behavioral economics relied heavily on evidence generated to predict behavioral consumption by experiments. More recently, however, behavioral economists have moved beyond experimentation and the full range of methods are employed by economists. The experiements played a large role in the initial phase of behavioral economics because experimental control is exceptionally helpful for distinguishing behavioral explanations from standard ones.

Suppose we observed this phenomenon in these any one of cares, in the form of failures of legal cases to settle before trial, costly divorce proceedings, and labor strikes. They are phenomenons of human' behaviours are caused by costs and benefits measurement of result. It implies the married people or the legal compensatory amount or labor strikes compensatory benefits will evaluate whether thier economic benefit is more or loss is more to decide divorce behavior or legal trial behavior or labour strikes compensatory behavior . So, consumer individual psychological behavior and economic benefits has close relationship to cause how consumer who prefers to make any consumption of choice every day. As the failures of legal cases to settle before trial , the behavioural economy concept would be difficult to tell whether rejection of offers was the result of reputation-building in repeated games, agency problems (between clients and lawyers) confusion why the lawyer' client (appellant) who choose to continue to attempt to pay legal fee to find the lawyer to appellate the case if the case is fail at the first time . However, in these game experiments of failures of legal cases to settle before trial, costly divorce proceedings, and labor strikes. These explanations are ruled out because the experiments are played once, have no agents, and are simple enough to rule out confusion. Thus, the experimental data clearly establish that subjects are expressing concern for fairness.

Other experiments have been useful for testing whether judgment errors which individuals commonly make in psychology experiments also affect prices and quantities in markets, such as shareholder's individual investment behavior. The lab is especially useful for these studies because individual and market-level data can be observed. Although behavioral economists relied on experimental datato predict shareholder's individual investment behavior, however, behavioral economics subject is seen as a very different method from experimental economics. As noted, behavioral economists are methodological profession. They define themselves, not on the basis of the research methods that who employ, but rather their application of psychological insights to economics.

Experimental economists, on the other hand, define themselves on the basis of use of experimentation which is as a research tool. Also, economists have made a major investment in developing experimental methods that are suitable for addressing economic issues, and have achieving among themselves on a number of important issues. For example, experimental economists often make instructions and software available for precise replication, and raw data are typically shared for reanalysis. Experimental economists also insist on paying performance-based. However, experimental economists have also developed rules that many behavioral economists are likely to find excessively . For example, experimental economists rarely collect data like demographics, self-reports, reponse times and other cognitive measure which behavioral economists have found useful. Descriptions of the experimental environment are usually abstract rather than which are carried on experiment in the outside world because economic theory rarely makes a prediction about how a happen would matter, and experimenters are concerned about losing control over incentives if choosing strategies with certain labels is appealing because of the labels themselves. Finally, economic experiments also typically use "stationary replication", in which the same task is repeated over and over in each period. Data from the last few periods of the experiment are typically used to draw conclusions about equilibrium behavior outside the lab. When economists believe that examining behavior after it is of great interest, it is also obvious that many important aspects of economic consumption of individual behavior to every individual consumer. The consumer's individual consumption of behavioral choose is like the first few periods of an experiment rather than the psychological methods to predict behavioral consumption.

Supposing if we need to make decision of marriage, educational decisions, and saving for retirement, or the purchase of large durables like houses, sailboats, can cars, which happen just a few times in a person's life, a focus on behavior is clearly not warranted. All said, the focus on psychological realism and economic applicability of research promoted by the behavioral-economics perspective suggests the usefullness research outside the lab and of a broader range of approaches to laboratory research. So, economists realize that who have ideal opportunity to learn by trial-and-error, in a stationary environment, and uses the opportunity to learn how to carry on experimenting any psychology and behavioral researches in lab experiment environment.

● What is psychology of consumption behavior?

Psychology is the science of human behavior and mental consumption processes. In consumption process behavior, it is any consumption behaviors as well as consumer mental consumption process is consumer individual internal experiences, comparison with alternative products, products choice of the best, making decision to consume or not consume for the product. So, advertisers often persuade to influence consumers' behavior to attract them to choose to buy whose products.

Why businessmen need to learn consumer psychology? Because psychology can help businessmen scientifically to evaluate common consumer beliefs and misconceptions about consumption behavior and consumption decision making mental processes. Consumption scientific psychology has four basic goals: To describe , explain, predict and change consumption behavior and consumption decision making mental process. Consumption psychological information is based on evidence, this is information based on direct observation and measurements with consumption behavior with scientific method. How are typical images of psychology? Consumption psychologists need to use scientific method to help businessmen to think what predicts who own, make a list of words would who use to describe a psychological scientist and what use to describe a psychological scientist and what images the businessmen have.

However, consumption psychologists have difference ways of looking at the same problem for the businessmen, which is why there are so many sub-fields of consumption psychology. Consumption psychology's roots began in philosophy, but the focus changes to a scientific focus consumer.

Behaviorism is focused on consumer buying behavior that can be measured and observable. This returned the scientific approach to consumption psychology. Consumption behaviorist's believe consumers are controlled by their environment. Consumption behaviorism focuses on consumption observable behavior. However, consumption cognitive psychology believes that consumption behaviors are preformed because of the product ideas and thoughts. The cognitive perspective focuses on such consumer decision making and choice processes, such as perception, memory and thinking to the product.

The two categories of consumer's behavioral consumption of decision

The field of consumer's behavioral consumption of decision research, on which behavioral economics has drawn more than any other subfield of psychology, typically classifies research into two categories: judgement and choice. Judgement research deals with the processes people use to estimate probabilities. Choice deals with the processes people use to select among actions, considering of any relevant judgements who may have made. Everyday, we, such as consumers need to make probable judements. Due to judging the likelihood of events is central to economic life. For example: Will you lose your job in a poor economic environment? Will you be able to find another house you like as much as the one you must bid for right away? Will the government raise interest rates in this year or next year? Will a merger strategy increase profits? These questions are answered by some process of judging likelihood. The standard principles used in economic to model probability judgement in economic are concepts of statistical sampling, which are concerned probabilities in the face of new evidence. However, it requires a separation between previously judged probabilities and evaluations of new evidence. However, (consumers) people often overestimate the probability who previously attached to events which later happened. This leads to "secondguessing". For example, Monday morning quarterbacking and may be partly responsible for lawsuits against stockbrokers who lost money for their clients. (The clients think the brokers should have known). For example, anybody has tried to learn from a computer distance learning manual has seen the classroom learning of knowledge in action. Another example for making probability judgements is called "representativeness": People judge conditional probabilities like P(hypothesis /data) or P(example/class) by how well the data represents the hypothesis or the example represents the class. Representativeness is an economical shortcut that delivers reasonable judgements with minimal effort in many cases. For example, in judging whether a certain student (University customer) described in a profile is, say, a psychology major or computer science major, the student decides how well the profile matches the psychology or computer science career to the student generally. So, University can read the student profile to predict whether the student will choose to study psychology subject more prefer or computer subject more prefer to predict whose computer or psychology student numbers more accurate in the year.

Many studies show how this sort of feature-matching can lead people to underweigh the "base rate", in this example, the overall frequency of the two majors. Another byproduct of representativeness is the "law of small numbers": Small samples are though to represent the properties of the statistical process that generated them (as if the law of large numbers, which guarantees that a large sample of independent draws does represent the process, is in a hurry to work). Field and experimental studies with basketball shooting and betting on games that people believe that there is positive attitude that players experience the "hot hand", when there is no evidence that such an effect exists.

For example, how the government tax department can judge whether the company's financial report has not been misled from accounting auditor's moral behavior, how to predict consumer's brand choice behavior and how to control students' learning behavior in classroom . It is important to judge whether it is either a good attitude or bad attitude from the consumer's personal behavior in the past. A consumer's good attitude to the product or the service consumption provides good consumption experience, close to optimal, answers when time or capabilities are limited, but it also needs logical principles and leads to situations. So, optimal is largely a critique (a reasonable one) of the later applied research. Otherwise, a consumer's bad attidude to the product or the service consumption provide poor consumption experience to buy the product or use the service again. Thus, the consumer's good or bad past buying experience to the product or to use the service will have help to assist the businessman how to predict whose consumption behavior next time.

Assume that people misspecify a set of hypotheses, or encode new evidence incorrectly. For example, assuming that people believe hypothesis A is more likely than B will never encode pro-A evidence mistakenly, but will sometimes encode pro-B evidence as being supportive. For another example, investors will think there is wide variation in skill of, say, mutual-fund managers, even if there is no variation at all. (A manager who does well several years is a surprise if performance is mistakenly thought due to nonreplacement, so concluding that the manager must be really good.) A question concerns stock market, such as: Overreacts in the long term. In their model, earnings follow a random walk but investors believe, mistakenly, that earnings have positive attitude. After one or two periods of good earnings, the stock market can not be confident that exists and hence expects, but since earnings are really a random walk, the stock market is too pessimistic and is underreacting to good earnings news. After a good earnings, however, the stock market believes many investors are increasing. Since, it is not the stock market is too optimistic and overreact. So, investor's past experience to earn or loss from the share, which will influence whose invetment behavior to choose to buy the share next time.

For another example, valuable consumer products (A $100 wireless keyboard, a fancy computer mouse, bottles of wine, and a box of chocolate) are sold to postgraduate (MBA) business students. The students were presented with a product and asked whether who would buy it for a price equal to the last two digits of their own social security number (a roughly random identification number required to obtain work in the United States) converted into a dollar figure, e.g. , if the last digits were 99, then the postgraduate business students will accept the hypothetical price was $99 to buy any of it for a price to the last two digits of their own social security number . After giving a yes/no response to the question. Would you pay $99? subjects were asked to state the most who would pay (using a procedure that gives people an incentive to say what who really would pay). Although subjects were reminded that the social security number is essentially random, those with high numbers were willing to pay more for the products. However, many studies have also shown that the method used to elicit preferences can have dramatic consequences.

Nevertheless, when required to make an economic decisions-to-choose a brand of toothpaste, a car, a job, or how to invest, people do make some kind of decision. Behavioral economists refer to the process by which people make choices with ill defined preferences as "constructing preferences".

So, psychologic methods can be used to predict why the consumer choose to buy the product as well as any consumer seems who needs to evaluate whether who will earn more benefit or low to choose to buy the brand of product or use the service to achieve the best benefits. However, in classical consumer theory, preferences among different commodities are assumed to be invariant with respect to an individual's current consumption. Specifically, people seem to dislike losing commodities from their consumption much more than they like gaining other commodities. For example, the research of "contingent valuation" studies that attempt to establish the dollar value of products which are not routinely trades. Contingent valuation is often used to do government cost-benefit analysis or establish legal penalties from environment damage. These surveys typically show very large differences between buying prices (e.g. paying to clean up oil of beaches) and selling prices (e.g. having to be paid to allow beaches to be ruined) to reduce environmental pollution from the low cost method for government spending.

Nowadays, there are many USA manufacturers use behavioral economy methods to predict consumer individual behavior, a quarter of the wealth in the USA has more interesting opportunities to do behavioral economies. They find that motivated sellers should regard the price who paid as a sunk cost and choose at a nominal loss from the purchase price. Sellers' listing prices and subsequent selling behavior reflects to nominal losses. There are some cases in which no effect would be expected, such as when products , such as house or antique dealers' products are purchased for resale rather than for utilization. For example, Do art or antique dealers like with pieces who buy to resell? What about surrogate mothers who agree to bear a child for a price paid in advance? Reference points can also serve as social focal points for house or antique products or surrogate mothers whose behavioral judging performance.

For an interesting example from corporate finance. In general, when managers whose firms face possible losses (or declines from a previous year's earnings) are very reluctant to report small losses. As a result, the distribution of actual losses and gains show a very large at zero, and hardly any small reported losses (compared to the number of small gains). A manager who does not have the skill to shift accounting profits to erase a potential loss (i.e. has some earnings in his pocket.) is considered a poor manager. It seems that the bad performance manager whose behavior is bad to mislead public to believe his firm have better performance in this year. Hence, in the mental accounting view, people(accountants) set up mental accounts for outcomes which are psychologically separate, much as financial accountants lump expenses and revenues into separated accounts to guide managerial attention. Otherwise, mental accounting stands in opposition to the standard view in economics that it predicts, accurately , that people will spend money coming from different sources in different ways. So, a generalization of the notion of mental accounting (the accountant's mislead financial report performance) , which aims to let investors and consumers have more confidence to choose to invest or to choose to buy it's products or consume its service more easily. So, it explains why the accountant needs to mislead to report it's earns are more than loss in every year.

Explanation what are of Preferences over risky to behavioral consumption and utility function concept to company profit intention or government tax income intention

What is preferences over risky to behavioral consumption. Such as prospect theory is experimental choices more accurately than (EU) because it gets the psychological of judgement and choice right. It consists of two main components, a probability weighting function, and a "value function" which replaces the utility function of (EU) to any consumer when who needs to choose to buy any product or consume any service by more than one choice. The weighting function P(P) combines two elements: (1) The level of probability weight is a way of expressing risk and (2) Captures how sensitive people are to differences in probabilities. New information of any products can help any decision maker to feel better to make better final purchase decisions. These theories effect may explain demand for information in settings like medicine or personal finance, where new information usually does not change choice, but relieves anxiety people have from knowing there is something who could know to choose to buy the medicine or borrowing loan of low interest payment. So, new information of any products can reduce consumer individual risk to choose to buy.

However, the planning problem for economic agents who would like to behave in fashion and discussed the important time discounting for choice. Most big decisions, e.g. savings, educational investments, labor supply, health and diet, crime and drug etc. decisions use have costs and benefits which occur at different point in time. Thus, time discounting is basically standard time discounting plus an immediacy effect, a decision discounts delays in equally at all moments except the current one, caring differently about well being. This functional form provides one sample and powerful model of the taste to individual to make right or reasonable behavior economic decision. However, most analyses of choice assume that people integrate new consumption with planned consumption. It is infeasible and perhaps for this reason, descriptively inaccurate. When people make decisions about new sequences of payments or consumption, they tend to evaluate them in isolation, e.g. treating negative outcomes as losses, rather than as reductions to their existing money flows or consumption plans.

How to decide fairness and social preferences. The assumption that people maximize their own wealth and other personal material goals just self-interest is a correct simplification that is often useful in economics. However, people may sometimes choose to spend their wealth to punish others who have harmed them, reward whose, so who have helped, or to make outcomes more fair. Just as understanding demand for products requires specific utility function. So. on economic view point, utility function concept can influence consumer choice. if the consumer feels the product has more utility, then who will prerfer to choose to buy the product. Otherwise, if who feels the product has less utility, then who will not perfer to choose to buy the product.

Behavioral economy can also use to assist firms to choose right behavior to decide to do any matters. I show hypothesis to establish any reference level of consumer surplus and product profit. Both sides are entitled to any firm's levels of profit, so price changes which threaten any matter are considered unfair. So raising any product price, it will reduce consumer surplus and is considered unfair. But the cost of a firm's inputs rises, subjects said it was fair to raise prices. Because not raising prices would reduce the firm's profit (compared to the reference profit). Everyday observation that firms don't change prices and wages as frequently commonly.

For example, when the fourth hary potter story book was released in summer 2000 year, most stores were allocated a small number of books that were pre-sold in advance. Why not raise prices or auction the books off? It is possible that it concerned about customer goodwill and excess demand to cause book stores limit such book price increases. Offended consumers are often able to affect firm behavior by media attention or provoking legislation. For example, scalping tickets for popular sports and entertainment events (resulting them at a large premium over the printed ticket price) is constrained by law in most countries. For example, some countries have "anti-laws" penalizing sellers who take advantage of shortages of water, fuel and other necessities by raising prices after natural disasters. So, the countries' governments can protect which citizen benefits to balance the natural resource supply and demand to sell in the reasonable price fairly after the natural disaster occurrence. This is utility function concept. Because the book store believes the fourth hary potter story book will be excess demand and reader goodwill is good. So the books' utility function is enough to prepare to sell to readers, which do not need to raise price to attract readers to read. Also, scalping tickets for popular sports and entertainment events will rise ticket price to be limited level because the popular sports and entertainment players believe who have attrative ability to attract full ticket buyers and whose numbers will exceed seats demand. So, the ticket numbers utility are enough and which are not need to raise ticket price too much. Also, shortages of water, fuel and other necessities by raising prices after natural disasters, because government make whose citizen has limit number of water, fuel and other necessities supply to keep enough utility function to satisfy whose needs. So, the nature resources do not need to raise price when natural disaster occurs.

A few years ago, responding to public anger at rising CEO salaries when the economy was being restructured through downsizing and many workers lost their jobs. Otherwise, some countries passed a law prohibiting firms from deducting CEO salaries for tax purposes beyonded $1 million a year. However, because some countries need to earn much tax income from these high salary CEO income every year. So, these countries do not suggest to pass a law to probibit firm from deducting CEO salaries for tax purpose. So, utility function can be applied to company benefit. If the company hopes to limit the CEO salary, then it will limit whose CEO 's duty (reducing utility funtion to whose duty). Aim to avoid to pay more salary expenditure to the CEO , when the country's economy is poor and it believes there are less consumers prefer to consume more. Otherwise, if the company does not hope to limit the CEO salary, then it will not limit whose CEO'duty (increasing utility function to whose duty). Aim to hope who can help whose company to earn more profit, when the country's economy is good and it believe there are many consumers prefer to consume. On the other side, if the country tax department hopes to earn more salary tax income, it will choose not to pass a law prohibiting firms from deducting CEO salaries for tax purposes beyonded $1 million a year. In the behavioral economy concept, the government tax department hopes to earn more salary tax when the economy environment is not good or it is worse to compare last year's economy environment. Thus, behavioral economy concept will be applied to company profit intention or country income intention or individual consumption intention.

How can behavioral game theory apply to company income intention?

How can behavioral game theory apply to company income intention ? Behavioral game theory has rapidly become an important foundation for many areas of micro economic theory to any organizations, such as bargaining in decentralized markets, outsource contracting and organizational structure. The descriptive accuracy of game theory in these application can be questioned because equilibrium predictions often assume strategic reasoning and direct field tests are difficult to any organizations. In fact, behavioral game theory uses any experimental evidence and psychological research to generalize the standard assumptions of game theory to any organizations how which choose to make profit intention.

One component of behavioral game theory is a theory of social preferences for allocations of money to oneself and others. Another component is a theory of how people choose in one shot games or in the first period of a repeated game. For example, in share buying and selling market, shareholders shall buy or sell shares from their judgement in the economic cycle market everyday. So share investment is seemed as allocation of game to these shareholders. Also, shareholders whose mind can influence whose psychological behavior to decide how to invest whose shares in their share investment economic activities. The component of behavioral game theory can include a model of learning to either individual or a population. Also, game theory is one area of economy in which serious attention has been paid to the process by which can equilibrium comes about. Many learning theories have been proposed and carefully tested with experimental data. Theories about population never predict as well as theories of individual learning through who are useful for other purposes. So, behavioral game theory can be applied to these complex environments. e.g. consumer supermarket purchase, share market etc. for these business organizations research.

How to apply behavioral game theory to macroeconomics and saving aspect? Many concepts in macroeconomic probably have a behavioral style that could be influenced by research in psychology. For example, it is common to assume that prices and wages are in nominal terms, which has important implications for macroeconomic behavoir. Behavioral economics suggests some ideas for among consumers and workers, perhaps it is influenced by workers' concern for fairness.

An important model in macroeconomics is the life cycle model of savings or permanent income hypothesis. This theory assumes that people make a guess about their lifetime earnings profile, and plan their lifetime earnings profile, and plan their savings and consumption in each period has diminishing marginal utility; and preferences for consumptions streams are time-separable (i.e. overall utility is the sum of the discounted utility of consumption in each separate period). The theory also assumes people lump together different types income when they guess how much money who will have (i.e. different sources of wealth are different). So, why many young people won't spend too much money for unnecessary expenditure, e.g. entertainment easily. Because who plan to save for their old age to use in their long time life time.

A behavioral life cycle theory of savings in which different sources of income are kept track of in different mental accounts. Mental accounts can reflect natural perceptual or cogitive divisions. For example, it is possible to add up the travellers' paycheck and dollar value of whose frequent flyer miles, but it is simply unnatural to do so. It is important to note that many key implications of the life-cycle hypothesis have never been well supported ,e.g. consumption is far more closely related to current income than it should be according to theory. However, predictions can be improved by introducing utility functions with habit formation in which utility in a current depends on the reference point of previous consumption, and by more carefully accounting for uncertaining about future income.

For example, in the accountancy (economic) professional view point mental accounting is only one of several behavioral approaches that may prove useful. Economics is money illusion, it is the tendency to make decisions based on nominal quantities rather than converting those figures into real terms by adjusting for inflation. Money illusion seems to be pervasive in some domains. So, it appears that employees don't seem to mind if their real wage falls as long as their nominal wages doesn't fall.

How can behavioral game theory apply to company income intention? Labor macroeconomics is involuntary unemployment. Why can some people not find work beyond of switching jobs, or a natural rate of unemployment? A popular account of unemployment pushs that wages are deliberately paid above the market clearly level, which creates an excess supply of workers and hence unemployment. But why are wages too high ? As efficiency wage theory shows that paying workers more than who deserve is necessary to ensure that who have something to lose if they are unemployed, which motivates them to work hand and economizes on monitoring.

How Another viewpoint indicates that employer and worker is such as into a gift exchange relationship. Employers pay more than who have to as a gift and workers repay the gift by working harder than necessary. They show how gift exchange can be an equilibrium and show some of its macroeconomic implications. In labor economics, gift exchange is clearly evident of experimental labor markets. In practical working environment, firms offer wages; workers who take the jobs than choose a level of effort, which is costly to the workers and valuable to the firms.

For example, firms and workers can enforce wages, but not effort levels. Since workers and firms are matched for just one period, and do not learn each other's identities, there is no way for either side to build reputations or for firms to punish workers who chose low effort. However, self interested workers should shirk, and firms should anticipate that and pay a low wage. In fact, firms deliberately pay high wages as gifts and workers choose higher effort levels when they take higher wage jobs. It seems that it has strong relationship between wages and effort is stable over time.

For another example, standard life-cycle theory assumes that if people can borrow, they should prefer wage profiles which maximize the present value of lifetime wages. Holding total wage payments constant, and assuming a positive real rate of interest, present value maximization implies that workers should prefer declining wage profiles over increasing ones. However, in fact, most wages profiles are clearly rising over time which is such as a phenomenon. Rather, workers derive utility from positive changes in consumption, but have self-control problems.

If any company has any good wages profiles would prevent them from positive changes in consumption, but have self-control problems that would prevent them from saving for later consumption of wages were more front-loaded in the life cycle. In addition, workers seem to derive positive utility from increasing wage profiles, it is perhaps because rising wages are a source of self-esteem and the desire for increasing payments is much weaker for non wage income. The standard life-cycle of labor supply also implies that workers should substitute labor and leisure based on the wage rate who face and the value who place on leisure at different points in time. If wage fluctuations are temporary workers should work long hours when wages are high and short hours when wages are low. However, because changes in wages are often persisting and because work hours are generally fixed in the short-run. So, it is difficult to tell whether workers are substituting. So, if the company can have good method to decide when to rise salary or wage level , even reduce salary or wage level, as well as how much rising or reducing salary or wage level is the suitable in different time. If the wage fluctuations are reasonable in the most suitable time, the labor turnover numbers will not be reduced easily.

How can behavioral game theory apply to individual business income intention? For example, taxi drivers who target daily will drive longer hours on low income days and will drive less hours early on high income days. This behavior is exactly the opposite of substitution. Also inexperienced taxi drivers support the daily targeting prediction. But experienced taxi drivers don't have negative elasiticies, either because target minded drivers earn less and self select or taxi drivers learn over time to substitute rather than target. Perhaps the simplest prediction of labor economics is that the supply of labor should be upward sloping in response to a increase in wage. Suppose to the inexperienced taxi drivers will attempt to drive long hours if who can feel or predict the taxi passengers number will reduce on the low income day. Otherwise, the experienced taxi drivers will attempt to drive less hours if who can feel or predict when the taxi passengers number will increase on the high income day. So, these experienced or inexperienced taxi drivers whose decison of driving long hours or less hours is depended on whose feeling of taxi passengers number who is high or low.

How, behavioral game theory applys to investor behavior. In finance, standard equilibrium models of asset pricing assume that investors only care about asset risks if who affect marginal publicly available information to forecast stock returns as accurately as possible the efficient markets hypothesis. When those hypotheses do make some accurate predictions and some investors in assets have limited rationality of behavioral finance. Also, in share stock market, it is common, shareholders should not want to trade with them, but the volume of stock market transaction is large. So, it presents data on individual trading behavior which suggests that the extremely high volume may be driven, in part, by overconfidence on the part of investors. Thus, if the company's share numbers buying and selling transactions are very large in the year. Then, it will influence many investors have more confidence to be encouraged to choose to buy the firm's shares in the year. Otherwise, if the company's share numbers buying and selling transactions are less in the year. Then, it will also influence many investors have less confidence to be encouragd to choose to buy its' shares in the year.

For another example, behavioral game theory applys to property agent's behavior. Property agent's individual behavior is similar to share agent's individual behavior. In the economy view point , property agent bases a list price for a house on the selling prices of nearly houses that is similar ("comparables"). Every nearest neighbour techniques bases on similarity is also used in credit scoring and other kinds of evaluations. Also, one firm whose every share sale on the selling price is comparable to its similar firms whose every share price in its same business industry. The shareholder will evaluate whose every share issued sale price in the stock (share) market. Otherwise, in behavioral economy view, for example, property or share buyer who has risky choice to decide to buy in the property or share market. It is a process of comparing the similarity of the probabilities and outcomes in two gambles and choosing on dimensions which are dissimilar.

As we mentioned above, behavioral economics simply includes an interest in psychology. In fact, we believe that many familiar economic distinctions do have a lot of behavioral content, they are implicitly behavioral, and could surely benefit from more explicit ties to psychological ideas and data. However, some people do not feel psychology and economy which have close relationship. Such as, substantial debate is ongoing in psychology about whether knowing the precise details of how the brain carries out computations is necessary to understand functions and mechanisms of driving car skill at higher levels, (knowing the mechanical details of how a car works may not be necessary to turn the key and drive it). So, the drivers who concerns more safe to their families and themselves, who will prefer to pay more money to buy the more safe vehicle to driver. Otherwise, the drivers who disconcern safe and concern money save, who will choose to pay less money to buy the less safe vehicle to drive.

Behavioral game theory can apply to price behavioral elasticity for how firm's price decision. For example , it is the distinction between short run and long run price elasticity which concerns behavioral economy. In fact, economy needs have theories concepts to support any evidence to prove any matter has happened. Concerning short run and long run price elasticity cause and effort issue, with a casual suggestion that the run is the time it takes for markets to adjust, or for consumers to learn new prices, after a demand or supply stock. Adjustment costs undoubtedly have technical and social component, but probably also have some behavioral factors influence in the form of gradual adaption to loss and learning. So, if there are many consumers who believe the product is reliable to use and the brand is famous, the product's price won't be push down often and it has less price elastic. Otherwise, if there are many consumers who do not believe the product is reliable to use and the brand is not famous, the product's price will be push doen often and it has more price elactic tendency.

Another macroeconomic model which can be interpreted as implicitly behavior is that business cycles can emerge if it is not general price inflation, so why the consumers shall not decide to buy this kind of product in the competitive market. So price when the market price inflation, consumers will not choose to prefer to spend to buy more food to eat or products to use. Otherwise, when the market price is stable, consumers will choose to prerfer to spend to buy more food to eat products to use. So, inflation will influence consumption of behavior.

Behavioral economic simply includes an interest in psychology. In fact, we believe that many familiar economic distinctions do have a lot of behavioral content, they are implicitly behavioral and could surely benefit from more explicit ties to psychological ideas and data. However, some people do not feel psychology and economy which have close relationship. Such as psychology is about whether knowing the precise details of how the brain carries out computations is necessary to understand functions and mechanisms at higher levels. (knowing the mechanical details of how a car works may not necessary to turn the key and drive it.)

Most psychology experiments use indirect measures like response times, error rates, self reports and natural experiments due to brain has been fairly successful in codifying what we know about thinking. However, pessimists think brain scan studies won't add much. The optimists think the new tools will lead to some discoveries and the potential is great that they cannot be ignored. However, economy needs have theories or concepts to support evidence to prove why any matters had happened. An example, is the distinction between short term and long term price elasticity. This distinction, mentions between of them, with a casual suggestion that long run is the time it takes for markets to adjust, or for consumers to learn new prices, after a demand or supply shock. Adjustment costs undoubtedly have technical and social components, but probably also have some behavioral factors influence in the form of gradual adaption to loss and learning.

However behavioral economy theory can be applied to organizational behavior, organizational behavioral theory concerns that organizatonal contracting are shot through with implicitly behavioral economics. Some economists motivate the incompleteness of contracts as a consequence of rationality in foreseeing the future, but do not tie the research directly to work on memory and imagination. For example, agency theory begins with the presumption that there is some activity the agent doesn't like to do. Why markets are better at making dramatic changes than managers influence cost. So, influence costs are the costs managers preform for projects who like or personally benefit from like promotion or raises. A lot of influence costs are undoubtedly inflated by optimistic, each division manager really does think their division desperately needs funds and social comparison of pay and benefits. Otherwise, why are salaries kept so secret? In all these cases, conventional economic behavior has deeper psychological questions of where adjustment costs, effort and influence costs come from. So, it beings these questions: Could these phenomena surely produce surprising testable prediction? Is psychology regularity an assumption or a conclusion?

Behavioral economics generally begins with assumption rooted in psychological regularity and asks what follows from those assumptions. An alternative approach is to work backward, regarding a psychological regularity as a conclusion that must be proved an explanation that must be derived from deeper assumption before we fully understand and accept it. The alternative approach is caused by a fashionable new direction in economic theory and psychology too, which is to explain human behavior as the product of evolution. However, we may not believe that behavior of intelligent, modern people lived in socialization and cultural influence can only be understood by guessing what their lives were like and how their brains might have adapted generally. There are other models that treat psychological regularity as a conclusion to be proved rather than an assumption to be used. Such models usually begin with an observed regularity. However, I think economic factor can influence consumers to make who feel the more reasonable psychological decision to make the more right behavior. Thus, economy and psychology has close relationship to influence consumer individual decision.

Economists have for deriving behavior from first principles and rationalizing apparent irrationality. Theories of this sort are useful behavioral economics and what fresh predictions do they make. However, critics have pointed out that behavioral economics is not a unified theory, but is instead a collection of tools and ideas. This is true. However, some economists believe that economic models do not derive much predictive power from the single tool of utility maximization. The goal of behavioral economic is to develop better tools that, in some cases, can do both jobs at once.

Economists like to point out the natural division of labor between scientific disciplines: Psychologists should concern to individual minds, and economists to behavior in games, markets, and economies. But the division of labor is only efficient if there is effective coordinaton, and all too often economists fail to conduct intellectual trade with those who have a comparative advantage in understanding individual human behavior. The only question is whether the implicit psychology in economics is good psychology or bad psychology. We think it is simply unwise, and inefficient to do economics without paying some attention to good psychology.

● Can predict consumer behavior with web search?

In behavioral economy view point, it can be applied to predict why consumers buy products from internet. Recent work has demonstrated that web search volume can "predict the present", meaning that can be used to accurately track outcomes, such as unemployment levels, auto and home sales and disease prevalence in near real time. Consumers are searching what for online can also predict their collective future behavior days or even weeks in advance. For example, specifically businessmen can use search query volume to forecast the opening weekend box-office revenue for feature films, first month sales of video games and the rank of songs, finding in all case that search counts are highly predictive of future outcomes from online google research. Finally, businessmen can reexamine previous work on tracking trends and show that, perhaps surprisingly, the utility of search data relative to a simple auto regressive model is modest.

Nowadays, people increasingly use the internet for news, information and research purposes. From this perspective, it is a short step to conclude that what people are researching for today is predictive of what who will do in the near future. For example, consumers may search to prepare to buy a new camera, moviegoers may search to determine the opening date of a new film, or to locate cinemas showing it and individuals planning a vacation may search from a places of interest, to find airline tickets, or to price hotel rooms. So online can aggregately count of search queries related to retail activity. Movie going or travel might be able to predict collective behavior of economic, cultural, or political interest. Determining the nature of behavior that can be predicted using search, the accuracy of such predictions and the time scale over which predictions can be usefully made are therefore all questions of interest.

Researchers have focused on the observation that search " predicts the present". For example, Ettredge et al (2005) found that counts of the top 300 search terms during 2001 to 2003 year were correlated with US Bureau Of Labor statistics Unemployment Figures; Cooper (2005) et al found that search activity for specific cameras during 2001 to 2003 year correlated with their estimated incidence and Eysenbach (2006) found a high correlation between clicks on sponsored search results of flu-related keywords and epidemiolopical data from the 2004 to 2005 year Canadian flu season.

Thus, motivated , I indicate one example how investigates whether search activity is a systematic leading indicator of consumer activity by forecasting. For first example, supposing to opening weekend Box-office revenue for 119 feature films released in the united States between Oct. 2008 year and Sept. 2009. For second example, supposing to first month sales of video games across all gaming platforms, e.g. Xbox, Play station etc.) for 106 games released between Sept. 2008 and Sept. 2009 year. These search data can be collected from yahoo using research rank from the current and previous weeks.

Can online search also predict the near future? A finding that may apply usually to a wide range of consumer behaviors , e.g. airline travel, hotel vacancy rates and auto sales and economic indicators , e.g. real-estate prices, credit card and confidence indicators. It seems all research based predictions simply models to build on publicly available information. For movies, baseline predictions can be used a linear model that includes production budgets, the number of screens on which each movie opened and box office projections from the Hollywood Stock Exchange (HSX) (hsx.com) on online, play money prediction market that is known to generate information prediction. For video games, many of the key indicators of revenue, including production budgets and initial available. Thus, it seems that businessmen can attempt to use internet (online) search technological method to search past information to concern whether what number of customers will be estimated.

● Can firm's conduct and behavior factor influence consumption of behavior ?

In behavioral economy view point, it can explain how firm conduct and behavior factor can infuence consumption of behavior. The usual assumption about the objectives of firms made by economists is that firms seek to maximize profit. The means that firms feel that who are protected against the possibility of new entrants, and proceed to maximize short-run profits. Firms feel that the barriers against new entrants ensure that their profits won't induce new firms to enter the industry and to reduce competitors enter to industry to raise consumers' choices to buy any similar products.

A major challenges to the profit maximization objective has come from proponents of the view that modern larger corporation are under a managerial control, which it is argued leads to the pursuit of other objectives, such as growth. The pursuit of non-profit objective is not unique to managerial-controlled firms, although the growth of such firms and of theories about than have emphasized these types of objectives.

Another view has focused on the controllers of the firm, whether owners or managers, having a wider range of objectives and that the achievement of profit maximization and the cost minimization requires considerable time and effort by the controllers. Thus, the controllers have incentives to forge profit maximization, unless who are forced to do so. Under oligopoly, firms can earn profits above the normal level, e.g. one country has only two electricity power companies are existing in the country's energy supply market. They may change a profit maximizing price, but actual reported profits may be less than potential profit.

This could raise from technical inefficiency or from higher than necessary payments to the factors of production. The technical inefficiency can arise since it takes effort by the controllers to reach full efficiency and which may be willing to make necessary effort. The higher payments can involve higher salaries to the controllers of the firm. For either reasons, company needs to concern how to report profit fall below true profit of the firm, with the difference used to finance inefficiency and higher factor payments in fair business conduct behavior. Particularly, company also need to concern how to carrying on fair business conduct behavior, e.g. none mislead advertising information, correct profit differentiation financial information, product reputations of the existing products presentation, none mislead consumption motives performance (which favor the established over the unestablished) and lower trade-in values of second –hand products of entrants (particularly in the car market). So, it seems that any one firm none mislead conduct behavior factor can influence consumer choices to increase or decrease to buy the firm's products in fair buying and selling transaction.

Another view point, for same products differentiation none mislead conduct factor is also important to influence each consumer behavior. For example, cars don't have a common prototype and each manufacturer must design its particular model. In constant , for a product like sugar , there is a common prototype, and differentiation through branding is within the discretion of the firm involved. This for some good product differentiation may be benefit whereas, for other products differentiation depends upon the activities of the firms involved, although the costs and benefits to the existing firms varies between profits. However, the height of the barrier to entry by product differentiation is likely to be influenced by the conduct and behavior of the firms involved, and thus in the case , there is an element of firm's behavior and conduct can influence any consumer buying behavior of choice to its products.

How to apply behavioral economic principles to assist policy makers or decision makers to make more reasonable decision.

Behavioral economics theories can also apply to assist any policy makers to make right and reasonable decision in right time. I shall indicate new principles to recommend and I also shall give any psychological cases to explain how policy makers can apply behavioral economic theories to judge how to make their any decision is the most right and the most reasonable.

Behavioral economy is an independent and demonstrates real economic well-being. It aims to improve quality of life by promoting innovative solutions that challenge mainstream thinking on economic, environment and social issues. Also, behavioral economy is different branches of more alternative economies into a form that is useful primarily for policy-makers. I think behavioral economy can be given an aid to policy makers how who use economic tools to the broader policy making community by providing a theoretical behaviour for many policy approaches to be used. The standard economic analysis assumes that humans are rational and behave in a way to maximize their individual self-interest. This rational man assumption indicates a powerful tool for analysis. However, it has many shortfalls that can lead to unrealistic economic analysis and policy-making. Also, I think behavioral economics and psychology has these principles to influence human behaviour. These principles include, such as below:

In common, people do many things by observing others and copying; people are encouraged to continue to do things when they feel other people approve of their behaviour. People do many things without consciously thinking about time. These habits are hard to change. There are cases where money is de-motivating as it undermines people's intrinsic motivation. People want their actions and commitments to be values usually. People put undue weight on recent events and who can't calculate probabilities well and worry too much about unlikely events and who are strongly influences by how the problem/information is presented to them. People need to feel effective to make a change, even just giving who the incentives and information is not necessarily enough in any environment usually. So any policy maker ought concern about what the acceptable degree is when who choose to decide to make any new policy in whose country. If who can predict whether whether whose country's citizen will or won't accept whose new policy implement and know why some won't accept whose new policy implement and why some accept whose new policy implement, then who can decide to do any economic activities more reasonable, e.g. investment to build public hospital or public school in the location; spending this expenditure to education or medical more.

In fact, much of our behaviour is strongly influenced by other people's behaviour. Social learning is a process by which we take in the behavior of others to learn how to behave. In more complex situations with which we are unfamiliar, we consciously watch and learn from the behavior of others. For example, when use a new library for the first time. When we make a conscious decision on how to behave, our sense of social identity is important, we think: how would other from my group behave in this situation? So, the policy marker will need to make to compare the economic benefits to choose to build either library or public school between of them to satisfy readers need or students need more in the location.

In situations where there is high social capital. i.e. where there are strong networks between people and a high level of mutual trust, so its seems other people's behaviour and our sense of social identity may be extremely important in influencing our own behavior and policy makers ought need to know how to judge their behaviour whether their behavior is either right and reasonable or wrong and unreasonable in any learning process of environment. The standard economic theory is tried to explain where people's preferences come from, so it does not take account of the direct influence of the people's behaviour and social norms on our behaviour. The theory assumes we independently know what we want and that our preferences are fixed. This standard theory is very good at explaining short-term decision making for policy makers only. In decision marker view point, for example, I want green vegetables and choose fruits as they are on special offer in short term, but it cannot explain longer term changes in preferences. Now, I only choose organic food for long term because orgnic food can have more clean and no pollution to compare general green vegetables and fruit. Thus, the learning process environment will influence the food consumers who prefer to choose to buy organic food more than general green food in supermarket.

For driving example, it would require too much effort to look up all the rules when driving in a new country, to find out all the fines/punishments for failing to meet the rules, to work out the probability of being caught and the possible costs, before deciding how to drive there. Instead we just copy other people, and perhaps adjust our behaviour according to the feedback we receive. However, some psychologists indicate to see people how to behave, especically in crises situations and when others are experts. These psychologists have identified that we are open to influence from people in authority or people we like. When we are influenced by authority, an expert, someone with legitimate power to direct our actions, someone who can either reward or punish us. The effects are less likely to be lasting than we are influenced by someone we like. Thus, learning process of environment can influence any person's psychological behavior change easily. However, some people's psychological behaviour is similar to economic behaviour to judge to make any decision. For example, why do you wear a seatbelt in your car? Most of us wear seatbelts as it has became normal behaviour, everyone does it. We neither evaluate the likelihood of having an accident, nor the chance of getting caught without our seatbelt on and incurring a fine. The enforcement of seatbelt wearing is now hardly necessary, as it has become a social norm.

What does this mean for policy makers? Policy makers focusing only on economic analysis may often devise a system that has an immediate effect. In psychologists view this issue point, knowing that there is a fine for speeding and a high likelihood of getting caught, the driver will probably drive more slowly, but who will drive just as fast one who realise the chance of being caught is low. However, of policy makers can change the social norm, perhaps in this case by encouraging us to frown on others who drive dangerously fast with campaigns against dangerous driving, then less enforcement will be needed after the change. In other words policy makers might want to take preferences as fixed in the short term, but they should consider shifting preferences in the medium term.

An example where policy appears to have successfully changes people's preferences in the US and Singapre and Hong Kong is banning smoking in public places. This change appears to reduce the social proof of the amount people smoke in private places and public places both also. It seems that government policies can influence the decreasing numbers of consumers require to buy cigeratte to smoke habitually, due to fine and punishment is regulated to be ban effectively. Such daily routines quickly became habits. Even when we consciously think about what we do, it can be difficult to change our behaviour. Perhaps I think it is a good idea for people to use public transport, but I do not know where the bus stop is or when the bus runs. I think to use private car to drive to work place is more preference choice. The reward feeling , my journey by car was easy and free to reinforce my old bad habit. Psychologists theories on changing habits generally involve raising it to a conscious level where we can consider the merits of alternative behaviour.

In our learning process in environment, this is followed by adopting the new behaviour, which, with time, becomes frozen as a new habit. Thus, I think that we need have regulation to control my behaviour, then we can change my behaviour to be new habit from old habit of behaviour easily, such as consumption behavior. For example, human blood sale is an economic product, due to paying donors for blood would increase supply. Supplies would be provided at a cost advantage in the future, if demand continued to rise. Such as supplies to hospitals for blood will has cost from donors when there are many patients need much blood to use to treat any diseases in any hospitals. Otherwise, if there are not many patients need much blood to use, but there are many donors have effort to provide blood to any hospitals, then it will be economic inefficiency and it is highly wasteful of blood. Thus, the hospitals need to predict when there are many patients need much blood or there are less patients need less much. Then, hospitals can pay cheap cost to donors for blood supply. Thus, the learning processing for donors for blood supply is needed for hospitals.

For shareholder behavioual learing process in share investment environment example, if you hold some shares in a firm that has gone down in value. What do you do? Many people hold on to their shares in this situation, in the hope that they will recoup their losses. Conversely, when shares have gone up in share, people are happy to sell them to realise their gain, A similar behaviour is also observed for professional traders who tend to hold on to shares with a loss for longer than those with a gain. The traders who exhibit this type of loss to a lesser degree tend to be the more successful ones.

For another learning process environement example, this is a case where the theory is directly applicable within economic cost-benefit-type analyses that include valuations of no-market products, such as valuations of pollution damage. Policy makers have a choice as to whether-to-accept, and as these may vary by up to a factor, the outcome of such an analysis many well depend on which value is chosen. When a policy maker reasonably has a right to something that might be taken away from them, the willing-to-accept value would be used. On the other hand, when the policy maker only reasonable has a right to the status quo and an improvement is proposed, then the willingness-to-pay is the correct value to use. Thus, for valuations of pollution damage, policy makers need to learn whether pollution damage cost is higher or pollution bringing benefit is higher to make reducing pollution decision for long term. In generaly, people are expected to rationally make the best choices given their preferences, independent of how these choices are presented. Therefore more information and choice is always considered good. Using this theory, policy makers should ensure that people always have as much information and as many things to choose between as possible, the process of introducing policy is irrelevant. Thus, gathering information can assist policy makers to choose right decision for pollution damage benefit or cost behvioral choice to their society for economic benefit.

So, a participatory approach not only improves policy, it also makes to any policy makers more happier. In most cases these principles cannot be used directly as part of any mathematical economics analysis, but highlight situations where this standard analysis will not accurately describe human behaviour and therefore might have unintended consequences when implemented in policy. However, that the policy implications could be quite powerful as the behavioural approach provides quite different lines of analysis to the standard economic model. It is heartening to see policy makers focusing more on the psychology of behaviour when devising policy. So behavioral economics is a relatively new field of economics that attempts to incorporate insights from psychology into economic models and analyses. As above cases seem any policy maker's economic activities which are relative to whose psychology's decision.

However, psychologists are often interest in understanding at the level of individual or social group of behaviour, the primary interest in economic is usually in understanding how behaviour and interactions play out in a system to shape economic outcomes. Economists are interested in system-level outcomes, such as the level and path of wages, the effect of taxes on economic output, how rates of savings respond to interest rates etc. However, those economic outcomes depend on complex interactions of individuals. So, behavioural economy concerns to how to judge individual to do the reasonable or right behaviour to hope to get the reasonable economic result as well as it's goal rather to help improve any policy makers to understand their behaviour in ways that allow economists to make better predictions and suggest better economic policies. However, new elements about information processing or individual preferences might impact economic models and analyses in any learning process environment.

Is psychology influencing all field of economics? It is possible that behavioral economy needs theoretical contributions and laboratory evidence to support to make any reasonable or right decision to any policy makers. This type of work generally uses existing observational data and estimates relationships between variables of interest by either using naturally occurring variation in the data i.e. natural experiment.

Perhaps more than any other field, behavioral economics has had a large impact on finance to the point that behavior finance is often considered a separate field as opposed to being of behavioral economics. Also, public economic is the study of how government policies in fluence economic markets. A primary emphasis of public economic involves the topic of taxation. Otherwise, the biggest impact that the behavioral approach has had in economic is the analysis of retirement saving to influence any employees' decisions about their retirement savings. However, when employees can do make any active savings choices to prepare their retirement. If employers can assist whose employees to design any methods to allocate fund, then accumuates interest and is tax free until the retirement funds are withdrawn to every retirement employee. The tax advantage make effort to save for retirement.

Behavioral economic is in understanding how individuals do or do not smooth consumption over time. Smoothing consumption is a standard economic models. It suggests that individuals should borrow or save in order to consume a similar amount throughout one's lifetime. For example, a teacher who is paid a salary 12 months a year, who should not spend all whose salary within one year. Rather, the teacher should smooth whose consumption over the 12 month period. How to allocate to spend paychecks, food and social security payments which concerns the teacher decide to spend whose salary efficiently. Hence, who needs to plan how he shall spend whose one year salary to be reasonable use in the future.

Public economic is to understand how people respond to taxation and social benefit programs. This has been an area that has seen an explosion of behavioral work in recent year. i.e. how taxpayers can experience over-withholding and receive tax refunds from tax department. Policymakers and insurers are also increasingly turning to psychology for approaches to improve health behavior. Traditionally health-policy focused largely on information provision, assuming that as long as individuals were well informed, their decisions would maximize their health choices. For example, influential work on the effects of smoking taxes, however, well being of smokers appears to increase with higher taxes to influence health behaviours are not completely rational.

Behavioral economic has also had a small impact on the study of criminal behaviour. For example, individuals are not less likely to commit a crime when who are 18 age and the pubishment of doing so increases dramatically. However, some economists explain the motivations people have for giving to charity and who understand the psychological motivations for charitable giving. So, it seems that charity award giving has probable to reduce 18 age people who choose to do crime behaviour easily because who feel who have effort to assist charity in their life time.

Industrial organization economists study why firms exist and how which function and compete with each other. Insights and psychology and behavioral economics have made a significant contribution to develop that model the interactions of profit maximizing firms with their customers. In fact, firms often need to evaluate whether their products if prices are needed to set what of price of level is the most reasonable and attractive to customers to choose to buy their products.

For cell phone plan sale example, individuals choose cell phone plans with fixed minute allotments and steep charges for going over the minute limits, but frequently exceed their plan limits. This behavior is the best explained by a model in which people overestimate the precision of their demand forecasts. So, cell phone firms need to research how cell phone plans with fixed minute allotments and steep charges of cell phone call fee charge plan is the most acceptance method to cell phone clients generally. However, cell phone call charge plan and various cell phone product features and the way cell phone clients allocate their limited attention affects cell phone products markets which are external important factors can influence any cell phone clients why who will choose to use the cell phone call plan because any cell phone will be very large durable product to any cell phone consumer after who choose to buy the cell phone product. Hence, who will not often choose to use the old cell phone firm call charge plan if who feel it provides the excellent cell phone call service and reasonable phone call plan to use to compare other cell phone call plans in the cell phone call market.

Hence, the cell phone call firm needs to make marketing research why consumers need to choose to use which cell phone call plan among of other cell phone call plans in the cell phone call market. Also, researching the cell phone buyers' choice behaviour why who choose to buy the cell phone to use issue, which will have influence to the cell phone buyer why who choose to use the cell phone call charge plan because expensive cell phone is needed to use excellent quality of cell phone call service usually. Otherwise, cheap cell phone is needed to use poor quality of cell phone call service usually. So, cell phone call plan is needed to follow the cell phone quality and price to be used and they ought have direct relationship to influence why the cell phone buyer who chooses to use the cell phone call plan.

Finally, behavioral economy can also apply to be used to labor supply as a motivating in negative or positive labor supply elasticities in taxi driving example. For example, it is possible that taxi drivers work fewer hours when wages are high-consistent with a model of daily income targeting. This finding is that when wages are high (perhaps it is raining and thus it is easy to find people who want a taxi ride), taxi drivers are able to hit their daily target quickly and then go home. However, when wages are low, taxi drivers are not able to hit their target quickly and thus work additional hours in order to hit their target. It means taxi driver's behaviour produce the effect that taxi driver works more when wages are low than when wagers are high. This work has resulted to analyze taxi driver of labor supply decisions with daily reference points in non taxi domains. So, instead of the weather and client numbers and taxi charge factors, the factors of taxi drivers' hours worked and the quality of service is produced is another important factor to influence any taxi drivers' numbers to supply to the taxi market.

Behavioral economic has also influenced the understanding of how staffs can impact worker productivity and job satisfaction. For example, it is possible that poor cooperation can cause worker productivity decreases and it can also cause poor job satisfaction to the worker. So, when working environment can impact productivity, social comparisons can have an impact on job satisfaction as well as the worker's job satisfaction and search intentions are affected by knowing about the salaries of their peers in whose firm. Hence, the worker's positive or negative psychological feeling to whose employers which will have effort to influence whose working performance and productivity to whose firm in possible.

Behavioral economic is increasingly being used in the field of development economics or low income countries. Such as, how Philippines can offer commitment to individuals who wanted to save money in whose country or how Philippines can change to smoking behaviour when commitment devices were offered to Philippine smokers. So, Philippines policy makers need to concern resource scarcity and resource allocation issue to solve how to let its low income level householders can raise to the middle income level to achieve the high income level householders and the low income level householders whose income level is not distant very much.

Have behavioral economy and psychology methods close relationship.

Finally, I shall analyze whether it has close relationship between the discipline of behavioral economy and psychology which two branches are totally opposite or if the behavioral theories is only complement that mainstream economics. I think study of economy is the behavior of the complex human beings; this science examines how people choose to act and allocate resources in different market situations. So the economic analysis, is based on the implications that arise from a series of simple assumptions (which are sometimes cited as unrealistic) regarding the human nature. However, in psychological view, the individual is characterized by unlimited rationality and by the ability to follow time consistent, in every situation, his self-interest. In these conditions, behavioral economic attempts to consider a field of analysis in the study of economic phenomena.

Because economics deals with the study of human behaviour on the market, it highlights the human character of the science and the fact that, besides of all the patterns and models, the analysis refers to the real individual. It is also behavioural because it attempts to combine approaches from several sciences mainly from economics and psychology, and also from sociology, philosophy, anthropology or biology. This is not an easy mission, in the conditions in which these various disciplines have adopted in time different approaches that became, in many ways, contradictory. So, behavioural economics is that a multidisciplinary approach will increase the explanatory power of economics.

On one hand, there are specialists two argue that behavioural economic is a field of economics that continues the hand, there are others who see it as a distinctive school of thought, which proposes a new paradigm. However, behavioural economists propose a multidisciplinary study, criticize certain assumptions on which the traditional model is built (such as rationality and self-interest, in their unlimited form), resource to experiments (the classical method of psychology) to validate some assumptions, propose new theories (such as the prospect theory) and advance different interpretations of the economic behaviour, e.g. how to maximize consumers satisfy their needs. This issue is concerned to concern consumption of psychology and social economic situation research aspect.

Also, I think that behavioural economics can help the economic science by describing more realistically the utility functions of the individuals. This field of study is based rather it is a natural extension of the basic approach. However, it is can be claimed that behavioural economics is also built on the premise that psychology methods and assumptions are equally important. Also, models of behavioural economics, allow the utility to depend on the differences between one's own level and a reference level. People are sensitive to changes and preferences are not stable in time. The vision of behavioural economics concerning the inter-temporal choice (which assumes that individuals prefer immediate gains and delay unpleasant activities) seems to be more appropriate to the human behaviour that the one of the traditional model (which assumes that utility is updated over time). I shall give below suitations to explain how to apply behvioral economy method to predict consumption behavior.

● How can consumer debt management psychological factors influence consumption behavior?

In behavioral economy view point, it can be applied to explain why consumer debt management psychological factors can influence consumption behavior. Some consumption psychologists had investigated several psychological variables which have been suggested as causes or effects of debts. Economic and demographic factors can predict debt category well to support this influence of factor. How can consumer manage money skills to pay debt which can influence when who plan to consume? Debtors were more likely to buy cigarettes and Christmas presents for children than non-debtors. Conclusions must be qualified because of low return rates, but the results suggest that a complex of psychological and behavioral variables affect debt and are affected by it. It is argued that these variables are linked to the psychology.

In general, economical environment is poor, it will cause many unemployed people, even some people will loan debt to pay daily essential expenditure from banks. If those debtors can't manage whose debt to be better to spend. Whose behavior will cause who do not have more spending desires often. Because these debtors will feel themselves as being in a community where debt was more common and more tolerated than non-debtors. The whole question of the classification of products a necessities or luxuries and its consequences for purchasing behavior is of current interest in economic psychology. Since debt is associated with poverty and poor people tend to give external reasons for economic phenomena, such as poverty and unemployment, causality may run the other way. In either case, however, there should be a positive correlation between external control and debt. There have different variables offer explanations of debts at different levels. One factor may be a consequence of another, or the mechanism by which it takes effect (for example, different patterns of economic socialization might generate different attitudes towards debt).

Some debtors need to borrow debt (loan) for house purchasing need. So, if the house loan debtors who need to pay back whose house loan to bank for long time. It is possible that their house loan will influence to reduce to spend much of daily consumption behavior to buy non luxury and daily essential products for long time. Thus, the result is these house loan debtors will reduce every day essential expenditure, such as food and soft drink, entertainment etc. to consume too much to compare to non house loan debtors for long time. It seems that retailers can attempt to apply debt management behavior to predict consumer shopping of desires.

In conclusion, I shall indicate two theories to explain why economy and psychology has close relationship to influence human do any behavioural economic activities daily. For example, through the prospect theory, behavioural economics adds new parameters to improve the mathematical modelling method, which was advanced by economists for decisions taken under uncertainty. However, the theory also proposes a slightly different interpretation. The results are interpreted by the individual as positive or negative deviations from a reference point, which has a neutral psychological value. Last but not least, in addressing social preferences, behavioural economics adds parameters that increase the concern of decision-makers to also assess their utility function in relation to others. For another example, the choice theory; secondly there is not a common consensus between the specialists of behavioural economics regarding the variables that should be included; and finally, many variables that affect the behaviour are not quantitative, but qualitative, and cannot be precisely measured. The findings of behavioural economic are relevant and can help the mainstream theory by providing a more realistically base of study. However, this argument has contributed to the development of behavioural economics, because there are a large number of phenomena that cannot be entirely explained by the mainstream economics.

So, why in the beginning, I indicated why behavioural economics does not imply the totally exclusion of the neoclassical approach and the most studies in this area try to provide a more realistic base of the standard theory. In the concluding, I believe that in time, behavioural economic models will replace the simplified ones, based on unlimited rationality. Also, economists have provided a great importance to the quantitative structures, departing from the human nature. However, behavioural economics can become truly revolutionary only it will always be receptive and will provide a critical insight to their own theories and perspectives, and especially the ones regarding the aspects that they reproach to the traditional economic theory. However, I also feel that the individual's behaviour on the market is determined only be economic factors. In brief, individual choices and, by this, the demand variation are explained only and the variations in the prices of products/services and the available personal income. Am important discussion in the field of determine directly the economic behaviour of an individual (like the sociological and psychological of factors) are actually active elements in the process the reshaping of the utility functions. Finally, in my view, I believe that the conduct of the market phenomena, as it occurs in reality. In this sense, the research of behavioural economics aims to see how the neoclassical model could be improved, using mainly psychology concepts. Although, there are some specialists who argue that behavioural economics can be an alternative to the neoclassical theory.

Finally, most findings, of my study conducted in this book, modify some of standard economical assumptions, in order to provide a greater psychological realism. However, the additions proposed by behavioural economists simply recognize the human limitations on (mentally) calculations, will and self-interest. So, I think psychology and economy has close relationship to assist any policy makers or decision makers to do any economic psychology daily. Because the purpose of economics is to better understand and explain the conduct of the economic activities as which occur in reality. Otherwise, human being is complex and its behaviour and constitution is studied by all the social sciences. Consequently, multi and interdisciplinary approaches can bring real benefits to the economic science, by providing a more realist foundation to cause any policy makers or decision makers how to decide to make any behaviours or economic activities by behavioural economic activities support daily.

● Can price change influence consumer behavior?

In behavioral economy view point, it can explaine why price change can influence consumer behavior. In general, under short –run profit maximization,

the price was seen as a mark –up marginal cost with the marketing determined by the elasticity of demand. However, economists have used these methods to determination of how prices change behavior. The first is the indicated prices are determined relative to costs by firms in the pursuit of objectives. In the view point, the first is firms are price-makers and let prices in a way which think will achieve these objectives. Subject to constraints arising from demand and cost conditions. The second is theory of perfect competition, firms are effectively price-takers and the interaction between demand and supply in the market set price. So, firms are regarded as price-takers, and hence not in position to set prices, such as price-adjuster . The third is the idea of observing the process of price decision-making and seeking observation is on the prices of price determination. Their view is expressed as price is based on full average cost , including a conventional allowance for profits and full average cost . Is determined as follows? price or direct cost per unit is taken as the base, a percentage addition is made to cover overhead or on cost or indirect cost, and a further conventional addition of percentage is made for profit. This, it seems price change behavior can influence consumer individual consumption behavior to any products.

● Can constructive consumer choice processes influence consumption behavior?

Consumer decision making has been an interest in consumption behavior research, e.g. how technological changes, an information explosion factor can influence consumer individual choice decision to buy any products. Due to limited processing capacity, consumers often don't have well-defined existing preferences, but construct them using a variety of strategies contingent on task demands. Rapid technological changes for instance, has led to multitudes of new products and decreased product lifetimes. In addition, new communications media, such as the world wide web have made amounts of information on options potentially available (Alba et al. 1987). It seems time pressure, such as fast product lifetimes and new communications, media, internet advertisement can influence consumers how to make decision to buy any thing which is the best to them, e.g. choice of gathering products of advertisement information to buy products from internet (electronic shopping) instead of traditional visiting shops consumption behavior. So, new information advertisement media, e.g. internet advertisement consumer information media will influence consumer individual decision tasks. For example, a consumer may be fairly certain about the values of some of the attributes to choose to buy which kind of mobile phone from electronic shopping easily at home. However, the consumer may not have information for all of the mobile phone options on some attributes (e.g. reliability information would not be available for a new mobile model) from internet advertisement. In addition, some attributes, such as safety may be difficult for consumer to trade off; making trade off requires possibly accepting a loss on such an attribute with potentially threatening consequences.

What is characteristics of consumer decision strategy in product choice process? It includes the total amount of information processed, the selectivity in information processing, the pattern of process, (whether by alternative brand or by attribute). First, the amount of information processed is very a great deal. For example, a mobile phone choice may involve detailed consideration of much of the information available about each of the available mobile phone, as implied by more rational choice models, or it may have a consideration of a limited set of information (e.g. repeating what are choices last time). Second, different amounts of information can be processed for each attribute or alternative (selective processing), or the same amount of information can be processed for each attribute or alternative (consistent processing). For example, suppose a consumer considers the mobile phones to decide that life time is the most important attribute, processed only that attribute and chooses which mobile brand, with the famous brand value on that mobile phone attribute. Third, choice process would involves on that attribute. This choice process would involve highly selective processing of attribute information (since the amount of information examined differs across attributes), but consistent processing of alternative mobile phone brand information, since one piece of information is considered for each mobile phone. The fact that working memory capacity is limited effectively requires selective attention to information, e.g. internet advertisement media.

In general, the more selective consumers are in processing information, the more susceptible their decisions may be to factors that influence the salience of information, some of which may be irrelevant, such as different mobile phone brands of product life time comparing information. Information may be processed primarily by alternative, in which multiple attributes of a single option are processed before another option is considered, or by attribute, in which the values of several alternatives on a single attribute are examined before information on another attribute is considered. For example, a consumer might engage in attribute processing by examining the price of each of the mobiles, concluding that mobile brand (A) was the most expensive, another mobile brand (B) was the least expensive, and the another mobile brand (C) had a very good price . However, the consumer could process in an alternative-based fashion or is design by examining the reliability, price, safety of mobile phone brand (A) in order to form an overall valuation of that mobile phone brand (A).

Finally, an important distinction among strategies in the degree to which are compensatory. A compensatory strategy is one in which a good value on one attribute can compensate for a poor value on another. A compensatory strategy thus requires explicit trade off among attributes. Deciding how much more one is willing to pay for very good rather than average reliability or long useful life time in a mobile phone involves making an explicit trade -off between reliability long useful life time and price for examples. Thus, in general, constructive consumer choice processes attribute , such as the product's price, quality, life of time , reliability, design , brand information of media sources as well as electronic internet shopping or visiting shopping buying channels of these factors will influence the consumer to do the final decision to choose to buy which kind of product in the consumption market. Also, any retailers need to concern whether which is the major influence of attribute to the product. Because wrong evaluation of the major attribute of the product will influence the consumer to make final buying decision when who compares the retailer's product to other retailers whose similar products in the consumer's choice process.

● How can economical environment factor predict consumers consumption?

The dominant approach to industrial economics is the one which is usually described as the structure-conduct-performance approach. So, predicting the performance of an industry in terms of profitability and advertising growth can predict consumer consumption in possible. The structure of an industry covers factors like the relative and size of firms, involved the ease of entry into the industry and the elasticity of demand for the output of that industry. The conduct of firms covers the objectives of the firms, price setting behavior, and attitudes to competitors (actual and potential), and from that the performance of that industry predicted, particularly in respect of profitability.

What are the main features of the structure of an industry? Many consumption psychologists discuss on the structure-conduct-performance topic, the number and relative size of the firms and the extent of barriers to entry into the industry to influence the product suppliers to consumption choices in the market. The number and relative size of firms is usually placed under either the size distribution of firms or individual concentration. Most industries don't fit into the category of a large number of small firms or of one firm.

Barriers to entry into an industry comprise all the factors which lead to new entrants into the industry being at a disadvantage to the existing firms because consumers have more choices to buy the similar products from the competitors . The first factor is the existence of economies of scale which means that a new entrant would have to produce on a relatively large scale increasingly. The second factor, the brand of products are supplied by a significant amount and thereby depressing price a significant amount , differentiation and advertising, so that a new entrant has to incur costs to overcome the loyalty of consumers to existing products. A third factor is the ability of existing firms to produce and distribute at lower costs than new entrants. Although, for example, access to cheaper new materials, accumulated knowledge of the industry etc. So, these external marketing environment factor will influence consumption behavior choices. For example, if the industrial structure determines or influences performance, the governments concerned with aspect of industrial performance (particularly aspects like price changes, technological progress and employment levels).

Consumption psychologists have often been assigned that the level of concentration in an industry is largely technological determined and that increases in concentration reflect impact of technological advance with increase the desired size of factory or firm. For example, mobile phone manufacturing industry, if the brand of mobile phone manufacturer had technological advance to manufacture any new model to attract consumers have more buying choices from their mobile products. Then, technological factor will influence consumers have more choices to buy the brand of mobile phone products. Other some psychologists believe the way in which unit costs change with the scale of production (cost conditions and economies of scale) factor which can influence consumers choice behaviors. When public policy favor active industrial intervention to change industrial structures, some indication is required as to whether the minimum efficient scale is small or large relative to the total market to supply their product numbers to influence consumers' behaviors. In the former case a policy favoring small units would be indicated, whereas, in the latter case large units may be favored.

Increasing returns to scale and economies of scales are usually defined as a situation when all inputs into the productive process are increased in the same proportion the volume of output increases in a greater proportion . How can economies of scale influence products supplying numbers? For example, that is the scale of output increases the degree of capital intensity rises. But within that change the type of the capital equipment is likely to be varied. Further, the balance between skilled and unskilled or between manual and non-manual labor may change. Thus , it is necessary to adopt a view of both increasing and decreasing returns.

The definition of unit costs of output declining with increased output. This must refer to all costs(including capital costs, and can only relate to a particular set of relative prices for inputs from which the unit costs are calculated. It would include any change in the price of input usage, such as mobile phone products which need to use different materials to manufacture any mobile phone products Thus, if a mobile phone firm had to pay more wages as its use of labor increased, that would have to be included. It is generally assumed that, for any scale of output, the firm is combining the impacts in an efficient manner. This efficiency includes economies efficiency (choosing the least cost combinations of inputs) and technical efficiency (producing the maximum feasible output from given inputs). The measurement of returns to scale under this definition may be only relevant to a particular economy, as it depends upon the particular relevance prices used.

Such as, each mobile phone product price will influence consumer individual behavior of choice to buy only one among the different brands of model mobile phones. So, mobile phone manufacturers need to concern how to reduce cost to gain economies of scale input to raise mobile phone output. For example, from a reduction in the effective price of an input to the model of mobile phone, as the volume of the styles of mobile phones purchases increased arising from an increase in monopsony power. For example, three mobile phone plants, A, B, C are assumes to have a fixed mobile phones output, and initially produce with unit costs A1, B1, and C1. Respectively. Supposing plants A and C would make subnormal profits and plant B super-normal profits, when capital costs are based on the historical cost of the mobile phone plant. Now the capital values of plants A and C are, it is argued, unlikely to fall and that of plant B to rise , for the amount which another mobile phone firm could be prepared to pay for a plant will reflect its profit prospects. If the decline in capital value fully reflects the initial deviations for normal profits, unit costs shift to A2, B2 and C2 respectively. Thus, there is a tendency at work towards mobile phone constant unit costs being observed. How far this tendency operates depends upon the based on which mobile phone firms value their assets. When the value is based on historic cost, the tendency does not operate. But the tendency does operate when the value is based in some way on the assets' profit prospects. Thus product manufacturers need to concern how to earn economic of scale to cost to avoid each product price will be changed often to influence consumer choices to other competitors more easily.

● How can auctions or online experimentation respond to predict consumer behavior and sale forecast accuracy?

Nowadays, in UK suggests that consumer buying behavior has changed significantly. Consumers caan buying different things, at different times and through different channels. As a result, forecast accuracy is very poor and many companies feel automated forecasting systems can not predict buying behavior more accuracy and relying on analysts to predict buying behavior by psychological methods. Automated forecasting systems weaknesses are such as: Historical data alone can't be used to predict feature sales in times and drawing together a wider range of internal and external data would help improve forecast accuracy. The impact on revenue manager varies widely. When sales forecasts are important, adjustments to revenue management system outputs are needed to retain credibility. When customers' behavior are poor to understand, there may be a need to sell from auctions or online experimentation to predict the market response. So, these automated forecasting system have these weaknesses to cause companies feel technological method can not be better than psychological method to predict further consumption behavior for whose products.

In psychological consumption of prediction view point, learning how to predict changes in consumers' attitudes and behaviors which is important to any companies. For example, in part behavior has changes as a result a recent major disruptive events, such as recession and exchange rate changes etc. economic factor, but there are other non economic factors to change consumers' attitudes and behaviors. For example, consumers are becoming smarter in their use of the internet to research products based on previous customers' view, seek out the best, deals and offers and then buy online, with a corresponding increase in the number of price comparison sites. So , companies are percentage seeing the rise of the strategic consumer who observes the dynamic of supplier pricing and adapts their buying strategy in response. However, some observers suggest that these changes to consumers' attitudes and behaviors are fundamental long, lasting and likely to continue to be disruptive.

Some consumption psychologists feel sales have become less predictable. In general, sales forecasts based on historical patterns in time series have become less accurate and hence less useful in the past year in many industries, not just these traditionally served by revenue management. Does forecast accuracy easily? For some revenue managers may be not too much, in some businesses prices are set by reference to the main competitors and forecasts have limited impact on operating and decisions about capacity. Marketing forecasting is aim to setting prices, maximizing revenue and managing operations.

However, forecast accuracy is very important to find why changing consumer attitudes and the implications for customer segmentation and forecasting of buying behaviors are not just relevant to revenue management. They are also fundamental to sales, marketing , brand management, customer loyalty, product design and beyond. Perhaps it has an opportunity for revenue managers to take a lead in influencing thinking of their colleagues in these areas. Some consumption psychologists forecast the future, who concern the historical data of companies collection before the recession, it can no longer be applied to forecast consumer behavior during the recession or after. At the opposite extreme, companies can simply continue to between auto prediction system to predict when the market stability will return soon and how to influence consumer behavior.

Sales are likely to depend on the economic situation, the competition and consumer behavior. However, these are external environmental factor to influence consumption of behavior. If it is possible to separate out these effects, then the forecasting model can take account of them by either building the economy/market into the model or segmenting consumers in an economy/market invariant way. External data, for example on the economic situation can also provide a good indicator of future sales. For example, internet (online) web site research technology is one possibility for combining and processing data from different sources on the web using automated tools. If buying behavior is changing and every consumer demand is becoming elastic, not only to increase revenue, but also to improve knowledge of the customers. For example, online auctions are mainly used in the travel and hospitality industries for offloading surplus capacity have been shown when facing only uncertain consumer demand. However, analyzing external economy environment factor is not effective to minimize risk to the sellers. Because sale forecasts are never going to be completely accurate and there is an argument for moving the focus away from being smarter with existing data towards making the business less dependent on sale forecasts. For example, taking close look at increasing flexibility in the supply chain or operations or re-examine the strategy for setting price.

What the current situation really emphasizes however is that there is certainly a need for forecast accuracy to be taken seriously by revenue managers and reported on by revenue management system. Thus, revenue managers need to concern how to predict whose consumers' psychological emotions to find why the reasons can influence whose consumption attitudes and behaviors changing to cause their product sale numbers had been falling. So, it seems that consumers' emotions can be influenced whose buying behavior by online auctions factor.

CHAPTER THREE

Behavioral economy method of organization consumer behavior prediction

How to apply behavioral economic psychology methods to predict consumer behavioral consumption to earn economic benefit? I shall indicate how to apply behavioral economics psychological methods to assist enterprises to predict what are clients' preferable choices to increase more attractive effort to win competitors. Enterprises include Walt Disney entertainment theme park how it applied knowledge management psychological method to attract more visitors ; Universities why need to consider campus building location and course teaching methods to attract students' choices ; airlines why need to consider how flight gas or oil price influences to passengers' choices ; underground train enterprises why need to consider route location influences to passengers' transportation choices ; Finally, environment protection product firms why need to consider what environment pollution benefits to society to influence businessmen decide to buy environment protection products of choices.

3.1 Apply knowledge management method to predict Walt Disney entertainment theme park behavioral consumption

In behavioral economy view point, I shall indicate health food consumers' eating consumption behaviors are similar to Disney entertainment theme park visitors' entertainment consumption behaviors. Concerning health food consumers who will prefer to choose health foods to eat more than unhealth goods. Their eating consumption behaviors are similar to theme park entertainment visitors who will compare which theme parks are more fun to attract who choose to visit either Disney theme park or other similar entertainment theme parks.

Disney has these characteristics to attract visitors to choose to play. Expecting to spend less time to queue of Disney visitors who only prefer to choose the entertainment facilities to play which only need them to spend less time to queue in Disney theme park. So, their consumption behaviors concern behavioral economy theory. Such as , the Disney expecting short time queue time of visitors who expect to spend less time to queue in order to play any many Disney entertainment facilities. In economic behavior view point, Disney visitors will feel queue time is same to money, who feel to wait long time to play any entertainment facilities in queue, who will feel to pay tickets to enter Disney, the ticket prices are not reasonable and unfair to them.

In economic behavior view point, such as for health food consumers, who will feel waste money to spend any unhealth foods to eat. Excess weight is significant societal problems, mindfulness may encourage healthier weight and eating habits. Some health psychologists found a positive relation between mindfulness and healthier eating. It causes some consumers concern health eating behavior, such as reduced calorie consumption and healthier snack choices, who also find causal effect of mindfulness healthier eating who found evidence that mindfulness is affected eating behavior by encouraging attitude preferences for generic mindfulness-based strategies which could have benefits for encouraging healthier eating behavior.

Excessive weight has several causes including physical inactivity, over-consumption of convenient food behavior. Mindful people experience their environments allow positive and negative thoughts and feelings to occur with less judgement. Mindfulness is associated with better mental health, relationship satisfaction and self regulation (Brown et al , 2007). Self regulation strength way, however play a role in other contents. Where mindful individuals face greater temptation, unhealthy eating may often result from a lack of self-regulations, which should be reduced by mindfulness. Thus, any one habit health eating behavior consumer will concern to choose what kind of health food to buy only choice health food to eat. So, it has limit health food demand to this habit health eating behavior consumer. Otherwise, any one inhabit health eating behavior consumer won't have any limit food choice. So, a variety of food demand is much to inhabit health eating behavior consumer to compare to habit health eating behavior consumer as well as a health food choice will be the concerning health food consumers' economic behavior model (attitude).

Walt Disney entertainment thems park had ever applied psychological methods to find what factors had caused its visitor numbers to be decreased. As Harriet Griffey (2010) stated that "sometimes, boredom can give disadvantages to reduce staffs' ability to motive to work and reduces positive emotion , such as happiness. Thus, it causes people (staffs) lack motivated reasoning to unconsciously evaluate evidence in ways consistent with whose preferences. This type of bias can hinder a company's ability to learn from mistakes and to build successful strategies." However, Disney needed to implement knowledge management strategy to satisfy visitors demand after who entered .Disney demanded cleaners to repeat to remember any information to prepare to answer visitors' enquiries. It will train every cleaner memory to remember any information to be long term from short term memory successfully and every cleaner won't feel bore to do only cleaning job duty. When every one feel places are clean, who will concentrate on answering any visitors enquiries as the same time. Even, if they can give excellent service performance to serve visitors to let who to know how to go to any places in the short time. It is possible that visitors will appreciate whose service performance to let their manager to know, so that every cleaner will have chance to raise salary. Besides, waiting time and queues are daily problem for Disney theme park. Fast lines or priority queues appear as a solution of efficient queues for clients. Disney understood fast ticket line system affected visitor attendance numbers. Disney entertainment facilities long waits leaded to lower service evaluations and greater customer dissatisfaction. Efficient queue waiting time management can improve Disney visitor satisfaction and the willingness to recommend the service. Disney analysed of theme park visitor behaviour in relation to pay the higher ticket price to select to pay more for fast queuing line ticket than common queuing line ticket. In fact, Disney fast queuing line ticket system choice gave potential queues to any waiting clients . In general, Disney visitors don't like to wait long time in every entertainment facilities queuing line, who will feel a waste of time and waiting can lead to negative emotional response like frustration, impotence, tension or irritation .In fact, Disney amusement theme park needed visitors wait long queues and delays which were a frequent occurrence in every entertainment facilities line. Disney theme park as sets of rides, spectacles and leisure mechanisms are intended to entertainment and spark the imagination of clients, allowing visitors to escape their daily routing. In result, waiting is often a problematic issue that can influence Disney visitor experience and that can appear as one of the principal motives for complaining. As Disney visitor demand fluctuates constantly and demand patterns are often difficult to predict. It caused extra staff needed for the extra line. Finally, priority services such as fast line system facilities segmentation of its amusement park. When Disney offer the possibility of purchases a fast line, which are creating two different group. Disney visitors who are highly sensitive to waiting times are willing to pay to avoid or reduce lines or visitors that are highly sensitive to price that prefer to wait rather than to pay extra money. Also, Disney provides extensive training opportunity for participants through its own Disney university. The question of whether their training opportunity can lead the improve human resource activities. On the third hand problem, Disney are also worried that employees may leave it and join other competitor to serve their parks after training. Disney shows a trend of increasing depending on human capital other than physical capital. It thinks human capital is the knowledge, skills, ideas and commitment of its employees. It explains that investing in training and development is essential to its client service growth. In fact, Disney had owned enough entertainment facilities, restaurants, hotels, shopping centres within theme park, but its visitor numbers are increasing to need to be served satisfactorily. However, it needs to train cleaners, entertainment facilities service staffs, queuing service staffs, hotels, restaurants, shopping centres service staffs, instead of it's entertainment facilities attraction.

Disney observes that spending on training and development is typically regarded as consumption, instead of investment. On job training usually can't be replaced by formal education, therefore Disney chooses to make contribution on providing further training and development to employees. Disney paid salary for staff training, which included classroom, seminars, symposia or conferences; computer based training, on site training, book and periodicals reading, formal mentoring and informal mentoring program opportunities to meet its old staffs and new staffs both needs of motivate factors to achieve advancement , achievement, personal growth responsibility and achievement and recognition to raise its business performance effectively and efficiently. However, Disney's amount of training has a positive influence on intrinsic motivation of its employees. Job satisfaction, salary, working condition, its policies, administration, relationship with supervisors, peers and subordinates are Disney factors to influence it's human resource activities performance. Disney training contents include these functional area: Raising excellent service performance include that hotel food and beverage service delivery, shopping center, merchandise sale, restaurant service, entertainment facilities queuing waiting service, cleaning and enquiring how to go different locations in Disney, cashier service etc. They are very important to influence visitor numbers. Disney implementation of knowledge management solution to improve queuing waiting line process. The use of Disney front line service staffs as human capital combined with knowledge of customer preference has made the fast pass an innovation solution to enhance queuing in the Disney theme parks. Disney ability to capture customers in virtual queues when giving them a pleasurable waiting experience has made them a leader in knowledge management initiatives in the service industry. Disney's emphasis on human capital within their theme parks, combined with traditional queuing theory to create more pleasurable waiting environments. Hence, Disney showed the value of tacit employee knowledge integrated with traditional queuing theory to reduce loss of customer satisfaction to enhance, goodwill and profitability. Knowledge management expresses itself as human action in form of evaluation, attitudes, points of view, commitments, motivation etc. It seemed that Disney agreed that human capital (people, knowledge, ideas, creativity) maybe today's most valuable commodity.

Knowledge Management Strategy was used to queue control from Disney. Disney managers have long understand the pressure of waiting time and revenue; who know that every minutes spent waiting in queuing is a minute that the client is not generating revenue. So, Disney managers have processed with design of a reservation system recognizes that guests can be freed from physically standing in the actually and perception of waiting by allowing guests to engage has arrived. Cope et al., (2008) showed that" the system was first tested at Disney in 1998. Managers assessed the system by surveying guests who used it. Results were positive and indicated that guests spent substantially less time in queuing, spent more per capita, and saw significantly more attractions, satisfaction level sky rocketed.The system was expanded in 1999 to include five of the most popular park attractions and was named FASTPASS. The system has since been expanded to all Disney theme parks worldwide, and is now in use by over 50 million guests per year .That guests have two options .Namely, they can choose to

Obtain a FASTPASS ticket and come back a later, designed time or Wait in a traditional queuing. Guests are assisted in making their choice by information regarding estimated waits of both options. Thus, can decide to wait in the traditional queuing, or take a FASTPASS ticket and return it a later time with no further wait. Once an assigned FASTPASS time is generated and provided to a guest, it is valid for the 60 minutes beyond that time, creating a window in which guest can return."

There are numerous benefits in allowing park guests to return to an attraction within a designed time frame. Queue Waits involve managing two major client issues:

1. How long Disney visitors actually wait every time queue.

2. How long Disney visitor think they are waiting by whose psychological feeling every time queue.

Thus, if they feel that who spend much time to queue, it will cause they feel angry and they also feel admission ticket price is paid too high to them unfairly. In general, clients were allowed the ability to see two attractions during the time they would have previously been able to see only one. This can viewed as an implementation of a multi-phased system, depending on the attraction picked, each queuing may be single channel attractions, the guest creates whose own multi phase system. Obvious, results, were that guests were able to engage in more revenue producing activities, saw more of the popular attractions and began to par take care, in other less utilized attractions . Wiig defined(1993)" Knowledge management in different ways and from different perspective. The emphasis is on human know how and how it brings value to an organization. Intangible asset contributes to corporation objective may be immeasurable and isn't simple to evaluate the impacts of knowledge management." However, Knowledge management may not be only factor influencing organizational performance. In fact, Disney refined technology utilization to improve the user design of all human resource related systems, improving timeliness (queue waiting time deduction), setting elapsed time goals and monitor performance towards those standards, considering to use of automated fast queue waiting system, evaluating staffing levels, a close examination of adequacy of current staff level is warranted, beyond to improve visitors satisfaction. Clients holding fast pass tickets may choose to visit a gift shop or any park concessions. Thus, Disney has ability to co-branded products and service. Disney's approach combining queuing and human capital. Dunn, J et al., (2002) showed "The use of fast pass provides an insightful application of the combination of techniques of queuing and human capital to strategically leverage knowledge management principle .When waiting lines are an part of the Disney experience, park guests build magical memories through innovation. It is Disney's recognition of front line service staffs that transforms that employees into knowledge who multi task in their roles.For example, an attraction host or a street sweeper may be a valuable Source knowledge to park guests. In addition to their primary roles, they may have a wealth of information about attractions for guests. They may be able to give directions, provide schedules, and offer helpful suggestions from their daily observation. This is the first stop to increase knowledge management . Next, Disney improves its clients' perception by minimizing the perception of waits. The use of the fast pass enables Disney not only to enhance the psychological aspect of waiting lines, but also to capitalize at the same time." Instead, Disney needed to give people specific tools designed to help them to do their job and solve specific business problems. Thus, after Disney learned how it applied the knowledge management method to solve its challenges, e.g. Human capital and queuing theory provide two very different valuable assets to raise its competitive abililty. Then, its visitor numbers was increasing largely and quickly.

It seems Disney understand what which visitor's individual psychological needs, who needs to pay reasonable ticket fee and who also dislike to need to wait long time to queue to play any entertainment facilities. Disney also understand cleaners have extra time to serve visitors when who can answer any visitor individual enquiries immediately. After the cleaners will feel satisfactory and happy if who can give positive feedback from any visitor individual enquiry. The cleaner will feel more valuable to Disney employer, due to who can do any enquiry duty during whose working hours. The most important, who have chance to get higher salary and promotion. Thus, Disney can predict visitor and staff individual psychological needs, then it can raise new and keep old visitor numbers and keep old staffs to choose to stay to it's organization to work for long term. It can earn more economic benefit for long term after it can predict whose staffs and visitors whose psycholgical needs successfully.

● Disney market research method

In behavioral economy view point, it can explain why market research can predict consumption behavior for Disney consumers. Disney can use market research method to predict what consumer behavior trend. In general, consumer will have choice behavior, when who needs to do decision to buy automobile among of more than one product choice or with the determinants of such consumer behavior as buying life insurance, putting money in a pension plan, using credit cards etc. actions. By comparison, questions about behaviors that involve a choice among less or more options are usually studied at a lower level of generality. Thus, consumption psychologists may be interested to know why consumers buy one second of automobile rather than another, why who choose one type of medical treatment over another, or why who fly one airline rather than another. So, consumption psychologists must clearly define the action, target, context and time elements of the behavioral alternatives to predict whose consumption behavior. For example, the decision to buy tickets on one airlines rather than another can be affected by the destination (target element): A consumer may prefer one airline for overseas flights , but another for domestic flights. Similarly , choice of insurance company may vary depending on whether who buy life insurance, automobile insurance or property insurance.

Why will decisions under uncertainty cause? In consumer choice process, who has chance to encounter decisions under uncertainty. For example, the attributes of each product were assumed to be known with certainty. Thus, the consumers knew the price, picture, quality, reliability and visual appeal of each product type. All consumers need to do was to be importance weights and subjective values to these attributes and then derive a weighted average. In many of choice alternatives are not known with certainty ahead of time. Often, the outcomes are produced by decision depend on the state of the world at the time and the decision is made. For another example, a LCD television can produce a high -definition picture only of the service providers transmit high-definition programs. To take this uncertainty into account, the consumer has to judge not only the value of a high-definition display , but also the likelihood that this attribution will be available.

Perhaps, more readily recognized are the risks and uncertainties inherent in investment decisions. The investment outcomes of a decision to invest in a fixed interest certificate of deposit or a stock market mutual fund depend on future market conditions. Whereas the CD produces a known payoff over a given time period, the amount and probability of possible gains or losses to be expected of the mutual fund can only be estimated.

Thus, advertising can reduce decision uncertainty to consumers' choices. If the product advertising can attract to consumer's consideration

, it will persuade the consumer to choose to buy the brand of product. Clearly, information about the decision making process, in general, as well as about decisions of particular relevance to consumer behavior. Thus, it seems advertising information can reduce consumers' choices processes under uncertainty to decide to buy the brand of product preference choice.

Why businessmen need to divide customer segment(s) to decide who is target customer group to predict consumer behavior. Nowadays, consumers are unique in themselves. A comprehensive knowledge of consumers and their consumption behavior is essential for a firm to succeed. In order to understand and predict consumption patterns and behaviors within segment(s), market research becomes essential.

Why businessmen need to concern market research with consumer behavior. Each individual is unique himself/herself and needs and wants vary from person to person. Markets identify segments and target one or few of these segments and target one or few of these segments and thereby fulfil the qualifications of the marketing concept. First, marketers need to identify customer needs and wants and then, deliver product and service offering, so as to satisfy the customers more efficiently and effectively, than the competitors.

Such as Disney, in order to understand and predict each visitor consumption pattern and behavior within segment(s), e.g. young, adult, old age, rich and poor segment. It seems Disney has many different age , student or working people customer segments. So, market research becomes essential to assist Disney to predict what different market segment needs. Such as young age segment needs excitement, e.g. entertainment facilities to play . Otherwise, old age segment needs not excitement entertainement facilities , this old age segment needs to walk in Disney garden or go to shopping centre or sit down to watch Disney movies etc. not excitement activites to. Market research defines to gather information about market and the customers. The environment of a firm, such as Disney may be grouped as the micro and macro environment both. The micro environment firm comprises forces to close affect the firm directly. For example, the firm's internal environment, the founder/leader and whose vision and mission, clients, competitors, suppliers and channel intermediaries. The macro environment, on the other hand, companies forces in the environment that first affect the micro environment and thought that which affect the firm, in other words, which affect the firm indirectly, including the demographic factors, socio-economic factors, political factors, technological factors, cultural factors, natural factors etc. The micro environment is studied in terms of strength(s) and weakness and when the macro environment is studied in terms of opportunities and threat(s) analysis of both comprises the SWOT analysis.

Thus, Disney market research can help which to understand the specific marketing situation facing . Identifies the needs and wants of Disney different age client segment(s), identifies variables age target segment(s), serves them better through formulation of appropriate marketing strategies a mix of the 4(p)s. It's goal is to achieve maximum efficiency and effectiveness to meet customer needs and wants and client satisfaction . Thus is obtained through a conscious attempt at understanding " what" the disney young or old age target needs, "why" who needs, "when" who needs, from "where" who needs, "how" much who needs and "how" often who needs during who are staying in Disney theme park at the staying time. Thus, the integration of Disney market research with Disney visitors behavior: Disney marketing research can understand and predict any different age segment behavior as well as Disney consumer research is a process and tools to be used to study what consumer behavior is or who expect to buy when Disney visitors are staying in Disney theme park.

Marketing research objective is to study the marketing environment and the clients who are a part of it, as well as to study consumers as individuals as groups. It focuses to establish trends and identify opportunities and threats in the environment, to study the market and forecast potential and to predict buying patterns based on modeling and , to understand consumption behavior and consumption patterns. Besides, consumer behavior research has tradition approach and current approach has traditional approach and current approach.

Traditional approach divides positivist and interpretivist both approaches. Positivist approach refers to as modernism is the earliest approach to studying consumer behavior and trends the study as an applied science. It lays emphasis on the causes of consumer behavior, these causes are directly related to effects. Thus it treats consumer as "rational" human things, who make purchase decisions after collecting information and weighing all alternatives. The process of consumer decision making, it seems of rationality, rational decision making and problem solving is the key. It is based on certain assumption, consumer actions based on cause and effect relationship can be generalized, who can be objectively measured and tested. If researchers could identify the reasons behind consumption behavior, who would be able to predict it, and if who could predict consumer behavior, who could influence it.

The methods focus on prediction of client behavior, including surveys, observations and experiments. It aims at drawing conclusions a large samples. The positivist consumer actions can be objectively measured and tested. It focuses to predict consumer behavior, e.g. large samples of quantitative methodology. Otherwise, the interpretivist consumer action is a cause and effect relationship can't be generalized , consumption pattern and behaviors are unique, these are unpredictable. Consumer actions are unique and different both between two consumers, and/or within the same consumer at different times and situations. It can't be objectively measured, tested and generalized. It focuses the act of understanding the consumption rather than predicting the act of purchase, e.g. methodology small samples of qualitative methodology.

In consumption psychological view point, the current approach is the term " dialectics" , considers all forms of human behavior, thus the current approach to the study of consumer divided into four approaches: materialism approach implies that consumer behavior is shaped by the material environment, e.g. money, possessions etc. , change approach means consumer behavior is " dynamic" in nature, it is always in a process of continuous motion, transformation and change. Totality means consumption behavior is " interconnected" with other forms of human contradiction means views changes in consumer behavior as arising from their internal contradictions, like moods, emoting etc. The approach studies the consumer as a complex total whole and views consumer purchase as well as consumption processes.

The current approach to studying consumer behavior uses both the quantitative as well as qualitative approaches. There are three broad research perspectives in consumer behavior: they are as follows:

Decision making perspective, the experiment perspective and behavioral influence perspective. According to decision making perspective , the buying process is a sequential in nature, with the consumer perceiving that there exists a problem and that moving across a series of logical and rational steps to solve the problem; stages being problem recognition, information search, evaluation of alternatives , purchase decision and past purchase behavior, it emphasizes rational , logical and cognitive approach to consumer decision making and purchase process.

The experiential perspective believes that not all buying may be rational and logical, in some cases, buying results are from a consumers' desire for fun and fantasy, pleasures, emotions and moods. The perspective emphasizes that consumers are feelers as well as thinkers. The behavioral influence perspective holds that forces in the environment stimulate a consumer to make purchases without developing beliefs and attitudes about the product.

In general, quantitative research is used by the positivists and qualitative research is used by interpretivists. How to use quantitative research in consumer behavior? It comprises (i) research techniques that are used to gather quantitative data over large samples randomly and (ii) statistical tools and techniques, e.g. survey, observation and experiments techniques. Thus type of research is descriptive in nature. It is primarily used by the positivists when studying consumer behavior with a focus on prediction of consumer behavior and techniques are also used by " dialectics" approach.

How to use qualitative research in consumer behavior? It comprises (i) research techniques that are used to gather quantitative data over small samples techniques , e.g. depth interviews, focus group of study is subjective in nature. The focus is on understanding consumption behavior and consumption pattern . the objective is to gain an understanding of consumer behavior and the causes marketing situations are unique, and hence the finding can't be generalized to marketing situations. It is primarily used by the interpretivists when studying consumer behavior. However, the qualitative techniques are also used by " dialectics" approach.

Today, both approaches and are used to study consumer behavior. In some causes, qualitative research may act as an indicator to qualitative research through case studies and other qualitative measures. Qualitative research is very often a prelude to quantitative research are used to prepares scales for surveys and experiments.

Brand image attention of behavioral consumption of prediction method

Brand is one good behavioral economy method to persuade Disney consumption. Disney can apply brand image prediction method to attract visitors visiting choice. Disney is one famous entertainment theme park in the World. The application of disney visitor consumption psychology, and in particular to Disney branding, has gained popularity over the past decade in academic research and business practice. What neuroscience can bring to advance Disney entertainment theme park understanding of the consumer psychology of brands choice of behavioral consumption. The Disney brand preference formation over time has four basic components: (1) representation and attention, (2) predicted value , (3) experienced value and (4) remembers value and learning.

First, on representation and attention component, it means that the amount of information consumers are exposed to is enormous, yet consumer's processing capacity is limited. How Disney consumers represent, attend to, and perceive incoming information may have a profound influence on their behavioral consumption , i.e. Disney brand identification. Representation is the first process in entertainment theme park industry brand decisions , which involves forming the representation of the choice alternatives, that is brand identification. For example, different beer brands provide different options for choice are identified to consumers. At the same time, the entertainment theme park consumer needs to integrate information on internal state , (e.g. thirst level) and external states , e.g. (location , social context) that drive attention. For example, when faced with a choice between a entertainment theme park consumer's choice is likely to depend on whose own level of entertainment theme park playing facilities (an internal state) and level of entertainment facilities chooses to play (an external state). However, the entertainment theme park brand image is a visual system allows for rapid entertainment theme park brand and entertainment service performance identification. One of the key questions at this stage is what entertainment theme park consumers pay attention to (i.e. focus on) once who are exposed to a number of rapidly identified entertainment theme park choice alternatives (i.e. theme park images).

Attention is the mechanism responsible for selecting the information that gains preferential status above other available information for researching on entertainment theme park image. Thus, if the enteaintment theme park brand image is attractive, then it will be probable attract the initial eye movement of entertainment theme park consumers and thus may have a profound effect on related theme park consumer behavior. For example, Pieters and Wedel (2007) showed that ensuring that consumers pay attention to the brand displayed in a print ad. It is the most effective way to ensure that who will transfer their attention to other elements of the print ad. So, entertainment theme park image of attractive visual selection and eye movement can enhance the quality of incoming information to consumer individual behavioral consumption for the entertainment theme park of choice. The suggestion of eye-tracking is as a useful tool for determining the extent to which entertainment theme park consumers find different entertainment facilities images extensions plausible. In sum, representation and attention are complex processes that influence all subsequent steps in our brand decisions framework.

Next, the step is predicted value, it is of each (entetainment theme park image) brand that is available for choice to represent the entertainment theme park consumer's belief about the experienced value of that brand at same time in the future. In other words, the predicted values involves the consumer's evaluation of how much enjoyment who will desire form playing theme park facilities among of different theme park of entertainment service choice. For example, clothes are at different retail stores (e.g. H&M vs. Zara), consumer who are loyal to a store as measured by real purchasing behavior. (i.e. amount spent, frequency and recent of purchases based on loyalty card data) show more activation in the compared to consumers who are less loyal. The cloth brand inviting loyalty card holders who will be persuaded by the brand . So, the loyalty card of the brand, e.g. Disney loyalty card of park's visitors can be the predicted value to the Disney image of the entertainment facilities to persuade the Disney loyalty card holders to choose to pay admission fee to enter Disney theme park to play.

Next, the step is experienced value , it is based on the pleasure derived from consuming a brand, such as Disney entetainment facilities service. It is a concept of motivational value to the consumer. Motivational value is a concept that is related to how predicted and experienced values interact is the motivational value or incentive of an option to the consumer. So building good brand image memory us important to influence consumer psychology. For example, the information of channel ,.e.g. ad. can build brand image memory to consumer more easily. Thus, good brand image can build good memory to consumers to prefer to choose to buy the brand of product easily. Otherwise, bad brand image can build bad memory to consumers to not prefer to choose to buy the brand of product easily. Thus, manufacturers or sellers can not neglect how to build good brand image to attract any consumer individual attention by attrative advertising because good brand image has close relationship with psychological consumption for shopping. It seems brand loyalty of famous degree can help businessmen to predict whether consumers are accepting or are not accepting to choose to buy their products or consume their service provision more accurate. For example, if the product brand is very famous long term, it seems consumers are accepting to choose to buy the product. Otherwise, if the product brand is not famous long term, it seems consumers are not ccepting to choose to buy the product.

Can scientific research method predict Disney visitors behavior ?

Using scientific research methods to predict Disney consumption behavior phenomena in this field, some experts had attempted to do research in predictive validity to evaluate whether a measure of scientific achievement to consumer behavior. There are three groups thought to have varying knowledge of and ability to predict consumer behavior are academics, marketing practitioners and consumers in general. Academic groups use their scientific knowledge of consumer behavior as a basic for such activities as teaching, consulting for corporations, and testifying in legal and regulatory proceedings. In contrast, marketing practitioners are likely to be as familiar with this scientific literature. However, practitioners gain expertise through their experience. This expertise might help them to make accurate predictions of consumer behavior. Finally, when few studies on consumer behavior reach the general public, consumer's personal experiences should help them to predict certain aspects of customer behavior. So, it seems that whether Disney ought choose to do consumer behavioral psychological method to predict consumer behavior, such as personal experiences (psychological feeling) method is more accurate than to scientific method, such as marketing research method.

In this discussion, I shall imply two hypotheses about why Disney experts ought measure consumer behavior by behavioral psychological method predictions more than scientistic method, such as marketing research method . The first hypothesis, experts can make more accurate predictions than novices as well as the second hypothesis, academics can make more accurate predictions them practitioners. Thus, these hypotheses bring the questions and asked the subjects to predict whether each hypothesis tended to be true or false. For example, whether the more frequently an adolescent interacts with peers about consumption matters is the greater the tendency to use peer preferences in evaluating products? (Moschis & Moore, 1979). Will a person be more satisfied with their recently purchased car if the car met or exceeded whose expectations? (Westbrook 1980). Hence, using behavioral psychological prediction method , it will ask these these questions to gather the data to attempt to analyze what factors can influence whose satisfied feeling during who play any Disney entertainment facilties. These survey questions can include: Will a disney visitor feel more satisfied to play any Disney entertainment facilities with who recently visited Disney if the Disney entertainment facilities met or exceed whose expectation? Whether the more frequently Disney entertainment facilities a player with whose friends who have more satisfied feeling to play any Disney entertainment facilities to compare the less frequently Disney entertainment facilities another player alone or no any friend?

A long term survey research indicated that a consumer reserch result for the practitioner group, who worked with marketing problems, but who were unlikely to be familiar with scientific research on consumer behavior. For exampl, systematic sampling was used to select 100 practitioners from the 1984 year American Marketing Assocication Membership Directory (academic addresses were excluded), a self addresses envelope was enclosed in the original mailings, and two postcard reminders were sent. Replies were received from 20 academics and 13 practitioners.

Subjects were asked whether who had previously read each of the studies. Two academic had read most of the studies because few of their predictions were usable (three or fewer), all responses from these subjects were excluded. Two academic respondents said that who did not understand all of the hypotheses, so who were also excluded. This left 16 academics. Other practitioner was excluded because who said that who did not understand the instructions, which reduced the number of practitioners to 12. Six academics and one practitioner reported reading one or more studies and their responses for these studies were excluded. Finally, the predictions by expects and native subjects showed that the prediction of consumer research percentage is larger than academics experts. For example, by assuming that researchers typically found what who were looking for and as a result, predicting

" true" for all hypotheses a subject would have been correct for 74.2% of the predictions, subjects who gave a higher percentage of these answers would be expected to achieve higher level of accuracy. Thus, consumption psychological prediction method is more effective to compare marketing research. Such as Disney entertainment theme park needs to use psychological method to predict whose visitor consumption behavior to gather what the factors can influece whose satisfied feeling to be poor after who played Disney entertainment facilities. Otherwise, in general marketing research method can only find its similar theme park competitors' strengths and weaknesses, so this method can not get the actual Disney visitors' feeling more easily.

Can intentions Disney visitor behavior be predicted by survey research ?

How can be survey research measured that is applicable to intentions, attitude or satisfaction data to predict consumer behavior? Whether surveyed consumers will be predicted how consumers behavior are more easier than non surveyed consumers. Most academic studies of satisfaction use consumers' intention to repurchase as the criterion variable (for an exception, see Bolton 1998), and most companies rely on consumers' purchase intentions to forecast their adoption of new products or the repeat purchase of existing ones (Jamieson and Bass 1989).

In practice, some consumer psychologists' studies adjust the intention scores by analyzing that actual purchase behavior of consumers whose purchase intentions have been measured previously. For example, the popular ACNIELSEN BASES model forecasts aggregate purchase rates by applying conversion rates to measured purchase intentions (e.g. it seems that 75% of consumers who checked the top purchase-intentions box will actually purchase the product). To obtain these conversion rates, BASES uses previous studies that measured the purchase intentions of consumers and then tracked their actual purchases. However, investigating whether survey research is useful to measure consumer behavior. It has a weak point, a limitation of these studies is that companies (businessmen) focus on the internal rather than the external accuracy of purchase-intention measures. That is, the company studies measure the improvement in the ability to forecast the behavior of consumers whose intentions who previously measured for survey research experiments, not the behavior of consumers whose intentions who did not measure. Therefore, the studies assume that the companies can predict the intention-behavior relationship of non-surveyed consumers on the basis of the relationship that surveyed consumer exhibit.

It would suggest that studies measure the strength of the association between intentions and behavior on the same sample of consumers overstate that external predictive accuracy of purchase intentions by survey method. This would explain why so many new products fail even after which are performed well in purchase-intention tests by survey method. I shall suggest survey framework distinguished between two sources of measurement reactivity. The first is self-generated validity effects, it is as a strengthened relationship between latent intentions and behavior, due to the measurement of intentions from post-survey research. The second source includes all measurement effects that are independent of latent intentions, such as those that social norms or post-survey intention modifications create.

I also suggest a two stage procedure to detect whether the act of measurement alters the strength of the relationship between a latent construct that is measured through surveys, experiments or observations and its consequence (e.g. intentions-behavior, attitudes-intentions, attitudes-behavior, satisfaction behavior) and to determine the time relationship in the absence of the difference between non-survey and survey consumers behavior measurement for Disney. For example, prediction of Disney visitor's entertainment facilities choice behavior intention to find why the kind of entertainment facilities can attract more visitors choose to play in Disney theme park. Disney survey method can measure to any machine entertainment facilities. So, Disney can show the strength of the relationship between latent intentions and visitor entertainment facilities choice behavior is stronger for surveyed consumers than for similar non surveyed consumers in order to find the reasons why more visitors choose to play which kind of entertainment facilities.

I also suggest the Disney survey questions can concern to compare with other inputs factors of entertainment facilities choice decisions. e.g. personal entertainment tastes, mood, other similar entertainment theme parks' competitive environment. In order to make subsequent visiting Disney behavior is more than one time with prior intentions for every Disney old visitors. For example, Feldman and Lynch's (1988) survey method predictions, Fitzsimons and Morwitz (1996) found that measurement of general intentions to purchase automobiles increase the likelihood that buyers will repurchase the automobile brand that they also previously consume and that first time buyers will purchase brands will large market shares. Under the assumption, if the survey's result showed the automobiles brand-specific purchase intentions. Thus, Fitzsimons and Morwitz's results suggest that the measurement of general intentions increases the association between latent, brand-specific intent and brand choice. So, brand is a factor which can influence consumers to choose to buy which automobiles. In conclusion, it seems Disney can attempt to use survey method to investigate visitor entertainment facilities choice behavior to predict what factor is the most influential to attract every Disney visitor to choose to play the entertainment as well as what factor is the most influential to every Disney (re-visitor) old visitor to choose to visit Disney theme park again.

Can food consumption for trust cooperation influence family or friend Disney client group ?

Some consumption psychologists have attempted to do research to prove that food consumption with strangers who are assigned to eat similar food cooperating more in a labor negotiation and therefore earning more money. I image meeting for coffee with a colleges that just met. Is it possible that eating the same snack could increase your trust in that person? Similarly, could eating the same snack as a salesperson increasing your trust information about the similar food.

In general, people prefer to gather to share in a meal with others rather than eat alone, cultures define themselves partially through shared tastes and cooking traditions, and religious improve food regulations and restrictions meant to increase bonding among in-group members. Some psychologists had examined the relationship between food consumption and social connection. Development research finds that attraction increases similarly in food preference and also that similarity, in food preference increase attraction. Whereas, past research focused on the outcome of goods for food choice and consumption behavior is possible that group's food consumption results in social connection as increases liking and smoother interactions, presumably leading to interpersonal closeness. If the psychologists' research of social group similar food consumption is proved which can influence the people like to consume more than one person alone eats dissimilar food consumption, then restaurant businessmen only need to arrange what kind of similar food can attract group customers to eat as well as what kind of dissimilar food can attract one person customer to eat alone by their design food product advertising information.

We define incidental similar food consumption as group people choose to consume similar good more than dissimilar food with one restaurant table that is assigned and unrevealing of either preferences or prosocial intentions. Such that people eating together could become closer and more similar, with benefits for work performance. Eating may thus serve as a strong cue for signaling liking and closeness and more importantly trust and cooperation.

Our main focus is on understanding how food can be used as a connecting device that increases consumers' cooperation and trust. To the extent that similar food consumption promotes closeness and liking, it follows that it would increase trust and cooperation, and this would be particularly true for strangers who can't rely on past behavior to establish trust. Unlike preference , such as taste in music or political beliefs, some food consumption psychologists feel that the role of food consumption on trust and cooperation is influenced by food product information. Thus, consumers can be strategic in food who consume, utilizing food when eating dinner on adapt or when out for lunch with a colleague . Similarly, marketers can use incidental similar food consumption to increase trust in product information when advertising a non-food product. Some food psychologists believe that similar food consumption lead to increase in cooperative behavior, such that those who consume similarly will be better at resolving a negotiation conflict than those consuming dissimilarly. Additionally, who also believe consequences of similar consumption for trust in product information. So, some food psychologists predict group close friend or family relationship consumers assigned to eat similar food as a product advertiser will like the advertiser more, which will translate into increased trust in the information presented about the similar food product.

Summarize incidental similar food consumption should increase closeness and liking, when group people are absence of dissimilar food choice, when people are influenced to consume similar food by food product information. Thus, the increase in closeness and liking should subsequently lead to an increase in trust and cooperation for the group of consumers who consume similarly. So, some food psychologists predict similarity in food consumption serves as a storage cue of trust compared with other incidental similarity and is therefore an important domain for examining implications of similar food consumption. These food psychologists suppose to consumers who eat the same food as product advertiser will trust information about the similar food product is more consumption as well as consuming similar food can increase cooperation resulting in a faster resolution of a labor conflict and more beneficial outcomes to both parties. Finally, who indicate similar food taste includes, sweet food ,e.g. sweet bread or ice cream or cookie as well as salty food , e.g. potato or chip etc. So, restaurant food shall divide sweet or salty taste similar food. If one person chooses to eat the restaurant food, the restaurant can advertise dissimilar sweet and salty taste food both product information to let the person to choose. Otherwise if one group people chooses to eat the restaurant food, the restaurant can advertise either all sweet taste food or all salty taste food product information to let the person to choose.

Hence, it seems that Disney one individual visitor or one group visitor whose entertainment facilities choice decision is similar to any restaurant's one consumer or one group consumer whose food taste choice decison. Disney one visitor with families or friends who can be influenced from whose families or friends to choose to play which kind of their entertainment facilities. Otherwise, one visitor without any friends or families who can not be influenced from anyones to choose to play which kind of entertainment facilities.

3.2 University campus choice and teaching method choice psychological prediction

University campus location factor

University can attempt to predict student individual psychological needs to avoid student turnover numbers increasing and campus location factor can influence students' studying choices. Whether University location can be a competitive advantage to attract students to study? The school (university) location means that the proximity of city center and the proximity of students home. To increase the occupancy rate, the university location is needed to provide as a model and resources based view which will be used to explain why the school location is a kind of competitive advantage for universities. According to Porter theory, it is a part of factor, which has some advantages against the treat of entry. It can decrease the treatment of rivalry. However, a good place has a certainly positive effect for attracting staff and more students. For resource-based view, the location is one of the internal resources for long term economic benefit production of factor. It can be accepted as one of the physical and tangible resource of a university.

I shall apply the first attractive factor of Porter five forces and resource based model to analyze my opinion to explain why school (university location) can influence students to choose the university to study. This view is represented by the opportunities and the threats. The university of thought is the resource based view which is represented by the strengths and weaknesses of the firm. Porter's five force model of competition elements include threats of entrants or substitutes, bargaining power of buyers or suppliers and competition rivalry. A firm's resources include brand name, in-house knowledge of technology, employment of skilled personnel, trade contract, machinery, efficient procedures and capital etc. Such as, both tangible and intangible assets are considered a firm's resources. For a university, customers can be thought as a students, suppliers can be thought as staff. In higher education industry, the good transportation infrastructure and well-connected universities have some advantages against the treat of entry to attract good staff and more students. The place of a university can decrease of treatment of rival and a good place has certainty positive location is an opportunity for universities to attract the students.

The resource based theory of university location competitive advantage
Students choose any one university to study who will judge whether economic cost is reasonable to decide to study the school, e.g. school fee, transportation cost etc.According to the Porter's theory, the resource based theory can apply competitive resources to be identifies to higher education institutions. For higher education institutions, such as resources might include the reputation of certain departments, the grouping together of areas of specialist expertise and the development of technical patents etc. Also higher education resources may not be imperfectly mobile, as the competitive resources of a university identifies tangible, intangible and organizational assets. So, the tangible resources might include campus location, building capacity, conference facilities and medical research facilities. Intangible resources generally include such items as patents, teaching and research performance, service levels and technology and the geographical location of a service. In a university, such intangible resources might include some of the above and may also include employees/ associates, e.g. experienced professors, renowned authors and distinguished teachers. Also, the location of a university can be accepted as physical and tangible resources of a university. However, I believe location is shown as an important factor to affect the students' university enrolment selection decisions.

To sources of competitive advantages are thought to be the reputation of the institution, the curriculum and educational standards, school fees (tuition), location and student activities etc. different factors. Moreover, any university's general client segments include such as, high school graduates, elderly students and international students, that have been influenced by several factors when selecting the best university to study. One of these factors is again location, the proximity to home and easy transportation is critical factor in selecting a university. Presumably, institutions that are located along well-established public transit routes have a competitive advantage over those with poor transit links. Due to the efficiency of innovation activity increased in easily accessible locations with a high density of economic activity. The existence of education and research institutions as well as easily available information is suggested as a reason for this increase. Also private higher education institutions desire to benefit from these flows by locating itself nearby. Therefore, together with other factors, such as existing capital global flows should be existing capital and population, level of income and location decisions of foundation universities. The location, social life campus, proximity of campus to the city center, exchange programs, the curricula infrastructure, languages medium of instruction and activities are the most significant factors to influence students to choose which university to study. By the past statistic indicated that the location has 94% rate, the proximity of campus to the city center has 84% rate. So, it seems the proximity of campus to the city center factor is more prior choice to compare with the school location is close to the student home factor.

Huang (2012) stated that " the right location attracts more students and ensures the revenues of the institution. The location of an educational institution might influence its future prospect of growth. A good location attracts not only more students, but also excellent teaching staff". Because of job opportunities areas, the students are able to get a part-time job and earn extra money for their tuition (Huang, 2012). Marketing concept has four "P", it can apply to university educational business, such as educational promotion, tuition price, teachers of people and school campus location of place.

Finally, I shall give two assumptions to explain why if the university location is not popular to be accepted to the country's students in general, then it will cause who won't choose to study the university. However, even if the university's tuition is reasonable or cheaper or lecturers are famous or reputation or educational advertisement is attractive. In fact, the poor location factor will influence many local or overseas students who don't choose to study the university in the country. The first assumption is that most of students feel that the proximity of the university to the city center factor affects their university final choice decision and the another assumption is that most of students feel that the proximity of university to home affects their university final choice decision. There two assumptions are used to determine the importance of university location to attract the students. In Porter theory, either proximity of city center and/or proximity of student's home of a university factors have same advantages against the treat of entry. It can decrease the treatment of rival and a good place has certainly positive effect to attract teaching staff and more students. In resource based view, the location can be accepted a kind of internal resources. It can be accepted as one of the sustainable competitive advantages literature, location is a kind of advantage for higher education institutions.

The factor of student demand for alternative modes of course delivery

The factor of student demand for alternative modes of course delivery is another factor to influence the student who chooses the university to study. Any university's educational program includes program design, material production (both print and e-version), promotion, essay competition, school networks, budgeting, coordinating with various constructors, data base management and program evaluation etc.

Nowadays, university teaching methods may include face-to face, online and hybrid modes of course delivery. However, the several ways to students to deliver their course works ,such as full time, part time, internal/ non campus, external studies/distance education, summer school, winter school, semester study and trimester study. The multi site of a university , e.g. major provider of distance online education operates popular affordable learning for student to use internet to study. Although, students do not need to attend to university classroom to listen lecturer's teaching, but it can reduce face-to-face contact between lecturers and students in university classroom often.

Although, it is a technological and innovative and effective learning modalities. In fact, such new technological teaching modalities may be necessitated to the graduated or master degree or doctoral degree students. But, I feel the online teaching method is not suitable to the bachelor degree students. As the delivery of course content or the commoditization of knowledge must be re-thought to the bachelor's if the student can't enquire whose lecturer any questions to give feedback by face-to-face. Then, who will concern the course to feel more difficult possibly if who can't listen whose lecturer's opinion to solve whose challenges about the course any questions immediately in classroom often.

The second attractive factor of student demand for alternative modes of course delivery is another factor to influence the student who chooses the university to study. Nowadays, university teaching method include face to face, online and hybrid modes of course delivery. However, the several ways to students to deliver their coursework, such as full time, part time, internal/on campus, external studies/distance education, "summer school, winter school, semester study and trimester study." The multi site of a university, e.g. major popular provider of distance online education operates a flexible learning for student to use internet to study. It can reduce face to face contact between teachers and students into university classrooms. Although, it is a technological and innovative and effective learning modalities. In fact, such new technological teaching modalities may be necessitated to the graduated students or master degree or doctoral degree students. But, I feel the online teaching method is not suitable to the bachelor degree students. As the delivery of course content or the commoditization of knowledge must be re-thought to the bachelor degree students because whose knowledge level is limited if the student can't ask whose lecturer any questions by face to face contact. So, students will feel difficult to learn if who can't listen whose lecturers' teaching and to enquire any questions and to give feedback in classrooms immediately. It is possible that who will wait long time to ask many questions to prepare to wait lecturers to give feedback by email later if their lecturers use online teaching method. So it is essential that educators and administrators need to understand differentiated teaching demand to different knowledge level of students. Because student preferences may vary by age, cultural, background, degree types, learning style and matter etc. factors to decide whether whose students are suitable to teach by either online distance learning method between individual student and whose computer or face to face learning method between students and the lecturer in classroom face to face oral teaching educational method. In fact, working adults remain strongly associated eith interest in online delivery. However, the availability of evening/weekend choices is the second most important enrollment factor to adult students, due to who consider when enrolling in an institution to indicate the important of face-to-face traditional delivery at not convenient times. So, online education is most clearly suited to independent learners those individuals who are self-motivated and self reliant and those who have a problem solving orientation.

The 2006 year Eduventures survey found that students interested in associate, bachelor's and master's degrees were most open to whole online delivery, although who were also open to campus-based delivery. Similarly, Gartner's 2008 year e-learning survey found that complete graduate programs offered online continue online. For example, international student demand for Australian higher education is expected to exceed supply in 2020 year, and key 2025 year there will be a shortfall of 22,692 international places on projected demand of 290,848. There numbers imply that to meet demand, Australian universities may want to invest further in online degree/delivery options. However, recent statistics indicate dealing interest in fully online programs in South East Asia, and a survey of 469 transnational students in 2007 year found that a majority of students opposed online provision. These findings suggest that, when branch campuses are found to be prohibitively expensive, the future of transnational programs is in programs that include face-to-face interaction facilitated by an offshore partner of the educational provider. However, education consumers prefer to combine online delivery and geographical proximity. Some of students who are living close to university campus. So who can access to courses delivered in a traditional mode, but chose to take online courses for the flexibility to it afforded them. This is an increasing trend in U.S. institutions as well, whereas online courses are used to cater solely to non-traditional students at a long distance from the campus, increasingly such classes are made available to the mainstream student constituency.

Whether online and hybrid courses will influence to university students to choose the university to study.

How can the technology online teaching contributing improve student outcome? At least, learning outcomes for students in online and hybrid courses match those of students in traditional settings. When these are reasons to believe that the hybrid model would produce more effective learning outcomes than the fully-online model in theory. Also evidence suggests that e-learning continues to grow in popularity with the number of hybrid or blended courses increasing at the fastest rate, although online/ hybrid courses certainly do not outcomes courses presented the traditional (i.e. face-to-face traditional classroom) delivery method. These facts help to demonstrate that despite the popularity and increased availability of online courses. However, students still value traditional classroom methods and that online options may not significantly detract from on-campus enrollments.

Hybrid degree programs, also known as blended programs are courses of study that combine traditional classroom based instruction with significant amounts of online instruction, with each passing semester, hybrid degree programs become increasingly popular for students and universities alike. Such courses allow students to reduce time-consuming trips to campus when still benefiting from face-to-face teaching method allow colleges and universities to more effectively use classroom space and to reduce cost. For these reasons, hybrid courses are often praised as the best of both classroom and online teaching methods, it is possible that students have chance to go to classroom to listen lecturer's teaching and who also have chance to use internet to learn from online teaching method as the same time. These is no standard model for hybrid education. Some programs may have students split their time evenly between online and on-campus instruction; some may have students complete the majority of their work online with occasional intensive weekends of on-campus activity and some require students to enroll in a combination of traditional classes as well as strictly online classes. Nowadays, a major educational consulting group found that hybrid or blended learning was the most rapidly growing delivery option when online, hybrid and traditional delivery options were taken into acount. Because of the trend towards more hybrid programming, university officials concern on their potential impact on enrollment levels for on-campus degree programs. Some speculate that hybrid programs have the potential to overtake traditional programs, when others hope to use hybrid programs as stepping stones to attract more students to campus on a full time basis. The structures of different programs reflect institutions' intent to use hybrid programs to attract students from non-traditional areas. For example, Michigam State university's Master of social work hybrid program accepts roughly 25 students per year. In 2008 year, these students lived anywhere from 85 to 435 miles from the main campus, therefore frequent in person activities were not feasible. Gather in addition to completing online assignments, students attended a one-week-summer institute on campus in June and face-to-face instruction sessions in smaller groups organized by geography once per month during the fall and spring semesters. In short, hybrid programs do not necessarily replace on-campus offerings, nor do they commonly draw more students to campus on a full time basis. Rather, they complement existing program offerings by reaching out to new packets of students who have the mean to visit campus on occasion but not regularly.

In conclusion, any university ought follow its subjects, student age, school location and tuition, lecturers' repuation and school research facilities etc. factors to decide whether the course is suitable to be chose either online teaching or face-to-face traditional classroom teaching or hybrid (online and face-to-face both) teaching method to teach whose different degree level students. Because these factors will influence who to choose which kind of subjects to study. For example, if many first year students feel the subjects are difficult to learn. It implies that online distance teaching or hybrid teaching method is not suitable to be taught to them. The traditional face-to-face contact traditional classroom teaching method is more suitable to be taught to them. So, it is flexible to any one of these teaching method to choose to teach any subjects to university student. It is no absolute suitable teaching method to teach any one of subject in any one of university. Because any university is independent, it means that the teaching method is suitable to be taught to the students in the university. It doesn't mean that the same teaching method is suitable to be taught to the students to another university because every university's lecturer's reputation, school tuition fee, course's contents and qualities and student age segment and location is different among of them. It is very difficult to ensure which kind of teaching method must be suitable to be taught to the subject to all universities in any countries. Thus, if the university can predict which student individual psychology needs, then it can reduce its student turnover number successfully.

In conclusion, in behavioral economy view point, consumer decision making has long been of interest to research. Such as this university student choice factor, e.g. university location, course design etc. factors can influence students to choose which university to study. The most prevalent model from this perspective is " utility theory" which proposes that consumers make choices based on the expected outcomes of their decisions. Some consumption psychologists view consumers are as rational decision makers and who are only concerned with self interest. However, utility theory views the consumer as a rational economic man. Consumer behavior considers a wide range of factors how to influence to change the consumer behavior , and acknowledges a board range of consumption activities beyond purchasing.

These activities commonly include need recognition, information search, evaluation of alternatives, the building of purchasing intention, the act of purchasing, consumption and final disposal. Some psychologists regard man and rational and self interested, making decisions based upon the ability to maximize utility when spending the minimum effort.

It concerns economic man theory, in order to behavior rationally in the economic sense, as consumers must aware of all the available consumption options be capable of correctly rating each alternative and be available to select the optimum course of action. Some psychologists view point, behavior is subject to biological influence through instinctive force or drives with act outside of conscious thought. So, the consumption psychological behavior is determined by biological drives, rather than individual cognition, or environmental stimuli thoughts and feelings can be regarded as consumer behaviors.

Some psychologists feel environmental variables influence consumer behaviors. However, an influential role of the environment and social experience is acknowledged with consumers activity seeking and receiving environmental and stimuli is as informational inputs aiding internal decision making . Input variables are the environmental stimuli that consumer is subjected to influence to choose either to buy or not buy the product, e.g. brand, advertisement, price, sale channel, place, salespeople service, quality, loyalty, durability etc. different elements can influence consumer final decision making.

Some investigations indicated about the changes in consumer behavior are caused by external environment influences, e.g. globalization and development of information technologies. It can help to understand the specific factors what should be taken into account in evaluation of consumer behavior.

In macroeconomic environment view point, for example, the global trend of economic liberalization, new political geography, gradual removal of international trade barriers , rapid technological advancement these environmental factors are just a few of the factors that have had major effect on the business management practices nowadays. The most obvious impact on the practical level of doing business has these macroeconomic environmental factors intensified competition. So, these factors can influence micro economical consumer behavior indirectly. Consumer behavior is mix of elements from psychology, sociology, sociopsychology, anthropology and economic. Management process will identifies, anticipates and supplies customer requirement efficiently and profitably.

In consumption psychological view point, technical criteria concerns the cost aspects of purchase, durability, reliability, comfort and convenience. Economic criteria concerns the cost aspects of purchase, include price, running costs and residual values, e.g. a trade in value of a car.

In conclusion, economic environmental and consumption psychological factors can influence consumer behavior changing, so businessmen can attempt to do any surveys, experiment etc. research methods to predict how consumer behavior will change to attract them to choose to buy their products more easily.

3.3 How to predict passenger individual consumption choice for airline industry

How can airline gas or oil price influence passenger individual airline choice?

For airline industry, if the airline firm can predict global economy trend how to influence oil or gas price, then it can predict its passenger consumption of choice more easily. Due to we are entering globalization. In Special, airline transportation demands are also increasing, due to many travelers need to catch planes to travel as well as many cargoes need to be carried to planes to transport to different countries to sell. It seems aviation transportation industry is important to influence the health of the global economy growth nowadays. However, ignorance of internal or external market dynamics, catching travelers business can be detrimental to airline profitability more than carrying cargoes business. Because the demands of travelling different countries' travelers' consumption are still more than the demands of businessmen carrying cargoes in any countries every year. So, the passenger income sector is still have the important position to compare to cargo income sector in global airline transportation industry any countries nowadays.

How can negative social change influence any airlines' air ticket prices to be risen to influence cost raising? In fact, the increase in petroleum price can have chance to affect airlines in a negative manner because increased oil prices have resulted in the reduction of services operations, the number of airline schedules flights, even airline bankruptcies. Whether inflation, terrorism, oil price, bank interest rate etc. external factors have the most influential to cause the bad effects to cause airlines need to raise air ticket price to influence traveler numbers to be decreased.

To support this hypotheses, these are my research questions, such as : Does a combination of terrorism and price of petroleum significantly influence airline profit changing mostly? The alternative hypothesis was whether a significant relationship exists between terrorism, price of petroleum and airline profitability more than other factors, such as inflation, bank interest rate of these factors cause to ticket price raising. I shall indicate that the first assumption was that terrorism has a negative effect on airline profitability and another assumption was that only external factors as oil prices or terrorism affect airline profitability.

What is the relationship of oil price and terrorism to airline industry to influence ticket price increasing?

However the effects of oil price and terrorism on airline profitability was limited to a regional perspective, e.g. the terrorism attack of plane crash event to USA on 11 Sept. After the terrorism attack happened on USA 11 Sept. incident of terrorism attack was restricted to events of skyjacking, attacks on oil production, refinery and distribution. Other types of terrorist activities, such as attacks on financial targets or senior government officials could have an adverse effect on the petroleum and airline industry. I think the disruption of the production or distribution of petroleum because of incidents of terrorism was costly in terms of loss of business and the inflationary effect on fuel dependent products or services.

In fact, some airlines have adopted more fuel saving technology, so whose fuel consumption would not use more than other non fuel saving technology airlines, these own fuel saving technology airlines which do not need to increase ticket prices to influence passenger numbers to be decreased in possible. It seems fuel price increasing will not be the only factor to influence the airline industry's traveler numbers decreasing, in addition to terrorism external incident factor influence. However, due to some airlines which have fuel saving technology, so which can avoid to use more fuel to provide planes to use and which fuel costs will be reduced, then which can provide cheaper air ticket fare prices to compare the non fuel saving technology airlines. The result will cause some airlines will lose travelling customers in this global airline travelling market, also the non fuel saving technology airlines need to renew their fuel technology if which want to keep their competitive abilities to avoid to close down their businesses.

Also, I shall indicate the financial risk of airline industry evidence from Cathay Pacific airways and China airlines against key determinants of which include interest rate, exchange rate and fuel price risk for the period of January 1996 year to December 2011 year. During this period, these key external factors which were the most serious influence to cause these two airlines choose to change their strategic behaviors. Due to any these financial risks is difficult to predict and it was also changing often, these factors will also affect any airlines stock returns which arise from changing economic conditions, e.g. fuel price movements and fluctuations in exchange rates. These external unpredicted changing factors will attribute to the air tickets cyclical demand, capital investment, fixed costs of labor and landing rights to this global airline industry.

However, the relationship between fuel price and stock prices varies across economies. The effects of oil price changes in sub-sector indices, such as wood, paper and printing, insurance and electricity. In the past, on global stock exchange market was positively significant in 2011 year. Otherwise, with respect to the U.S.A. aviation industry, some economists suggested that global airlines stock returns were negatively to percentage change in fuel prices related to any airline firm value, e.g. Qantas and Air New Zealand were negatively share price growth to fuel price risk in the short term in the 2011 year. Thus, airline industy needs to concern whether the effects of oil price changes in sub-sector indices, such as wood, paper and printing, insurance and electricity influences to predict when oil price will increase or decrease because it will lead to influence its passenger travelling numbers indirectly and these sub-sector industries have close relationship to bring cause and effect influence to oil price to airline industry.

How can demand be caused by e-service transaction channel to predict passenger individual consumption choice for airline industry?

Electronic airline ticket shopping is one good example for passengers' consumption behavioral influence. In the past, if somebody wanted to buy a book, on little learned about from whose friends or relatives, first who had to go into more bookstores to see of that book exists and after to make some price comparisons in order to decide from where to buy it from one bookstore choice only. These activities were time and money consuming. The situation has changed how the person can learn about launching a book easily from social networks, and by simply accessing an online store, such as Amazon . com , readers who can purchase the book to save time and energy by pressing a button activity only. So, the process of buying a product simplified in terms of time and money spent, but because more difficult in terms of decision making which has become more complex. The main reason is people have too many options to choose from in terms of product or service, price, quality and time.

Can digital internet technological electronic service influence consumers to choose this shopping style when who is habit to spend time to play internet . Is lifestyle a tool for understanding buyer behavior? Consumption psychologists had examined to confirm that it has relationship between the consumers' general life styles and their consumption pattern and the brands of products are used by them. They concluded that consumers often choose products, service and others because who are associated with a certain lifestyle . The products are the building blocks of lifestyle, marketers should therefore, have a complete idea of these changing lifestyles. So, dividing to segment them and position their products successfully.

The lifestyle of individuals has always been of great interest to marketers. They deal with everyday behaviorly oriented facets of people as well as their feelings, attitudes, interests and opinions. A lifestyle marketing perspective recognize that people sort themselves into groups on the basis of the things groups on the basis of the things who like to do, how who like to spend their leisure time and how who choose to spend their disposable income. Lifestyle is an important concept used in segmenting markets and understanding target customers, which is not provided by the study of demographics alone.

Many researchers have focused on identifying the lifestyle of the consumers to have better information about them. This study used the lifestyle analysis to identify market segments. Otherwise, some consumption psychologists believe to apply life style analysis for market segmentation, the developed of product strategy and the developed of the most appropriate communication strategy. They suggested successful retailers based on general application of lifestyle analysis have begun to implement a portfolio management approach which focuses on the needs of the key target markets. So, lifestyle segmentation can provide a valuable insight into the task of creating an effective brand identity. The study of lifestyle often provides fresh insights into the market and gives a more dimensional view of the target consumers. The marketing managers may be able to develop improved multi-dimensional views of key market segments, uncover new product opportunities obtain better product position, develop improved advertising communications based on a richer more life-like portrait of the target consumer and generally improve overall marketing strategy. These consumption psychologists assume that the members of any target client groups are all similar. The first hypothesis is people differ in their lifestyle they can be grouped into segments and the second hypothesis is people belonging to lifestyle segments differ in their demographics.

Thus, such as airline ticket every consumer who can either choose to buy electronic airline ticket from internet or airline shop. In travel consumption environment, a travel consumer chooses a travel agent package or a airline brand , which indicates a maximum possibility of the definition of whose lifestyle identity. Alternatively, a travelling person makes a choice in a travel consumption environment in order to define actualize whose lifestyle identity if through the travel agent package products or airline brands chosen. It can be assumed that the travelling individual's consumption behavior can be predicted from an understanding of how who represents whose would be himself/herself of the details of choosing lifestyle system are known from internet survey or questionnaire method. Thus, digital internet is one good channel to research travel consumer lifestyle to predict whose consumption style.

In economic view point, demand is a model of travel consumer behavior. It attempts to identify the factors that influence the choices that are made by travel consumers. In microeconomics, the objective of the travel consumer is to maximize the utility that can be derive given their travel choice preferences, income, the airline ticket prices relates travel package products and services for which the travel demand function in derived.

Utility is the capacity of a travel package product or service to satisfy a traveller' want. It can explain the phenomenon of travelling value. Since utility is subjective and can't be observed and measured directly. The objective in microeconomics is to maximize the satisfaction or utility of traveller individuals given their travel package preferences, incomes and the airline ticket prices of travel package products or services who buy or consume in travel market. Thus, total travel utility of more or less travel satisfaction degree be caused by traveller consumer behavior. It is the traveller consumption psychological result (effect) and it has close relationship with travel agent service.

Are internet delivered electronic services being made available to travel consumers about how who are evaluated for travel airline potential adoption to predict travel consumer behavior? Some psychologists' past researches had focused primary on the positive travel utility gains attributable to information technology adoption. However, their results indicate that e-service is adversely affect primary be performance-based risk perceptions, when perceived ease of use of the e-service reduces risk perceptions. E-services are interactive software based information systems received via internet. E-services are important in travel agent/airline e-ticket business to consumer (B2C) e airline ticket-commerce because which represent ways to provide on travel demand solutions and improving travel customer satisfaction. So, it brings this question shows that whether travel agent/airline businessmen can predict travel consumer adoption of e-services.

It is important to distinguish the different between conducting basic travel e-ticket purchase transactions and adopting e-service. The travel ticket e-service adoption decision is essentially different from most typical travel ticket e-commerce purchases as which create a longer-term relationship between the travel consumer and travel service provider. Hence, even, if travel ticket e-services are an e-commerce application to which some adoption models exists. It requires a distinct conceptualization to travel e-ticket businessmen and traditional travel agent businessmen need focuses on the role of perceived risk on influencing on adopting intentions of travel ticket e-services. When travel ticket e-services are convenient and create efficiencies for travel ticket e-businessmen users. Little is understand about how travel consumers evaluate them for adoption. So, travel ticket e-service performance quality and the potential utility of the travel service usefulness is a difficult task for travel consumers, especially given the newness of the online e-ticket visa card payment environment. If the travel consumer feels e-transaction is not suitable to him/her to use for airline ticket shopping, then it is possible that it will reduce the chance to the travel consumer to choose to use the kind of e-transaction service to buy the airline brand of travel package products. So, this travel e-service transaction will include both risks (potential negotiations utility) and perceived usefulness (potential positive utility) to let every travel customer to feel either of high utility or low utility after who choose to use e-service to buy airline ticket shopping.

How important are risk perceptions to the overall travel e-services adoption decision? What types of risk are influenced and therefore important to the travel customer of e-service? Perceived risk is commonly thought of as an uncertainty regarding possible negative consequences of using a travel package product or service. It has formally been defined as " a combination of uncertainty plus service of outcome involved" (Bauer 1960, 1967) and " the expectation of losses associates with purchase and acts as an inhibitor to purchase behavior" (Peter & Ryam 1976). Their research's pilot test result have indicated some electronic service shoppers, such as airline e-ticket buyers concern for the theft of their private information, or simply its misuse by the travel businessmen collecting it. Members of a focus group drawn from the population studied to concern for the loss of privacy of personal financial information as an identify-theft. So, privacy risk was gathered and modeled as a deterrent to utility evaluations and the adoption choice to influence consumers choices to buy the product from this e-service sale channel.

Overall, some consumers will feel those perceived risks to influence who decide to buy the travel ticket package product from e-service sale channel. Such as performance risk, it means the possibility of the product manufacturing and not performing as it was designed and advertised and failing to deliver the desired benefits, financial risk, it means the potential monetary outlet associated with the initial purchase price as well as the subsequent maintenance cost of the travel package product (ibid). The current financial services include potential for financial loss , due to fraud, time with means travel consumers may lose time when making a bad purchasing decision by wasting time researching and making the purchased, learning ow to use a product or service only to have to replace if it does not perform to expectations, psychological risk means potential loss of self oneself. Travel consumers feel unwise if they experience a non-performing travel package products and may experience their feelings of harm to their self-image from the frustration of not achieve their buying goals, social risk means potential loss of status in one's social group as a result of adopting a travel package product or service, looking foolish, privacy risk means potential loss of control over personal information, such as when information about travel package purchase used without the travel customer's knowledge or permission. A travel consumer is carrying a criminal use whose identity to perform fraudulent transactions. Overall , when any one consumer feels one of those perceived risk will occur, then any one of these risks will influence who to choose to use e-service transactions method to buy travel package product from internet. So, travel package internet shopping seems have bad image to influence travel consumer shopping choice of channel as well as travel consumer demand of the travel package product will be reduced if who feel e-ticekt service transaction channel is not safe to whom.

Is online video and television service is to be affective in predicting technology adoption to influence consumption behavior choice? It seems online video and television and online e-ticket travel package service which are similar to behavioral economy analysis. Such as the online entertainment consumer who can use computer to watch online video and television in anywhere, e.g. library, at home etc. places. Even some online video and television service can provide free charge to let any entertainment consumer to watch any time from internet. So, who will feel no any expense. Online e-ticket buying service can let the travel consumer use whose computer to compare any airline companies' e-tickets prices and travel date and time schedule and travel destination from internet at home conveniently. So, who does not need to spend transportation cost or driver whose car to to to the travel agent or airline to buy paper airline ticket. Hence, both online video and television rent service and e-airline ticket consumption services can help consumers spend less time and expense to make consumption decision at home in short time. It is a popular online consumption behavioral economy model.

Nowadays, online video and television services have become one of the most promising activities in terms of advertising revenue. E-Marketer has estimated that online video or television advertising will soar at 56% to 70% in the next five years (Halleman, 2008). To predict user acceptance of online video and television services. Despite a digital growth in online video and television to service over the span of a few years.

What factors can influence consumers to choose to buy the product after who watch online video and television advertising? Some psychological experiments shows a greater influence of perceived behavioral control on intention to use this type of services. The effects of attitude toward use and subjective norm were positive, but more moderate. The lesser effect of attitude towards use may be explained by the evidence benefits of watching videos online. However, search recent consumer studies have confirmed that watching online videos and televisions has become one of the favorite online activities for internet users (Hallerman 2008. Mulligan et al. 2008).

Hence, airline ticket consumer individual behavior can apply e-service questionnaires survey channel to gather what who needs or expectation are chosen to buy any prefer airlines to predict how to satisfy or attract whom final travel consumption of decision more easily.

Can advertising influence travel consumption behavior?

Advertising is a subject on which people tend to hold strong and often opposing views, and economists are not expectations to this. Some economists regard advertising as one means by which firms concentrate on promoting whose tastes and opinions in the direction of their products and also more generally in favor of private consumption (consumer behavior). Other economists see advertising as an efficient way by which firms supply information to potential consumers. Otherwise, some economists see advertising as a barrier inhibiting new entrants into an industry thereby enabling the established firms to reap high profits, when others see advertising as evidence of competition and an aid to new entrants in establishing themselves. So, it seems advertising can influence consumer choices possibly.

Advertising relatives to sales varies considerably between industries. For example, the ratio of advertising in 1968 year varied from over 15% in the toilet preparations industry to over 10% in the soap and detergents industry to near is in a number of toilet preparation producer industries. A distinction is frequently made between information an persuasive advertising , and it is often suggested that some forms of advertising (such as classified ads.) are likely to have more informative content than other forms (such as television advertising).

What is the sale of advertising in the demand function? One response is that a firm can sell more of its products because consumers have more information on that product. The information may relate to its existence, price, quality etc. Thus advertising is seen as essentially supplying information to consumers how to choose the similar kinds of products to decide which is the suitable product to buy. The other response is that advertising seeks to persuade consumers to purchase with favored people or situations, repetition of the same message. This advertising seeks to promote tastes rather than to inform. One firms' advertising may not be successful through false judgement by that firm and its advertisers or because of the impact of the advertising of other firms. The difference between the two responses can be put in terms of the conventional; utility maximization approach top consumer demand theory. The first response regards consumers' taste (i.e. the utility function) as fixed and advertising informs the consumer about availability, price etc. So, that utility maximizing process can take place more effectively . The second response regards advertising and seeking to promote consumers' tastes and change the consumers' utility function in a manner favorable to the advertiser. So, different types of advertising have been as containing information and persuasion in varying proportions and varying in the degree of desirability. But for the firm, the intention is to sell its products, and it will present any information in a way which seeks to influence the consumer to purchase its products.

Some consumption psychologists believe utility maximization by well-informed individuals plays a central role in conventional micro-economies. However, advertising can be a part of the conduct of firms in that firms use advertising amongst many other things to seek to increase profits or whatever their objectives it. Finally, advertising can be a part of performance, influenced by industrial structure. Some consumption psychologists also believe the highly differentiated products are more suitable for advertising than undifferentiated ones. They suppose existing firms benefit from their past investment in advertising and new entrants have to overcome those advantage.

If advertising is a profitable activity for firms to undertake, then the question arises as to why other firms don't follow suit. If other firms possibly including new entrants did follow suit, then the returns to advertising are likely to be reduced. It is useful to discuss the returns to advertising in terms of the returns in increased sales per advertising message and the cost of delivering an advertising message. Increasing return would occur form a message of repeated showing of a particular advertisement led to the product demand increasing at an increasing rate. Thus, of the product demand per unit of time is same to the number of advertising message per unit of time, then increasing sale returns would be raised possibly. The implications of any increasing sale returns to advertising may depend upon whether the increasing returns operate for advertising of a single product or for advertising of a number of products. Thus, it seems advertising promotion behavior can create barriers to entry to reduce consumers have more choices from other competitors' similar products sale. Such as any airline businesses can attempt to use advertising to attract travellers to concern what they can give different or unique or excellent airline service to let travellers feel which airline service is more especial to compare other airline competitors, during external environment factor influence consumer travel desire , such as fuel rising or unemployment etc. external poor environment factor influence to global airline travel market. Hence, airline advertising promotion method can let travellers to feel why (what reasons) who ought to find the airline travelling service.

How can airline atmosphere environment influence traveller travel choice behavior?

On the one hand, some consumption psychologists suggest in-store variable factor can influence consumer emotion to feel either pleasure or displeasure of intended shopping behaviors within the store, thus these consumption psychologists who believe retail store environment can influence consumption behavior. On the other hand, some employment psychologists also suggest work environment can influence employee individual emotion to work, work environment include hospitals, schools and prisons etc. public work environment. It seems consumers and employees whose emotion will be influenced by environment factor. It brings this question. Can store atmosphere environment predict consumers buying decision?

These consumption psychologists feel the component of store image, physical in-store variable , such as aisle width, brightness and crowding, when clearly these physical variables are store environment's major factor which can influence consumption behavior will be changed. Some retailers have claimed large effects from manipulating store atmosphere via layout, lighting, color and music (Wysocki 1979; Stevens 1980).

Some consumption psychologists also show these avoidance behaviors can cause consumer individual shopping emotion. First, physical approach and avoidance, which can be related to store patronage intentions at a basic level. Exploratory approach and avoidance can be related to in-store search and exposure to a broad or narrow range of retail offerings. Second, Communication approach and avoidance can be related to interaction with sales personnel and floor staff. Third, performance and satisfaction approach and avoidance can be related to repeat shopping frequency as well as reinforcement of time and money expenditures in the store.

In consumer psychological view point, pleasure or displeasure refers to the degree to which the consumer feels good, joyful, happy or satisfied in the situation. Then, another degree to which a consumer feels excited, stimulated, alert or active in the situation. Thus, if the consumer feels the shopping environment is comfortable, joyful, happy or satisfied. The shopping environment, it will have more chance to influence the consumer chooses shopping. Otherwise if, the consumer feels the shopping environment is excited, alert, stimulated or active. The shopping environment will have less chance to influence the consumer chooses shopping. It seems each consumer individual emotion will influence whose consumption behavior as well as store atmosphere environment has close relationship to influence each consumer individual emotion also.

Thus, retailers need to concern how to design whose store environment, e.g. what kind of furniture color, style and size; how much area of the store. For example, the store area is either large or middle or small area to let many or small number of consumers to stay in the store at the same time. How to let consumers to enter or leave the store? For example, how to let consumers to feel to leave the store easily when the fire is happening in store, it can make the consumers feel more safe, so who will have more probable to stay in the store to consume. How to display whose products to let consumers feel to touch or see to find any products on the shelves more easily. Choosing what kind of music to let consumers to listen during who are staying to shopping in store, e.g. soft music or none any music (quiet environment). These different store external feeling factors will influence each consumer individual emotion to feel more comfortable or uncomfortable feeling to decide to spend more long time or short time to stay in the store. Thus, it seems store atmosphere environment can influence consumer individual shopping behavior, so retailers can not neglect how to design store atmosphere environment to let whose customers feel more comfortable and safe to stay in stores.

Hence, it seems that if any airline company which can design attractive service counter environment to let travellers feel the airline service counter comfortable and enjoyable. It will have possible to influence them to choose to buy any travel package service from the attractive airline atmosphere environment influence more easily. So, atmosphere environment has indirect factor to influence consumer to consume more easily.

How can airline counter servicer knowledge influence traveller consumption behavior?

Can model for understanding service encounter evaluation that can synthesize consumer satisfaction, services marketing, and attribution to influence consumption behavior to the retailer? Can airline servicer travel knowledge and service attitude influence traveller consumption of decison making ? These factors concern on the service industries how to influence consumption behavior, which focus on service encounter satisfaction and service quality to both the importance and the complexity of the issues. First and foremost, customer satisfaction depends directly and most immediately on the management and monitoring of individual service encounters (Parasuraman, Zeithaml, and Berry 1985; Shostack 1984, 1987; Sollmon et al. 1985).

What is the conceptual definition of service encounter? The model of service encounter evaluation relies on Shostack's (1985, p.243) definition of the term" service encounter" as " a period of time during which a consumer directly interacts with a service." The author identified all aspects of the service firm with which the consumer may interact, including its personnel, its physical facilities and other tangible elements, during a given period of time. I give this hypothesis, such as when an employee offers to compensate the customer for service failure, the offer may influence attributions. The employee performance will lead the customer to have negative beliefs about the firm, when the bad employee offer leads the customer to think bad image to the firm. So, the employee's bad service attitude can influence the offer is made to compensate for service failure to build bad service image to the company. Moreover, physical surroundings also are hypothesized to influence customer emotion in service failure situations. For example, if a customer experiences service failure in an organized , professional environment, e.g. lawyer, doctor, accountant professional services. The customer may not have more confidence to find the firm to serve to him again. In contrast, in a disorganized environment, the physical cues may suggest incompetence, inefficiency and poor service. In such an environment, the customer may attribute greater responsibility to the firm and be more likely to expect the same type of problem to occur in the future. Thus, any professional service firms, whose employees' service performance can influence customers' confidence to decide to find whose professionals to give any professional service opinions again. Thus, any professional service firm, whose employees' service performance can influence customers' confidence to the service firm likely.

How can the impact of personality and emotion on post-purchase service processes influence consumption behavior? Will consumption behavior be influenced to the retailer by consumer satisfaction or dissatisfaction and post-purchase service behaviors? Such as complaints, recommendations, and repeat purchase intentions, toward loyalty and word of mouth. Developing a new customer is expensive. Particularly in mature markets, competition is strong, product differentiation is low, and promotional costs have skyrocketed. So, understanding who these customers are, why who are dissatisfied, and how or even whether to market to them is an increasingly important issue.

That a customer's level of satisfaction affects much post-purchase behaviors, such as complaining and negative word of mouth is well documented. Satisfaction itself is influenced by comparing actual product performance to expectation. So, some consumption actual product performance will be needed to expectations by the product manufacuter or seller. So, some consumption psychologists began to research that the role of consumption based emotion in consumer satisfaction formation how to make recent personality research particularly concerning. It seems post-purchase processed can be a response to influence consumption- based emotions and consumption behavior to any retailers. The degree of satisfaction is a specific consumption experience, it has a direct impact on such post-purchase processes as repeat purchase intentions and complaining. So, any retailers need to concern on how predicting post-purchase consumer behavior will be.

Because personality should be an important predictor of consumption experiences, and thereby of post-purchase processes. Post-purchase processes can include either on positive consumption-based emotions or on negative consumption-based emotions. When the consumer satisfies to use the product, the useful of product expectation will be increased. Otherwise, when the consumer dissatisfies to use the product, the useful of product expectation will be decreased and the consumer complaint behavior will be increased. So, it seems post-purchase processes can influence consumers to decide to continue to choose to buy the products from the retailer again as well as how to reduce consumers have negative emotions to the products which is an important factor to influence any consumption behavior changing to the retailer. Hence, airline or travel agent counter servicer's attitude and travel knowledge will have either positive or negative influence to any traveller's final travel decision.

In -store consumer digital signage behavior how can influence consumer behavior

Digital signage is a new technology, where people broadcasting displays adapt their content to the audience demographic and features. In some shopping centers, retailers like to use machine learning methods on real-world digital signage viewer data to predict consumer behavior in a retail environment. Digital signage systems are nowadays primarily used as public information interfaces. They display general information, advertise content or serve as media for enhanced customer experience.

Interaction design studies show that the interaction level of users with digital signage systems will increase, including also the mobility of users around the display. Since digital signage systems can have a significant effect on commerce, which are also rapidly shopping centers ad retail stores. Retail generalization studies reveal that in-store digital signage increases customer traffic and sales (Burke, 2009).

Some consumer psychologists believe purchase decision processes can be described with five stages. The first stage is problem recognition, where consumer recognizes a problem is a need. The second stage is search for information via heightened attention of consumer towards information about a certain product, which can even resolve in actual proactive search for information. The third stage represents the evaluation of alternatives , which usually involves a comparison between various options and features based in the models of the expected value and beliefs. In the fourth stage of the purchase decision process, a provider, place, time, value , type and quality of the selected product or service and determined. The fifth stage are the final stage describes the post purchase use, behavior and actions.

Why will digital signage influence consumers choose to buy the product? It is possible that some consumers who like to use visa card to go to shopping as well as who like to use digital signage to confirm who are the visa card holders to let the businessmen to feel who are rich to let bank give trust to issue visa card to them to use. So, who do not need to bring much money to leave home to prepare to buy anything and who only bring one visa card to leave home safely. Thus, the digital signage systems are a new approach to automatic modelling of in-store consumer behavior based on audience measurement data. It is a unique machine payment method, which can also be used to predict more distinctive characteristics, such as an consumer individual's role in the purchase decision process. So, I believe digital signage audience measurement data can be used to model various user behavior for one kind of in-store consumer behavior prediction of method. Hence, it seems travel agent or airline can choose to apply visa card signature method to encourage travellers to make travel package purchase decision more easily by this electronic card payment method.

3.4 How does MTR (Mass Train Railway) need to
consider route design location of choice?

Nowadays, transportation and economic development have close relationship. Economic development stimulates transportation demand by increasing the numbers of workers commuting to and from work, customers traveling to and from services areas, and products being moving by lorries on the roads between products and customers. According to Bailey, Mokhtarian and Little (2008) indicated "transportation route is past of distinct development pattern or road network and mostly described by regular street patterns as an important factor of human existence, development and civilization. The route network combined with increased road transportation investment result in changed levels of conveniently reflected through cost benefit analysis, savings in travel time, and other benefits. " These benefits are noticeable in increased catchment areas for services and facilities , shops, schools, offices, banks and leisure activities by transportation route design of location choice.

Why MTR underground train transportation needs to know passenger behaviour

Understanding individual passenger behaviour is essential for the design MTR transportation, because who can choose to catch bus, taxi, tram, train ferry etc. different kinds of public transportation tools. Individual traveler who decides to catch which kinds of public transportation tools, it depends on whether the public transportation tool can provide real time travel information, liking link travel time schedule. So, any country's (MTR) mass transit railway transportation enterprises need to understand where it has terminal to give convenience to the local living areas of time travelers to choose to catch MTR easily. Although, MTR ticket fare is one factor to influence any passengers choice. But, those other factors can also influence them to choice. e.g. MTR any terminal location of convenience, short time travelling, none crowding in busy (peak) time, MTR platform waiting arrival time, none sudden MTR engineering machines broken accident events occurrence frequently etc. different factors, any one of these factors which can influence passengers who choose to catch MTR or other kinds of transportation tools.

Why route choice can influence passenger behavioural choice

Usually, the busy time passengers will regard the route choice as a coordination problem to influence them to choose to catch which kinds of transportation tools. The route choice is as an opportunity costs to influence any busy time passengers to decide to choose to catch which kind of transportation tool which is the best right choice in the right time among of them. In the short time, for example, it seems any busy time passengers will choose to catch bus to substitute MTR underground train transportation tool, due to who feels the bus can arrive any destinations to compare other kinds of transportation tools in the most short time. However even if the MTR can either charge cheaper ticket fare to sell full day or charge discount ticket fare to sell in the busy (peak) time to compare to bus fare. It is possible that the busy time passengers will still choose to catch bus, if between the bus terminal and the another bus terminal that distance is the shorter time route to spend time to arrive destination to compare between the MTR terminal to the another MTR terminal arrival time . Also, although the busy time passengers will feel to enounter traffic jam to influence sitting or waiting bus time to be longer time in possible and who also feel MTR can avoid traffic jam problem. However, usually any busy (peak) time passengers will feel the chance of traffic jam occurrence will be less. So, the short bus route choice is more potential factor to influence the busy (peak) time passengers still to choose bus to catch.

However, if anyone wants to investigate results of day-to-day route choice which can be transferred to more realistic environment. It is necessary to explore individual behaviour in an interactive experimental set up to ensure busy (peak) time passenger transportation behavioural choice. For example, a passenger has a choice between a main road (M) and a side road (S) for travelling from (A) to (B). (M) is faster if (M) and (S) are chose by the same number of passengers. So, this method can be researched whether MTR terminal station is located at the main road (M) or the side road (S) where is more suitable to accept to passengers generally.

Why trip time reliability and crowding factors can influence MTR passenger choice.

Other problem is MTR busy (peak) time's crowding in public transportation occurrence of MTR underground train transportation tool is becoming a growth to concern as MTR demand growth at a busy (peak) time. To capture the MTR passengers benefits with reduced crowding from improved MTR public transport service and image. It is necessary a identify the relevant dimensions of crowding that are meaningful measures of what crowding means to MTR passengers. Two main influences on MTR model choice that are growing in relevance are trip time reliability and crowding. It represents a benefit-cost framework. In fact, MTR passengers can be willing to pay more expensive ticket fare, it MTR can avoid crowding and short and the accurate arrival trip time between terminals is reliable to occur. How to measure of MTR crowding, e.g. weighting the gap between the busy time, the standard (i.e. objective) and the perceived (i.e. subjective) metrics. We are not in a position to definitely map the two dimensions, which is a crucial requirement for translating objective improvements into equivalent subjective gains that then can be applied, willingness to pay estimates MTR ticket fares to obtain the additional MTR passenger benefits of MTR public transportation investment to any terminal stations.

Because MTR crowding has a negative impact on passengers in terms of psychological on emotional distress. MTR passengers are willing to stand for up to 20 minutes of the service is fast and reliable usually. However crowding outweighed these benefits from a MTR passenger's perpective, experienced crowding leads a increased dissatisfaction. e.g. stress and less privacy during who needs to stand up in MTR. Due to there are no enough places to supply to them to stand up in MTR. If the MTR trip time was longer time between the passenger's terminals, who will feel more dissatisfaction and it will cause who feels whether who ought need to choose to catch other transportation tools to substitute MTR next time. e.g. bus, train, tram, ferry, taxi etc. So, from an operator's perspective, the MTR service frequency or MTR size is significantly influenced by the level of ridership, which sends a signal to respond if the monitored crowding level exceeds the benchmark standard in the busy time. e.g. in the morning time or at the night time, the students or employment people who need to go to schools or offices (working places). The locations of different places between MTR terminals and crowding are regarded as a key service attribute for MTR pubic transportation along with other factors, such as travelling time and reliability, e.g. service quality, none engineering machines are broken to cause MTR stops suddenly.

Given the increasing importance of crowding on both the disutility to existing MTR public transportation users and the influence to it. MTR passenger can choose to use either the MTR public public transportation or other public transportation. It is timely to review the MTR current measures of crowding defined by transportation authorities. MTR operators ought evaluate whether they apporpriately reflect MTR each traveler experiences and perceptions of crowding in busy (peak) time. I suggest that MTR needs to buy other underground trains to supply to the busy (peak) time passengers to let them have enough seats to sit down, so who do not need to stand up in any MTR underground trains when they catch MTR underground trains in busy time. It aims to let who are willingness to pay the estimation of reasonable ticket fares to compare the other kinds of transportation tools in the busy (peak) time.

How MTR can attract many passengers.

On the commuter departure time choice of any reference point researching hand, the departure time decisions of communters are of fundamental importance of peak period MTR traffic congestion. However, whether on the demand side, MTR underground train congestion relief measures, such as MTR ticket fare to every terminal station needs to be charged cheaper fare or discount fare in the peak (busy) time every day. To aim to attract many passengers to choose to catch MTR Underground train public transportation tools, substitute to choose other public transportation tools in the peak time.

Over the past decades, there have been very active research efforts in the departure time problem, both in econometric modeling and dynamic user equilibrium fields. Although, these works provide valuable insights into dynamic commuter decision making, they do not identify the commuters' response to gains and losses related to whole actual arrival time to reference points who may have relative. The appliability of the reference point hypothesis of prospect theory to the commuter's departure time decision making to obtain a better understanding of how departure time choice in MTR platform during their waiting underground train arrival time. However, every MTR underground train actual arrival time and deviation variables related to reference points (gains and losses) are the key factors in the departure time choice model. How the MTR underground train of every commuter's daily departure time decision can be modelled when the reference point hypothesis of prospect theory. The MTR underground train's schedule delay is defined as the difference between the preferred arrival time (PAT) and the actual arrival time (AT) for a given MTR commuter. In a daily MTR commute, a commuter in the indifference band actual arrival time is an essential feature of MTR schedule study. Two reference points are the earliest acceptable arrival time and the work starting time for a given MTR platform waiting passengers. In psychological view point, prospect theory proposes that the displeasure of a loss is perceived or greater than the pleasure of a gain of the same attitude and therefore, the value function is stronger for losses than gains.

To conclude, it seems that if MTR waiting passengers need not spend long time to wait underground train arrival in platform and it can provide seats to let them to sit down in the busy (peak) crowding time. It will make them to feel pleasure, even the MTR ticket fare is not fair and reasonable to charge higher fare to compare other kinds of public transportation tools fares. So the peak waiting time factor can influence the passengers to choose other kind of transportation tools to catch easily. Moreover, MTR's two reference points are the earliest role. Similarly a loss is observed when the MTR platform waiting commuter experiences or actual arrival time which is beyond that the MTR schedule time. Due to that a MTR waiting commuter is as an early side arrival of whose actual arrival time is earlier than whose preferred arrival time.

In general,passenger transportation choice consumption behavior is similar to alcohol choiceconsumption behavior.Because some passengers choose to catch the kind of transportation tool , it is habit cause. Such as some alcohol consumers who oftern drive the brand of alcohol , it is habit cause also.

Some consumption psychologists had attempt to research whether planned behavior can predict alcohol consumption. This research aims to quantify variables between theory of planned behavior variables and (i) intentions to consume alcohol in habit and (ii) reducing alcohol consumption reasons. They showed some drunken violence alcohol consumers who will reduce to consume much alcohol if who feel driving accident or causing death or violence behavior or alcohol poison causing non-health after who have consumed too much alcohol often. Thus, it is important to understand the psychological determinants of alcohol consumption.

A model of human behavior that has been extensively utilized to predict health-related behaviors, such as alcohol consumption in the theory planned (TPB; Ajzen, 1991). This model proposes that the most important determinant of behavior is a person's intention to perform the behavior. Three variables are identified as determinants intention, attitude, subjective norm and perceived behavioral control . Attitudes are an individual's positive or negative evaluation of performing the behavior. Subjective norms reflect an individual's perceptions of social approach or disapproval for performing the behavior. It represents an individual's perceptions of control over behavioral performance in the face of internal and external barriers. These results suggest the possibility that alcohol consumer behavior that are harmful to health, such as alcohol consumption, may yield different relationships when compared with results for behaviors that are beneficial to health. Specifically, individuals may wish to emphasis a lack of control over health risk behaviors, because these behaviors are not seen as socially , desirable and may need to be explained away be reference to external causes, such as peer pressure (De Visser & Mc Donnell, 2013).

It seems that the passenger will reduce times to catch the kind of transportation tool if who feels the kind of transportation is dangerous (not safe) , such as if the alcohol consumer feels the alcohol will cause unhealth to him/her. Then, who will also reduce times to choose to buy the brand of alcohol to drink.

Hence, it seems fear feeling psychological factor can influence alcohol consumers to reduce alcohol consumption in these situations, such as what action is being considered (e.g. heavy episodic drinking and the action is located (e.g. driving car) and what is the time frame for the action(e.g. needs car), the staff is a company driver when needs to drive car every day. Thus, whose action will influence to reduce whose alcohol consumption. Although, who has drinking alcohol in habit, but because who is one company driver, who is fear to cause accident to hurt himself/herself and whose staffs when who sit in whose company car together. So, who will choose to reduce to consume alcohol in possible. Hence, dangerous is one most factor to influence passengers who do not choose to catch it.

However, social mobile analysis is a good method to research what the main factors which can influence passengers to either choose to catch MTR or choose other transportation tools, such as bus, tram, train, ferry , taxi etc. Some consumption psychologists had using a data set involving on adults (26 couples) living in a community for over a year to find that social behavior measured via face-to-face interaction, call and SMS logs, which can be used to predict the spending behavior to explore diverse business because loyal customers and overspend. Their results showed the mobile phone bases social interaction patterns can provide more predictive power on spending behavior than personality based features. Interestingly , these consumption psychologists found that more social couples also tend to overspend. Obtaining such insights about couple level spending behavior via novel social-computing frameworks can be of vital importance to economists, marketing professional and policy markers.

The basic idea is that a person's attitudes and behaviors are influenced by several levels of society, such as culture, subculture, social classes, reference groups and face-to-face groups. Such as any passenger's transportation tools choice, which are also influenced by culture, subculture, social classes, near transportation tool place, transportion cost, transportation time schedule and transportation service etc. factors.

In Special finally, some consumption psychologists investigated whether the social behavior measured via face-to-face interactions, call and SMS logs can be used to predict the spending behavior for couples in terms of their propensity to explore diverse businesses, engage frequently with them and overspend. Their findings not only motivate in potentially new line of investigation into a spending behavior via mobile sensing , but also demonstrate the feasibility of passive (i.e. which don't require active user attention) method, for undertaking similar studies at a large scale in near future.

In recent years, mobile sensing and reality approaches have been used to understand multiple aspects of human behavior. Insights on a behavioral level (e.g. overspending, loyalty and diversity) have much longer term validity and can explain certain aspects of human behavior. To study spending behavior of couples, the consumption psychologists focus on three important behavior : exploration, loyalty and overspending behavior. The aim is to identify the couples that tend to explore diverse business, engages repeatedly and frequently with certain businesses and (or) spend higher amounts of income to them. For exploration, who calculated the diversity in vendors frequented. The exact method for calculating diversity scores is explained in the next section. For loyalty, who considered how frequently couples engage with their favorite businesses. Specifically, they calculated the percentage of transactions (out of a couple's total transactions), that were made at their top businesses. Lastly, to quantify overspending, they calculated the ratio of the amount of money spent by a couple to their self-declared discretionary spending budget. Hence MTR can use mobile to enquire what are the general expectation to any passengers in order to predict the reasons why who prefer to choose other transporation tools more accurate.

How to apply online psychological advertising method to predict passenger behavioral consumption?

Online advertising can give relevance information to represent the similarity between advertisement and queries. These existing online advertisement works mainly focused on interpreting advertisements clicks in term of what consumers seek. (i.e. relevance information) and how consumers choose to watch TV or magazine or online advertisement etc.

from different promotion media. (historically to know the product is selling on the market through advertising information). However, few of manufacturers or sellers attempted to understand why consumers chose to watch the advertising from TV or magazine or internet etc. different media.

Why can MTR can choose online advertisement to predict passenger behavior? Online Advertisement can be as a commercial search engine for manufacturers or sellers to gather data to concern how behavioral consumption is. The online advertisement's each observations motivate who to systemically model to test what each consumer individual psychological desire in order for a precise prediction on behavioral consumption after online advertisement promotion from internet media.

Today, internet is one kind of effective psychological advertising promotion method. For example, an online advertisement system, sponsored search has been one of the most important business models for commercial web search engines. It generates most of the revenue of search engines by presenting to users sponsored search results, i.e. advertisements (ads), along with organic search results. To deliver the most interesting ads to the users, a sponsored search system consists of technical components, including query-to-ads matching, online click prediction for matched ads, online click probability and auction to determine the ranking, placement, and pricing of the remaining ads. To aim to attempt to predict behavioral consumption for any kinds of product sale from online advertisement media.

In today's industry, generalized second price auction (GSP) is the most widely-used auction mechanism , in which the price that an advertiser has to pay depends on the predicted online click probability of the online buyers, whose own ads as well as the bid price and predicted online click probability of the ads ranked in the next position. The online sponsored search systems typically employ a machine learning model top predict the probability that an online user clicks an advertising from internet.

However, in practical sponsored search system. There are many ads without adequate historical click through data, even after query levels. Then online ads can been click improved prediction accuracy to consumer individual behavioral consumption when each click is occurred to the seller individual website. For example, online ads, such as : free Nike coupons ad. It shows " Go-Get_couptons.com/Nike, Download and print Nike coupons (100% Free)" ; another Nike-sales prices ad. It shows www.calibex.com, clothing, latest fashions and styles on sale. Buy Nike Fast!" ; another

Perfume.com official site ad. It shows "www.perfume.com, 10,000 + brand name perfumes and colognes-up to 80% off retail!" ; another Luxury English Perfume Ad. It shows " www.florislondon.com, shop online for luxury perfumes for men, women and the home". Above of these are example online ads. For two queries, "Nike" and "Perfume" , and two ads under the same query field similar relevance to the query.

Despite the usefulness of the relevance and historical of what users click and how users click. Specially, relevance information can indicate what relevant content users seek to click from online (internet) media. However, as it is well-known that users are not active to search for ads., the search engine, instead has to recommend ads. To users during their generic web search. Therefore, the relevance between query and ad can't perform as the key driver for click. In my opinion, in order for more click prediction, businessmen need to examine why users click.

Thus, MTR can use online advertisement to gather any passenger opinions concerning these questions: What will influence them to choose to catch other transportation tools, instead of MTR? What are MTR passengers expectations when who are catching MTR transportation tool? etc. different consumption psychologial questions.

How to apply psychological research to analyze of online user desire in sponsored search for behavioral consumption of reasons? First, according to literatures on consumer behavioral analyses, many factors will influence the decision making for consumption, including thought based effects and feeling-based effects. Though-based effects are basically win or loss analysis (e.g. trade-off between price and quantity), when feeling-based effects are more subjective (e.g. brand loyalty and luxury seeking). Note users online clicking the ad. Usually are with the intention to purchase something. In this situation, it is natural that the factors mentioned in consumer behavior analyses will influence their online click behaviors.

So, MTR advertisers can gather online advertisement data to choose how to design whose online advertisement to follow either is based on win or loss analysis, either focusing on MTR ticket price and MTR service performance quality features or is based on more subjective analysis , focusing on MTR brand loyalty and luxury(high income passenger segment) seeking features to attract any MTR passengers individual attention to choose to watch MTR online advertisements from online advertisement media more easily. So, it seems that online advertisement is a promotional and gathering data channel to persuade MTR passenger individual attention to predict these influence factor: how to change or improve MTR service performance or MTR station location choice or how to arrange busy time and non busy time MTR ticket price etc. influence factor in order to design MTR online advertisement to attract many passengers change their attitude to prefer choose to catch MTR transporation tools.

Does habit strength moderate the intention behavior to consumption?

Scientific evidence provides a sufficiently strong basis to justify the systematic development of intervention programs to increase healthy nutrition behaviors (World Health Organization, 2003). Such as an adequate consumption of fruit, a high consumption of fruit is associated with lower risk of cancer (Kremers et al., 2005, World Health Organization, 2003).

Will the concept of habit influence consumption behavior? Such as, fruit is a kind of health food. If the consumer has habit to choose to buy different kinds of fruit to eat everyday. Is habit as a factor to influence the consumer to choose to buy fruit to eat? Otherwise, if the consumer has no habit to choose to buy different kinds of fruit to eat everyday. Is non-habit as a factor to influence the consumer individual consumption behavior to choose any kinds of fruit to eat everyday.

Traditionally, habit has been measured by the number of times that behavior has already been performed in the past by an individual. Evidence to date indicates direct effects of past behavior on current behavior (Conner & Abraham, 2001). Some consumption psychologists had done experiment to research whether habit factor can influence fruit consumption. Their showed fruit consumption was assessed with a five item questionnaire, which was validated against seven day dietary records and biomarker for fruit intake (Bogers et. al 2004).

According to this consumption questionnaire result, it showed that intention is hypothesized to be the most immediate determinant of consumption behavior, yet several recent lines of research suggest that intentional control of behavior may be difficult to change, due to habit behavior consumption is caused to the individual consumer. Thus, it is difficult to change the consumer's behavior, when who have habit to choose to consume different kinds of fruit every week. However, results showed that the influence of intention on fruit consumption was weak and non-significant for those who had a strong habit toward fruit consumption. In constant, for those with a low or medium habit strength towards fruit. For those with low/medium habit strength, path analyses confirmed the reasoned, intentional process is for fruit consumption. In contrast, for those with high habit strength, it had the strongest influence on behavior. Thus, perceived control ability of fruit consumption seems to overrule the planned and intentional processes of fruit consumption for those with a strong habit. The environment behavior link also relates to the origins of habit, which are thought to originate from repeated performance of a given behavior in a stable situation. Thus, it seems environment can be one factor to influence strong habit consumers to buy fruit to eat every week as well as strong habit fruit consumer will buy much fruit to eat more than weak habit fruit consumer per week.

Hence, MTR needs to change any passenger's transportation tool choice of habit, after the passenger's habit has been changed. Then , MTR will have more passenger numbers chance.

3.5 Why environment protection product businessmen need to concern what the degree of quality of life to their potential buyers
Why environment protection product businessmen need to concern what the degree of quality of life to their potential buyers. Because if the potential buyers felt whose quality of life is good , so who will fell air or water pollution is not serious to influence whose health. Then, who will not have more needs to choose to buy any environmental protection products. Otherwise, if the potential buyers felt whose quality of life is bad, so who will feel air and water pollution is serious to influence whose health,. Then, who will have more needs to choose to buy any environmental protecton products. Some researchers have showed that human rights to identify the factors that need to be included in a quality of life measure. But, even if accepted as a starting point, that still does not point to clear to indicators or how which are to be weighted. So, a technocratic and unsatisfying device that is sometimes used is to recort to " expert opinion". So, it implies that if the country had any environment scientists prove the country's air and water pollution is serious, then the environment scientists' opions will be possible to influence the country's citizen consider to attend to buy any environmental protection products to protect those health.
I suggest environment protection products firms can use surveys methods to enquire whose country's citizen ideas concerning their feeling of quality of life. How to use life satisfaction surveys to measure human quality of

life? Some researchers had been carrying on researching a methodologically improved and more comprehensive measure of qualify of life satisfaction surveys. Surveys of life satisfaction is as opposed to surveys of the related concept of happiness, are preferred for a number of reasons, such as GDP statistic method. These surveys ask people the simple question of how satisfied who are with their lives in general. A typical question is on the four point scale used to the surveys studies. For example, on the whole are you very satisfied, fairly satisfied, not vey satisfied, or not at all satisfied with the life you lead? The results of the surveys have been attracting growing interest in recent years. Despite a range of early criticism, such as cultural non-comparability, the effect of language differences across countries, psychological factors distorting responses, tests have disproved as migitated most concerns. One objection is that responses to surveys don't adequately reflect how people really feel about their life. However, responses to questions about life satisfaction tend to be promoted, non-response rates are very low. This simple measure of life satisfaction has been found to correlate highly with more sophisticated test ratings by others who know the individual, and behavioral measures. The survey results have on the whole proved far more reliable and information then might be expected to measure quality of life.

Another criticism is that life-satisfaction responses reflect the dominant view on life, rather than actual quality of life in a country. So, life satisfaction is seen as a judgement that depends on social and culturally aspects, but this relativism is disproved by the fact that people in different countried report similar criteria as being important for life satisfaction, and by the fact that most differences in life satisfaction across countries can be explained by differences in objective circumstances. In addition, it has been found that the responses of immigrants in a country are much closer the level of the local population than to responses in their motherland.

In the view point of economists, who disagree to take the survey results completely at face value and use the average score on life satisfaction as the indicator of quality of life for a country. There are several reasons. First, comparable results for a sufficient number of countries tend to be out -of -date and many nations are not covered at all. Second, the impact of measurement errors on assessing the relationship indicators tends to cancel out across a large number of countries. But these might still be significant errors for any given country. So, there is a bigger chance of error in assessing quality of life between countries if we take a single average life satisfaction score as opposed to a multi-component index. Finally, and most important reason, although most of the inter-country variation in the life satisfaction surveys can be explained by objective factors, there is still a significant unexplained component which, in addition to measurement error, might to related to specific factors, that we want to net out from an objective quality of life index.

Instead environment protection product firms can attempt to use the survey results as a starting point, and a means for deriving weights for the various determinants of quality of life across countries, in order to calaulate an objective index. The average scores from comparable life-satisfaction surveys (on a scale of one to ten) can be assembled for 1999 year or 2000 year in a multi-variate regression to various factors satisfaction in many studies. Together these variables explain more than 80% of the inter-country variation in life-satisfaction scores. The surveys showed the weights of the various factors, included health, material well-being, and political stability and security. These were followed by family relations and community life. Next, in order of importance were climate (environment factor), job security, political freedom and finally gender equality. The surveys showed that the values of the life-satisfaction scores that are predicted by nine indicators represent a country's quality of life index or the corrected life-satisfaction scores, based on objective cross-country determinants. The method also means that the original units or measurement of the various indicators can be rely on the potentially distortive effect of having to transform all indicators to a common measurement also. The survey results indicate the determinents of quality of life factors, and the indicators used to represent these factors are: material wellbeing, health, political stability and security, family life, community life, climate and geography (environment factor), job security (unemployment rate), political freedom, gender equality. However, a number of other variables were also investigates but, upward trend in average life-satisfaction scores in developed nations, whereas average income has grown substantically. However, there is no evidence for an explanation that it has relationship between increasing incomes and stagnant life-satisaction scores: otherwise, the idea that an increase in someone's income causes enemy or disadvantage and reduces the welfare and satisfaction of others. In the researchers' estimates the level of income inequality had no impact on levels of life satisfaction , life satisfaction is primarily determined by absolute, rather than relative, status (related to states of mind and aspirations).

The explanation is that there are factors associated with modernisation that, in part offest its positive impact, such as crime, and drug and alcohol addiction, a decline in political participation and of trust in public authority, the erosion of the institutions of family and marriage. In personal terms, this has also been manifested in increased general uncertainty and personal risk. These pheonomena have accompanied rising incomes and expanded individual choice (both of which are highly valued). However stable family life and community are also highly valued and these have undergone a severe erosion. The survey results also showed that four of the indicators are forecast for 2005 yar (GDP , life expectancy, unemployment rate, political stabiliy); one geography is fixed and the remaining four, which represent slow changing factors and quality of life has relationship.

Thus, the researchers implied that GDP method is not accurate to measure human's quality of life. It ought have those other different methods to measure human's quality of life, such as survey method etc. as well as income is not only one factor to influence material wellbeing of human's quality of life; there are other different variable factor to influence human's quality of life, such as health, political stability, security, family of life, community life, climate and geography (environment factor), job security (unemployment rate), political freedom, gender equality etc. factors.

McGregor & Goldsmith (1998) explained that " quality is life is relative and difference between individuals, but it can be perceived as the level of satisfaction or confidence with one's conditions, relationships and surroundings relative to the available alternatives. The concept of quality of life is multifaceted. Quality of life consists of among other things: hope for the future, land, adequate food, clothing, shelter, income, employment opportunities, maternal and child health, and family and social welfare." The concept of quality of life is indeed multi-dimersional, complex and very subjective. For example, someone who has changed their consumptin habit to better ensure that their choices with make a better quality of life for themselves, the environment and future generations, may be seen by others as having a lower or inferior quality of life since which have removed themselves from the materialistic mainstream characteristics of our consumer society. Someone may feel that an absence of violence and abuse in their life and natural fresh air and clean water good quality supply can lead to even though who have fewer tangible resources, money or shelter; peace of mind and freedom from abuse has increased the quality of their daily life relative to what it was like before.

Otherwise, standard of living is often equated with quality of life, but it is not the same thing. A standard of life is a way of life to which a group of people are accustomed. Some people's standard of living includes only basic food, clothing, shelter and safety. Other people expect to eat at expensive restaurants, wear designer clothes, live in huge homes and travel extensively. Different people expect and want different things, who have different standards, which are very much shaped by values, goals, money, past experience and socialization. However, standard of living are most commonly assessed in terms of annual household income levels and to a lesser extent, wealth, community assistance, family contributions, special family needs, distribution of income within the family or household and geographic location.

Thus, it seems that standard of living or GDP alone is not a good measure of quality of life. Quality of life is a personal and inward looking concept that has both objective (factual) and subjective (perception) components. However, an individual's quality of life is also affected by external factors (build and natural environment; services and facilities) and this directly links quality of life to regional issues. The subjective aspect of quality of life is particularly important as if reflects how people feel about their situation and this can't be gauged from objective indicators. Subjective quality of life is often broken down into seven life domains: standard of living, health, achievements in life, personal relationships, safety, community connection and future security. For example, the measure of domain, such as standard of living includes as on income and wealth and housing aspect. The subjective measures: satisfaction with standard of living, distribution with wealth in the region, perceptions of personal income, wealth, housing affordability, housing density, green space and facilities near to homes. Objective measures may include distribution of income, welfare dependence, levels of housing stress. On health aspects, the subjective measures , satisfaction with personal health, region's health services, self assessed health status, needs and service usage. Objective measures may include services available per capita, suicide rates . It seems environment pollution factor can be one part to influence human quality of life.

Many studies of quality of life suggest that personal relations are an importnt aspect, or perhaps the most important aspect of quality of life. For example, Cornelia, B.F. (1999) found that change in interpersonal relations appear to contribute more heavily to satisfaction with quality of life than does either socioeconomic status or social participation. Who found that quality of life is not related of living, having choices is the productive work that you do is the most important dimension of quality of life. However, on environment aspect, rural development is most effective in increasing quality of life when it can increase diversity, both in the environment and in the economy,which can increase social capital, the norms and networks that provide for a collective identity and mutual respect. It can also increase standard of living. Efforts need to promoted standard of quality of life may have.

In fact, every American community with the problem of balancing environment growth with the need to maintain environmental and social health. For example, efficient agriculture to businesses get information about new technologies to present pollution. Increasing role of quality of life and standard of living took place in countries all over the world, especially nowadays, when numerous affects of the global crisis are felt all over the world. Emerging crisis caused many problems. thereby, in the current situation, it is interesting to examine the level of the quality of life and standard of living. After short overview of general development of concepts of standard of living and quality of life. The different indicators can measure quality of life or standard of living include GDP per capita, shopping basket, GFK basket, households' expenditures, poverty rate, income inequality, life satisfaction and happiness etc. indicators. The measures show an increase in the standard of living and quality of life. Hence, if the result showed the standard of living and quality of life. The high level of human development and the results of the level of satisfaction imply that human are moderately satisfied with their lives and enjoy a rather high level of happiness.

Standard of living and quality of life have been concerning issues in countries for many years, especially nowadays, when numersous effects of the global crisis are felt all over the world. The financial security and prosperity of the economic systems disappeared. The economic storm caused rising unemployment, falling incomes, increasing rates of poverty and declines in overall well-being. Thereby, in the current situation, it is interesting to examine quality of life and standard of living. However, standard of living is defined and the level of welfare available to individual or to the group of people. It concerns products and services, people are able to consume and the recources who have access too. It depends on the quality and quantity of available products and services and the way who are distributed within the population. Otherwise, standard of living is generally determined by indicators, such as real income per person and poverty rate. Quality of life indicates to the overall welfare within a certain society, focused on enabling each member on opportunity of accomplishing objectives. Unlike the concept of standard of living, quality of life refers to not only indicators of material standard, but also to various subjective factor that influence human lives, such as natural environment pollution challenges. However, in the estimation of standard of living and quality of life their are used two types of measures, objective and subjective indicators. Objective indicators are used to determine and to explain the economic segment, when subjective indicators are used as a descriptive indicator of the noneconomic segment of quality of life and standard of living.

Many researchers were done in the field of economics, psychology, clinicial medicine, health care, phiolsophy and social science to measure whether which kind of factors can cause human quality of life to be poor. The understanding of the concepts passed through a long period of evolution. Human need natural resources have enough supply to able to satisfy their needs. It concerns the physical circumstances, such as natural environment in which people live, the products and service who are able to consume and the resources who have access to. So, the good quality of life which depends on the quantity and quality of available products and services and their distribution within the population. Otherwise, the idea of standard of living requires a macro perspective and it is generally measured by standards, such as real income per person and poverty rate. The most common measure is national output per capita, measured such as GDP or GDP per capita. Other measures, such as income inequality and life satisfaction are also used. So, it can be feeling of human intangible measure, psychological feeling to measure quality of life to human. It seems that the environmental pollution can have close relationship to influence human quality of life. Thus, quality of life can be measured by objective as well as subjective indicators. One researcher, Felce and Perry (1995) who defined quality of life is as total welfare which includes objective and subjective evaluation of physical, material, social and emotional welfare, personal development and activity, all together evaluated throughout personal set of values.

What are objective indicators of standard of living and quality of life? Objective circumstances refer to the economic and material conditions which are important aspects of the standard of living and quality of life. In the assessment, eight different indicators were used: CPI, GDP per capita, shopping basket, household's expenditures, GFIC basket, poverty rate, income inequality and HDI. However, these indicators is one number measure. It can't measure anyone's psychological feeling, such as health, safe emotion. The challenge concerns whether environmental pollution factor, such as air pollution, water pollution can cause human's health to be poor, even goes down human's quality of life and economy loss. I shall indicate some evidences to give reasons to support my conclusion why I believe that environment pollution is a factor to cause human quality of life to be poor , even it can also cause economy will encounter loss too.

In general, measure of quality of life need include human's psychological feeling indicator. I shall indicate, Hong Kong, China countries air and water environmental pollution challenges how to influence these two countries' people quality of life to be poor, even, it will cause their economy loss. Nowadays, China and Hong Kong and India and Afria are encountering health problems arising from damage to lungs, heart and blood vessels. Hong Kong and India and Afria and China e.g. Shanghai city pollution is a significant cause of premature death from cardiopulmonary disorders. Present level of pollution cause injury to the immature developing lings of children and adolescents. This damage will lead to life-long health problems in many and a reduction in life-expectancy. Although, there is no evidence from analyses of trends in pollutants that pollution measures in recent years have reduced pollutant concentrations in a way which will benefits public health.

There are clear indicators that for some pollutants. The problem is worsening. In fact, air and water pollution is Hong Kong and China and Afria etc. developing countries' the biggest cause of social and environmental injustice. It harms not only citizens today, but because its transquenerational effects on the urborn and youngest members of the society, it will cause its will health effects well into the later years of this century, even environmental pollution challenge will cause these countries will encounter economy loss. Thus, these above countries can give more chance to any environment protection products to sell their products to any cities, which are encountering environment pollution challenges.

Human activities have created forms of air and water pollution, such as gases from fuels, uncontrolled emissons from fossil fuels and other chemical sources have long been recognized as a cause of ill health and premature death. For example, in December, 1930 year, a dense fog affected the Meuse Valley in Belgium. Beginning on December, 3 date, the fog intensified over three days and was associated with laryngeal symptoms, chest pain, coughing, and breathlessness. Some patients showed signs of pulmonary oedema. Overall 60 deaths were attributed to the episode. After a long investigation, the cause was considered to be emissions from high sulphur fuels, including suplhur dioxide and sulphuric acid.

What is the current threat to health? the migigration of air polluton following the introduction of clear air has been followed by a period of unprecedented economic development creating new forms of pollution from the combustion of fossil fuels. For example, in constrast to the relatively large tar laden particulates from burning dirty coal which caused episodes like the London city, UK. Smog , traffic pollution now genertes fine with a different size and composition and gases,such as which may cause injury to the respiratory system and the effects of other pollutants. Such as particulates and drive the formation of the secondary pollutant ozone. The effects of pollution will therefore to some extent reflect genetic, environmental lifestyle and behavioral factors to develop these distance in a population together with the existing prevalence of diseases which may be polluted. Hence, living in polluted urban environments is associated with increased levels of biological markers of inflammation compared with residence in a clean air environment. The damage is caused by air pollution manifests itself through a variety of common and recognized health problems, such as upper complaints heart and lung disease. Because of this, we can use statistical methods as well as clinical studies to detect the signal of changes in health problems and increased health care demands in the population. However, doctors had proved air or water pollution can cause these both curdiovscular or respiratory disease indirectly. Curdiovscular disease includes formation of arterial plaques, coronary artery, heart attacks, irregular heart rhythm, loss of heart rate variability, high blood pressure, stroke etc. disease. Respiratory disease includes inflammation of nasal, throat and tracheal airways with acute, lower respiratory tract inflammation and infection causing bronchitis, reduction long growth and function in young people. So, it seems environmental pollution can influence quality of life to human as well as environmental pollution and illness and poor health problem has close relationship.

On the other side, envionmental pollution can bring health risk, over it will influence social inequalities. Some researchers had found that the evidence has been compiled for six envionmental health challenges, such as air quality, housing and residential location, unintentional injuries in children, work related health risks, waste management and climate change. It seems human need to concern air and drinking water quality, waste management and climate change how to influence our environmental pollution challenge. Although, the evidence base on social inequalities and environmental risk is fragmented and data are often available for few countries only, it indicates that inequalities are a major challenge for environmental health policies. Irrespective of development status, environmental inequalities can be found in any country for which data are available. The valid for the exposure to environmental risk factor is also unequally distributed, and this unequal distribution is often related to social characteristics, such as income, social status, employment and education, even environment risk factor can influence human's quality of life.

(i) How environmental risk factor can influence different groups

However, environment protection product firms need to concern how environmental risk factor can influence inequally health outcomes to different groups. Such as, the first group is social determinants affect the environmental conditions of an individual and may contribute to the fact that specific individuals or population groups more often experience loss adequate or potentially harmful environmental conditions. The second group is the affected population groups could still be more exposed through e.g. the mechanism of education and health behavior. The third group is given socially disadvantaged groups could show more severe health effects of the social disadvantage is associated. The final group is social determinants affect health (what remains unclear is the relative importance of socially determined exposure to environmental risk factors). Thus, any manufacturers need to concern how whose behavior can lead environmental pollution to influence poor health to alive, due to whose productive process. Even, every country's citizen themselves can not neglect how to protect our natural environment to be clean issue. Due to environmental unhealth poor issue can lead our bodies to be unhealth and to be ill and we have no health to work to influence our job inefficiency and low productivity if we often need to see doctor to raise workload to my staffs often. Then, employers will be probable to consider to attempt to buy any environmental protection products to reduce or avoid pollution occurrence to influence loss of legal compensation from the different social groups' complain. Hence, employers will cosiderate environmental justice and environmental inequity issue, e.g. how to reduce indoor air pollution and occupational or exposure to environmental tobacco smoke pollution exposure to high traffic roads or to industrial plants pollution to influence different social groups' health challenges. So, the environmental protection product firms' clients , who can include social different target groups and any product manufacturers.

(ii) How Afria country environmental pollution influences

Surprisingly, most of above countries , among of them, although Africa is a green and natural environmental country, but Africa has encounted poor natural environmental quality to influence it has poor quality of life to its citizen and poor economy growth to its society both. Why does Africa encounter this natural environmental pollution challenge? Afican have now two potential sources of pollution: consumption and production . This looks reasonable to Africa, since maintenance is completely dedicated to improving the environment, when production generates pollution only as a " by product". Capital implies the possibility of a country being trappical in an economent poverty trap by both a bad environment and low longevity. Some countries (or regions) may even experience other time, both environmental degradation and decay in expectancy. The fact that, in some cases, environmental degradation doesn't imply lower longevity may be due to the fact that economic growth might , at the same time, worsen environmental quality, but generate additional resources that can help increasing (or preserving) longevity. However, these is also evidence of countries where environmental degradation is associated with a reduction in life expectancy. It seems worsen environmental quality will influence any country's economic growth and poor quality of life both. For example, McMichael et al. (2004) identify 40 countries that experienced a loss in longevity between 1990 year and 2001 year (26 between 1980 year and 2001), they also support that the resulting world divergence in terms of life expectancy might be explained by "…. (the growing) health risks consequent on large-scale environmental changes is caused by human pressur, by both bad environment and low longevity, biodiversity and sustainable energy".

(iii) How human adult consumption and environmental quality influences future environment for human survival probability of life expectancy.

I shall assure human adult consumption and environmental quality has relationship to influence the future environment (green preferences) to provide human survival probability, it depends on inherited environmental quality. Thus, human will increase or decrease in the survival probability when we need a higher or lower life expectancy. In general, we depend on these environmental conditions to live, which include quality of water, air and soils etc. and resource availability, biodiversity, forestry, fisheries etc.

It is interesting to analyze different possible strategies to escape from the environmental poverty trap as well as factors that could push some economies back to a low equilibrium characterized. To research whether environment factor has relationship to influence human quality of life. We need to give idea of explaining whether environmental care has relationship to an uncertain lifetime. However, I suppose that an environmental kind of factor can be instead of being defined in terms of GDP per capita, capital accumulation etc. economic factors. Poverty is now related to environmental quality. It should be clear, however, I focus only on one specific mechanism lying behind environmental traps. Just as under development traps may be related to a wide variety of factors, ranging from financial to technological ones, including human capital accumulation and life expectancy. So, I should use this assumption to explain why it has relatively between environmental quality and life expectancy.

This " synthetic" indicator (YCELP, 2006) indicated environmental health is defined by child morality, indoor air polluton, drinking water, adequate sanitation and urban particulates and ecosystem vitality that includes factors like air quality, water and productive natural resources, A key ingredient of our setting is that survival until the last period is probabilistic and depends on the inherited quality of the environments. This survival probability affects the weight of the future environmental quality in human's utility function to achieve interest aim. Final stage, human will have optimal choices depend on life expectancy: in particular, a higher probability to be alive in the third period boosts investment in the environment and reduces consumption. In this case, a given country may be caught in a high morality/poo environment if low income is associated with a deteriorated environment.

John and Pecchenino (1994) were the first to introduce the possibility of multiple identifying, case for a poverty cause characteristic by poor economic performance and environmental degradation, however, life expectancy is assumed to be exogenous and plays no role in their model. Such as soils deterioration are the like, are all susceptible of increasing human morality (thus reducing longevity). So, the existence of both environmental performance and longevity, with countries being concentrated around two levels of environmental quality and life expectancy respectively. The two-way causes are between the environment and longevity. If the causal relationship between environmental quality and life expectancy involves the existence of an environmental poverty, characterized by both bad environmental conditions and short life expectancy.

Human life stage will encounter generations of three periods to get utility from consumption and environmental quality. During adulthood, when all relevant decisions are taken, adult can work and allocate their income between consumption and investment in environmental maintenance: consumption involves deterioration of the future quality of the environment (through pollution and/or resource depletion) when maintenance helps to improve it. The dynamics of environmental quality may also be affected by external factors on more resourced communities. The most importance, unhealthy physical environments across the region adversely affect everyone, ever though who are likely to be most concentrated in more burdened community which also have less social power to change those environments.

Why life expectancy and the environment has close relationship to influence quality of life? Life expectancy and environmental quality dynamics are jointly determined. Human may invest in environmental quality, depending on how much , we expect to live. However, environmental conditions affects life expectancy. In particular, some countries may encounter in a low life expectancy / low environmental quality. This outcome is consistent with stylized facts relating life expectancy and environmental performance measures. Some expects to live longer, who would be willing to invest more in environmental quality, because who feel which have causal link between life expectancy and environmental quality. However, environmental quality is a very important factor affecting health and morbidity: air and water pollution, depletion of natural resources and quality of life.

(iv) Why social and physical environmental factors have close relationship to influence economic growth

I shall indicate reasons to explain why social and physical environmental factors have close relationship to influence economic growth, even human health of quality of life. The social and economic burdens of poor education, lack of affordable housing and less than self sufficient income affect, not just those individuals and families who have the fewest resources. The social gradient means that not only do whose in the bottom worse health outcomes to bottom of income group and the top income group whose will have poor quality of life influence. The higher rates of disease and disability and lesser productivity among many communities means a higher public and private burden of life years, particularly life expectancy once one reaches age 65. In recent decades, research and has increasingly shown how powerfully social and economic conditions determine population health and differences in health among subgroups, much more so than medical care. It seems that environmental factor can influence human's quality of life.

Los Angeles Country Department Of public Health (2016) indicated a country health rankings model, this department explained these three health factors can cause this health outcomes. These health factors include health behaviors (30%), it includes tobacco use, diet and exercise, alcohol use, unsafe sex; clinical care (20%), it includes access to care, quality of care; social and economic factors (40%), it includes education, employment, income, family and social support, community safety; physical environmental factor (10%) , includes natural environmental quality, built environmental quality. Then these factors can cause this health outcomes, such as morality (length of life):50% and morbidity (quality of life) :50%. SO, it implies that physical environmental factor can influence human's length of life. So, on our social environmental problems result is from a complex interplay of a number of forces. An individual's health –related behaviors , particularly diet, exercise and smoking, surrounding physical environment and health care (both access and quality) all contribute significantly to how long and how well human love. However , none of these factors is as important to population health as are the social and economic environments in which human live, learn, work and play. We refer to these factors can be as the social determinants of health to influence our quality of life. How do social determinants affect our quality of life? In the late 19th and early 20th centuries, public health concentrated particularly on the physical environment. Improvements in, for example, clean water supplies, healthier housing, sanitation, workplace safety and safe food lead to sharp increases in average life expectancy . Also our quality of life needed to be concentrated on expanded access to medical care, resulting in further expansion. So, the poverty tap is now characterized by those elements, such as low levels of : (i) environmental quality, (ii) life expectancy and (iii) human capital.

In fact, environmental degradation can have a significant impact on human health. De Hollander et. al (1999) & Melse & De Hollander (2001) showed that estimates of the share of environment, related human health loss are as high 5% for high income countries, 8% for middle income countries and 13% for low income countries. Air pollution and exposure to hazardous chemicals are important causes of the related burden of disease in countries. The transport and energy sectors are major contributors to air pollution, when important sources of chemical pollution are agriculture industry and waste disposal. Opportunities for reducing environment-related health risks are considerable. The benefits of many environment policies in terms of reduced health care costs and increased productivity significant exceed the costs of implementing those policies. So, the impact of environmental risk factors on health are extremely varied and complex. For example, the effects of environmental degradation on human health can range from death caused by cancer, due to air pollution to psychological problems resulting from noise. So it implies environmental factor can influence our quality of life in our societies. However, many factors can also influence human's health of a population, including diet, sanitation, socio-economic status, literacy and lifestyle.

De Hollander et. al. (1999) & Melse and De Hollander (2001) showed that total burden of disease, with estimated environment-related share expenditure, mid-1990 year. The average income group has 15 daily/1000 capita, the middle income group has 20 daily/1000 capita, the high income group has 10 daily/1000 capita. As regards both total burden of disease and the health conditions related to environmental; degradation. The result indicates the environment –related share of the burden of disease is greatly dependent on income, with higher-environmental shares generally occurring in lower-income countries.

On the one hand, it seems the large environmental share of health problems is primarily, due to factors related to poverty, such as limited to access to proper food, housing, health care and drinking water. Environmental determinants of human health in developing or developed countries are related. On the other hand, those to the exposure to air pollutants (particularly in urban areas and chemicals in the environment than to poor living conditions. Also sources of human exposure to chemicals are many and varied. Chemicals can reach the environments, for example, through emissions from industries, anti-fouling paints on marine vessels, pesticides in agriculture, waste incineration and leakage from waste disposal sites. When emissions of chemicals from industries and other point sources of pollution have lead to poor quality of life, source of chemical exposure. Intensive agricultural production uses chemicals in pesticides and fertilizer and in feed additives and medication for livestock. Residues remain in fruit, grains, vegetables, meats and daily products, all of which can reach the consumer.

Other sources of chemicals in food include bio-accumulative chemicals in the environment, such as heavy metals and persistent organic pollutants, which can be found in fish, meat and dairy products. So, environment pollution can influence human need to eat bad or unhealthy food to cause we have poor quality of life to live, such as the high income group or middle income group or low income group of families in our societies fairly. Other human health risks that have recently received considerable attention include unsafe livestock feeding practices through which toxins reach the food chain unintentionally. Dioxins that have accidentally contaminated poultry feeds that contain diseased animal remains can cause the so-called " mad cow disease" in livestock which has been linked to a new form of disease. The effects on health from exposure to chemicals and air pollutants vary from allergies to cancer. Although, the link between exposure and disease is often not clear, Even at low exposure levels, urban are pollutants can cause, asthma, allergies, respiratory diseases and cardiovascular disease if the exposure is continuous or long term. Heavy metals have been shown to cause neurological disorders and various cancers. In addition to , physical diseases, environmental contamination can also cause psychological problems. Noise, one of the determinants of the quality of urban life can have an impact on human health, decreasing the quality of life and potentially contributing to depression.

For Ireland, UK country example, this country politicians and policy makers believe the role of environment can be used to measure quality of life, concerning on either in its own right or relative to economic and social aspects of quality of life. Agreement on what measures quality of life and how it can be measured by the role of environment, not just in Ireland, but everywhere. The conventional approach is used for policy has been to use measure of gross domestic product(GDP) or regional valued added. However, it is acknowledged that such conventional economic measures have only a partial relationship with societal wellbeing. To the extent that economic measures are related to public products and consumption, there are also pressing issues in relation to public products and the sustainability of economic growth. However, the role of environmental factor can influence resource use and human's behavioral consumption.

Aspects to quality of life other than income include the environment, freedom, health, working condition, leisure, social and family relationship. Economists don't deny that these factors do play a role in quality of life. However, environment factor can be one role to influence other factors to influence our quality of life to be good or bad effect. For example, locations which might be desirable as paces to life (in terms of income earning opportunities or other factors) were also likely to have higher costs of living, particularly with regard to house prices or health or unhealthy air/water pollution of environment situation of the place to provide human to live. Alternatively, social indicators are based on normative ideals of literacy, low rates of premature mortality or a quality environment. Other measurement of people's personal evaluation of their quality of life, much depends on personal expectations and experience.

(v) How environmental factor can influence any country's house price.

I shall indicate that why environmental factor will influence any country's house price. For Ireland example, citizen average incomes and higher in the east of the country, house prices are lower in the west, who are also more able to afford a property of choices. There are more opportunities to purchase houses, where people own their own houses, who are more likely to have benefits from an appreciation is its value and to consequently perceive a higher degree of health. Generally, levels of property appreciation have been higher in the east. Unfortunately, young people and the more economically active segment of the population are more likely to be faced with rising entry level house prices and the prospect of large borrowings. So, the quality of life, such as education, crime and access to healthcare and living environment are not uniformly better in the west or the east regions. Indeed, many measures of social disadvantage are at their worst in the west regions. Some indicators of environmental quality are , indeed better in the west regions, but there are others, such as drinking-water quality or recreational access that are often worse.

Comparisons can often be reduced to an urban-rural dimension rather than a regional one. Factors such as incomes, house prices, crime levels, air pollution and congestion are all likely to be higher in urban areas in Ireland city, UK country. Why environment and housing price has relationship in Ireland to influence quality of life to its citizen? If Ireland's regional development policy is successful , it will bring with it greater competition in the housing market and greater pressures on the environment in Ireland. Because the forest will be decreased to build house, the natural environment will become wood and steel and stone of housing built environment. In fact, it appears that there is a fair of amount of agreement on the relative rating of factors influencing quality of life. Ability to own one's home and security of income were needed, but respondents also placed almost equal important on clean air and drinking water, low crime were differences. The Ireland's rural respondents appeared to place a slightly greater emphasis on key natural environmental attributes, when urban residents valued absolute incomes and social or leisure activity rather more.

In this respect, the analysis identifies three components to Ireland people of quality of life, each of which was evident in all three locations. There components can be broadly described as domestic security, social/leisure and aspects of the planned environment. The first of these includes indicators, such as security of income, absolute income, house ownership and low crime. As this component includes air and drinking-water quality, it suggests that these indicators may be associated with personal health and well-being. When the planned environment component includes those attributes that affect quality of life over which the authorities have a direct influence, for instance, a clean environment, traffic and reducing vehicle numbers on the roads in busy time. Hence, environmental protection product firms can find anywhere the houses price are going down, it is possible that the pollution factor influences who choose to live there. So it implies that the locations of house buyers will have more needs to buy their environmental protection products protect whose health if who need to live these locations.

(vi) How environmental pollution can influence social welfare

Environmental quality has an undefined impact on quality of life and various indicators are used to show regional variations in aspects, such as water quality . There are many measures of environmental quality , but is only for quality of life. Moreover, the measurement of societal welfare is important. Societal welfare is not simply , the sum of the parts, but varies depending on the individual in which people find themselves at any time in their life. In principle, it should be possible to apply weights to each element of societal welfare, but as preferences for each of these vary within the population. In the absence of a method with which everybody is satisfied, GNP and GDP are typically the most popular used measures for quality of life or standard of life. But, these are problems with the data itself to measure quality of life because quality of life is feeling or satisfaction of level to the country's citizen and it can not be seen by numbers or statistic method. For example, GDP ignores household production, such as the effort that goes into the rearing of children, the benefits that this provides for society and the public expenditure that is avoided. Neither are costs treated equally with the benefits. GDP counts all economical activities irrespective on pollution appears to increase. GDP even through it is a degree of double counting.

Otherwise, environmental products are good to be measured to quality of life. For example, many environmental products are unpriced. Consequently, environmental products that people value, or which are critical to the sustainability of development, are abused or depleted because of their public products have good characteristics and the absence of a market price signal. Environmental economists try to work within the economic model to measure quality of life. Rather than questioning the link between utility and consumption or choice, the preferred approach is to add an element into the utility function that represents the value of environmental products or the stock of natural capital. By one means or another , the preservation value of these environmental products is estimated in terms of willingness to pay to protect the environment or as willingness to forego other products in return. It seems the quality of people's environment can be represented by objective indicators. At another, their interpretation will vary and can be represented by subjective indicators. So, enviromental products can have economic benefits to provide social welfare to citizen to live in any countries.

Objective indicators come in two forms: (i) economic indicators and (ii) social indicators. The former depends on an ability to select the environmental products and services that are desires, in other words, the satisfaction of preferences . The economic argument is that people select the best quality of life, who can obtain commensurate with their resources and personal desires. By comparison, social indicators are based on normative ideals on what could be considered the food life. For example, would be infant morality, literacy, crime rates and social indicators are objective measures. Both have guided, much of the research on quality of life, particularly concerning with the urban environment. Quality of life can include natural a significant influence on local quality of life, for instance, natural beauty spots used for recreation.

For environmental quality concept, it concerns with health, safety, wellbeing, residential satisfaction and the physical sustainability can be considered to result from an when live ability can be considered to represent the interaction between the physical and the social domains. As with expenditure on the environment, investment in social capital contributes to quality of life. However, the benefits will again vary amongst individuals, depending largely on the security of their individual circumstance. As with the environment, the government can certainly adopt strategies that provide for public security by taking measures to reduce crime, a measure likely to be appreciated by everybody (except criminal) , at least to one degree or another. In other necessary to enhance social interaction, namely community centers or sports facilities. Furthermore, the creation of social capital has an statement which responds to general social trends to raise Ireland citizen's quality of life.

I shall indicate Ireland to explain whether environmental factor is the main factor to influence our quality of life and economic growth. Is environmental quality higher in the Ireland west regions? And if so, does this compensate for lower incomes in these regions? Is it bad that rural areas are characterized by higher costs of living in areas other than housing by environmental factor? In fact, in Ireland , UK country, population increase has a direct impact on the environment by placing demands on local natural resources, particularly open space and water. It also leads to a sense of crowding that reduces the utility associated with access to the environment. How can environment factor influence economy growth in Ireland? In Ireland, agriculture has gone through a period of significant change that has been accelerated reductions in the amount of mixed cropping and traditional land management. Indeed, changes in the expectations of young farmers will ensure that further change is likely to be characterized by increases in farm size and greater specialization with implications for landscape and wildlife. These characteristics of farm holdings are more familiar in the east regions of Ireland , UK country. As with likely to extend to the west regions as the older generation of farmers retires, although this will probably be accompanied by a trend to more farming of production needs to young farmers. So, good natural environment can provide Ireland young farmers to produce more agriculture to earn income, even who can export more rice, fruits, vegetable etc. agriculture foods to overseas. Hence, Ireland GDP will be raise if it can have good natural resource environment to provide Ireland young farmers to grow foods to sell to domestic and

/or foreign agricultural market. Given the rate of economic growth, and its concentration in the east of the Ireland, UK country, it would be easy to presume that the quality of the environment is higher the further away from the mid east one goes. Thus, good natural environment is an important factor to influence the farming industry development in Ireland , UK county to satisfy their needs and to raise their quality of life nowadays. It implies that environmental protective products have more needs to any farming to use in Ireland, UK country.

I shall indicate New Zealand and America two developed countries to explain why which are facing environmental pollution challenge to influence their citizen's quality of life and economic growth nowadays. The first country is NZ, although, New Zealand is a developed and natural environmental country, but it had been envountering air pollution annouance and noise annoyance to influence it's citizen's health-related quality of life. I shall indicate why which has this relationship between of them in New Zealand. Nowadays, New zealand population growth is an increasing demand for consumer products and urbanization have lead to concerns over the lived environments in many of the world's cities, such as Auckland, wellington cities in New Zealand. However, environmental quality is an important determinant of health, such as the bad influence of traffic-related air and noise pollution on health outcomes, specially with respect to at risk groups, both in relation to long term exposure as well as acute effect, from brief exposures. For example, cholesterol levels and in relation to myocardial infaction. Nowadays, New Zealand is encountering the high degree of air pollution and noise annoyance to influence it's citizen's quality of life. Air pollutants can be detected either visually, such as witnessing smoke emanating from a vehicles's exhaust, or by smell, such as when odorants stimulate olfactory receptors. The evidence linking air pollution to adverse impacts on human health.

Many air impacts on human health. Many air pollution health studies have focused specifically on urban area, and vehicle generated pollution in particular, as road vehicles are one of the major sources of pollution across much of the world. Elemental carbon, Nox and ultrafine particles an considered to be pollutants most strongly associated with road traffic emissions. In Auckland and Wellington cities, New Zealand , it has been estimated that 71% of summer and 21% of winter concentrations of fine particulate matter is attributable to motor vehicles. Moreover, poor town planning decisions in Auckland (and in New Zealand in general) over many decedes has meant that may people live in very close proximity to busy road and motorways within " road corridors" and so are the adverse effects of road traffic, including noise and air pollution as well as experiencing on potential for degradation in their quality of life. Such as, New Zealand is highly suitable for studies investigating the impact of roads on the health of its residents. For example, NZ, road traffic noise and aviation noist has been linked to cardiovascular disease, hypertension and ischemic heart disease. It influences NZ resident personal psychological and physical both health challenges. In fact, NZ noise increases morbidity and mortality independently of air pollution exposure, though air pollution constituted a greater burden of disease when arise exposure had a greater impac on quality of life, e.g. NZ road traffic noise and air pollution will be caused from drivers in busy time. Specially in Auckland and Wellington cities. It will influence urban and rural environmental pollution. Some retired old people who will feel annoyance when this road traffic occurs in Auckland or Wellington cities to close to their houses in transportation busy time every day.

Next developed country is America, this country's air pollution is also serious nowadays. Because traffic jam often occurs in New York, Washington, Boston etc. big cities in US. So, U.S. cities' parks and its trees have significant influence to produce fresh air to provide U.S. residents who are living in cities to breach for their body health. David J. & Gordon , M. (2016) indicated " In U.S. these urban parks are estimated to contain about 370 million trees with a structural value of approximately $300 billion." The number of park trees varies by region of the country, but which can produce significant air quality effects in and near parks, related to air temperatures, air pollution, ultraviolet indication and carbon dioxide (a dominant greenhouse gas related to global climate change). Additional open space and other vacant lands in cities, which may contain trees and other vegatation. Contribute significant additional benefits, effects of parks and open space at the city scale can vary significantly depending on the amount of parkland and amount of tree cover within the parkland.

The reasons why parks can reduce air pollution. Parks generally have lower air temperature than surrounding areas. Temperatures are usually cooler toward the center of a park than around its edges. At night, the center of a large park may be 13 degree cooler than surrounding city areas. The cooler air from parks often moves out into adjacent developed neighborhoods. This cooling of surrounding areas tends to increase with park size and percentage of the park covered by trees. So, cooler air temperature is provided by urban parks can have significant impacts on human health. During heat wave events, which can kill hundreds of people, park areas may provide city dwellers with some respite from high air temperture, particularly in the evening, during hot, sunny days tree shade can greatly increase human comfort. Because park influences on air temperature extend to developed areas outside of parks, local energy use for heating and cooling buildings is also effected. Although, the net around effect of parks on energy costs has been by reducing temperature is difficult to estimate at least in the southern United States the effect will usually be a net annual benefit. Futhermore, large park trees will reduce winds and may provide a benefit of winter heating of buildings near the park. Although, the overall economic effect of urban trees and parks on air temperature reduction is not fully billions of dollars annually at the national scale in terms of improved environmental quality and human health.

In fact, trees and vegetation in parks can help reduce air pollution both by directly removing pollutants and by reducing air temperatures and building energy use in and near parks. There tree effects can reduce pollutant emissions and formation. However, park vegetation can increase some pollutants by either directly emitting volatile orgnic compounds that can contribute to ocone and carbon monoxide formation or indirectly by the emission of air pollutants through vegetation maintenance practices, such as operation of chain and use of transportation fuels. David J. & Gordon , M. (2016) showed "Annual pollution removal and economic benefits by U.S. urbank park trees is estimated at about 75,000 tones ($500 million) or 80 pounds per acre of tree cover ($300 per acre of tree cover). Carton storage and annual removal by urban park trees and soils in the United States is estimated at about: carton storage trees: 75 million tons ($1.6 billion), carton storage (soils) : $102 million tons of carbon removal (trees): 2.4 million tons ($50 million)". Park management is recommended by U.S. environment protection department: considering that most of the effects of trees on microclimate and air quality are beneficial for park users and nearby residents; park designs that include a variety of land cover, areas of dense trees, scattered trees and lawn are likely to provide the greatest opportunities for optimum physical comfort of visitors; increase the number of healthy trees (increase pollution removal and carbon storage); sustain existing tree cover (maintains pollution removal levels) and (carbon storage); maximize use of low volatile organic compound emitting trees reduces ozove and carbon monoxide formation; sustain large, healthy trees (large trees have greatest per tree effcts on pollution and carbon removal); using long-lived trees (reduces long term pollutant emissions from removal; reducing fossil fuel in maintaining vegetation reduces pollutant ans carbon emissions)." So, if US had many green parks, then which can reduce air pollution, also it can assist many travellers who prefer to travel to US to raise GDP travelling income growth generally. It imples, USA park players and NZ road users will have more needs to attempt to buy any environmental protective products.

(vii) What is consumer neuroscientific research method to predict consumer behavior?

The key motivation has not been possible to directly observe the mental processes when subjects perceive marketing stimuli, such as advertisement or when who make purchasing decisions. Despite the long history of consumer research, little is known about the neural representation of how marketing stimuli affects consumers' perceptions, their decision-making processes and their consumption experience.

In the past, consumer researchers had to rely on varying the stimuli , e.g. prices or packaging and context factors, e.g. putting subjects in a good or bad mood in order to measure participants' reactions , e.g. choice behavior or brand preference. However, same researchers suggest scientific tools can observe brain activity to predict consumers behavior (Ambler et al., 2000 and Shiv and Fedorikhin, 1999 et al).

However, some consumer psychologists showed advertising research studies have often pointed out the important role of emotions for advertisement memorization (Ambler, 2000). In advertising research, who suggest that emotion and ratio are represented in different hemispheres of the brain. Research on the neural representation of stimuli-induced emotions, however, could show that emotions are not only processed in the left brain hemisphere, but are also processed bilaterally (e.g. in the left and right hemispheres of such cortical structure.

Customer loyalty is as an example, which can be defined as " a deeply held commitment to rebuy or a preferred product/service consistently in the future (Oliver, 1999). Consumer loyalty is a popular predictable consumer behavior topic for marketing researches, early research tried to establish whether customer loyalty has impact on aspects of business performance (such as profit margin and sales).

Loyalty is a psychological construct that develops over-time during a learning process of the consumer. Thus, loyalty research can benefit from insights in neuroscience and neuro-economics about how learning processes are represented in the brain. Some brain psychologists also explained how people learn to be loyal. They showed the following three processes in order to learn to be loyal.

(1) The brain should be able to memorize and retrieve positive and negative outcomes of former decisions, such as positive experiences after choosing brand A over brand B.

(2) The brain should be able to predict several outcomes of choosing between alternatives (buying A or B).

(3) The brain needs to integrate the information from processes 1 and 2 into the decision process.

Thus, it seems any environment protective product firm needs to concern how to develop loyalty and advertment promotion method and commitment to let environment protection product consumers to have more confidence to choose to buy whose products or learn how to use whose environment protection services more easily.

Whether design factor can predict consumer behavior for environment protection product

(i) Why environmental pollution and human right abuses has close relationship to influence quality of life and economic growth?

In fact, environment pollution and human right abuses has close relationship. It is clear that poverty situations and human rights abuses are worsened by environmental degradation. The result can influence poor human quality of life to the developing countries' people unfairly. There are these several abvious reasons: firstly, the exhaustion of natural resources leads to unemployment and emigration to cities; secondly, this affects the enjoyment and exercise of basic human rights. Environmental conditions contribute to a large extents to the spread of infections diseases. From the 4,400 million of people who live in developing countries, almost 60% lack basis health care services, a almost a third of these people have no access to safe water supply; thirdly, degradation poses new problems, such as environmental refugees. Environmental refugees suffer from significant economic, socio-cultural and political consequences. And fourthly, environmental degradation worsens existing problems suffered by developing and developed countries. David J. Nowak & Gordon M. Melsler

(2016) showed" Air pollution , for example, accounts for 2.7 million to 3.0 million of deaths annually and of these 90% are from developing countries. " Hence, our societies need to concern human right law to protect unfair treatment to developing countries people. Firstly, both disciplines have deep social root, even though human rights law is more rooted within the collective consciousness, the accelerated process of environmental degradation is generating a new " environmental consciousness". Secondly, both disciplines have become internationalized . The international community has assumed the commitment to observe the realization at human rights and respect for the environment. Thirdly, both areas of law tend to universalize their object of protection. Human rights are presented as universal and the protection of the environment appears as everyone is responsibility.

Human right and environment law can raise our quality of life because the first approach is one where environmental protection is described as a possible means of fulfulling human rights standards. Here, environmental law is conceptualized as giving a protection that would help ensure the well-being of future generations as well as the survival of those who depend immediately upon natural resources for their livelihood. So, the end is fulfulling human rights, and the route is though environmental law, the second approach places the two sphere in inverted positions, it states that the legal protection of human rights is an effective means to achieving the ends of conservation and environmental protection. Therefore, the presently existing human right is as a route to environmental protection. The focus is on the connection to influence any economy: health, food supply , housing, fresh natural air supply etc. aspects of quality of life issues. Hence, human right and environment law and human quality of life and economic growth has close relationship . We can not neglect to concern how to achieve human right law to protect our nature environment existing in our societies.

What are environmental factors affect human health in important way, both positive and negative? On positive environmental factor aspect, which can sustain health, and promoting them is preventive medicine. They include : sources of nutrition (farming, oil quality, water availability, bio diversity/ bio integrity, genetically modified organisms ; hurting, fishing: wildlife, fish populations; water (drinking, cooking, cleaning,sanitation); air quality; ozone layer (protection from cancers disease etc).; space for exercise and recreation, sanitation/waste recycling and disposal. On negative environmental factors aspect, which are threats to health, and controlling them is public environmental health. They include: environmental conditions favouring disease sectors (endemic and exotic sectors); invasive biota (visuses, bacteria etc.), their hosts and sectors; environmental disruptions: floods, droughts, storms, fires earthquakes, volcanoes; air quality: pollution landing to respiratory disease or cancers; water quality: biotic and abiotic contaminants ; integrity of water transport and intrastructure; monitoring and management of municipal, agricutural, industrial outflows to the environment (gases, liquids, solid waste), human changes of the environment that: create conditions that favour disease; disturb and release noxious levels of previously bound chemicals (e.g. mercury released becomes poison) or bioto (e.g. methane released from thawed peat contributes to climate changes, create temporary, intense, life threatening heat islands (e.g. urban heat waves exacerbated by climate change); result from nuclear; biological or chemical welfare or terrorism, disruption cased by other war and violense. So, it implies , such as India developing county, which have large population are living in this country and their health is bad, due to air and water pollution is serious. So, environmental protective product needs will have more.

(ii) What is space and environmental technology?

For example, Cananda is a developed country and it begins to concern environmental pollution challenge to announced \$3 million to support the initiative strengthening health and environment linkages: from knowledge to action. The initiative will bring together scientific, technical and socio-economic information on environment and health linkages, and transfer that knowledge to inform decision-making at the local, regional and national levels. Also, Canada is principally concerned with the health of Canadians. This involves health factors in Canada and in biologically shared health regions (shared geography or exposure through trade and travel). Supports international health initiatives, such as determining health risks throught environmental analysis of disease vectors in Africa or Asia.

How can the space and environmental factors affecting health? Environmental information and environmental management contribution to the maintenace and restoration of health. Space based environmental management factors and communications can play roles in: Environmental information is for optimising use of health resources; distribution of and access to health advice and treatment (i.e. to health staff treatment facilities; short range environmental prediction for avoidance of high risk, situations and to guide immediate health system responses. Managing acute risks, adopting to them (e.g. temporary moving of vulnerable elderly monitored; modeling of health impact of environmental parameters; prediction of long term health resource needs and environmental planning and mitigation and adaptation to global changes. Large benefits are possible from attention to environmental factors, e.g. asthma prevention, disease and epidemiology. Benefits need to be quantified. This is of particular interest and relevance to pandemics , such as malasia in underdeveloped countries, potentially saving thousands of lives.

What is space and environmental technology? It can contribute to and keep abreast of environmental health forecasts (using existing models and known parameters); prepare and deliver prospectuses for what space can do in anticipation or response; steer space programs according to real risks and real accumulative health benefits, as long technical investment, don't focus primarily on threats that may have high emotional impact , but are of low actual risk; position space technology and the canadian space program in people's winds, aggressively and realistically, as a first line contributor to foresight and preduction, long term maintenance of well-being and prevention of factors of ill-health ; ongoing delivery of health services and management of current health factors and potentially capable and ready to respond in health emergencies. Finally, making the full business case for environmental protective product investment in space technology and space program contributions relative to the full and public and private cost of health programs. This connects not only to GDP raising, but to indicators of quality of life to any countries.

(iii) Why does environment protective product need survey to enquire design questions?

In conclusion, environment protective product researchers are similar to design product researchers who can use interviews and questionnaires to measure consumer response to their both products? They have similar point, such as environment protective products and general products which need to be designed. If the design of environment protective product is very attractive to compare other environment protective product competitors. Then, its sale numbers have possible to be increased. Hence, face to face walking interview and questionnaires with pedestrians is one kind of consumer behavior prediction method.

In psychology view point, implications tests have been developed in an attempt to overcome and to obtain investigates the adaptation of implicit methods to measure how to design product preference. Two questions are for test. (I) establishing an acceptable methodology for tests using environment protection product images . (ii) determining whether response to design environment protection products can produce significant effects in affective experiments.

How can environment protection design researchers predict how to design their environment protectionproduct to be more attractive? Understanding how environment protection consumers experience to design environment protection products have important implications for environment protection design research and design practice. These questions are often investigated experimentally by presenting consumers with a range of environment protection products or design variants and measuring subjective response for future design development. Measuring environment protection consumer response to design environment protection product testing, e.g. survey methods, questionnaires, interviews and focus groups. Questionnaire methods are especially popular, and often feature attitude response, such as choice questions. Although, those explicit measures can provide helpful feedback to environment protection product designers, who are also subject to a number of limitations. Consumer survey responses to a product or predict future environment protection behavior, such as how to design environment protection product purchasing decisions in the environment protection marketplace.

In some cases, environment protection participants might be motivated to answer a questionnaire dishonestly, or in a way that seems most socially acceptable. However, the survey may not be targeting the same thought processes that a consumer faces in the environment protection product use scenario or in the environment protection marketplace. There is evidence that actual environment protection product-related behavior is affected by more spontaneous or processes, as consumers are often distracted or pressed for time when consuming actual environment protection products or making purchasing decisions. Other methods include psychophysiological techniques, such as eye tracking, brain imaging, heart rate measurement, and voice pitch analysis for an overview of these methods applied to design environment production product measuring to consumer responses.

(iv) Can implicit design questionnaire (survey) or /and interview methods can test consumer behavior for measuring consumer response to environment protection product?

Some design researchers often use interviews and/or questionnaires to measure consumer response to any product design method, such as environment protection product. In psychology, " implicit" tests have been developed in an attempt to overcome self-report biases and to obtain a more automatic measure of attitudes. Two exploratory studies have conducted to (i) establishing an acceptable methodology for implicit tests using product images, and (ii) determining whether response to products can produce significant effects in affection.

How to contribute design-research methodological developments for measuring consumer response. For example, product design research and conventional methods need to be gathered consumer feedback. How can consumer research in product design? Understanding how consumer experience designed products has important implications for design research and design practice. Thus, product manufacturers need to attempt to develop knowledge about the relationship between product designs and the responses who elicit from consumers, e.g. borrowing which product features can contribute to consumer preference by presenting consumers with a range of products or design variants and measuring subjective responses to them. This process can offer guidance for what products or design variants might be most preferred and can give useful clues for further design development.

Consumer response can be measured by questionnaires(surveys), interviews and focus groups. Questionnaire methods are especially popular and often feature attitude response. However, consumer survey responses may not fully capture reactions to a product or predict future behavior, such as purchasing decisions in the marketplace. This is evidence that actual product-related behavior is affected any more spontaneous or impulse processes , as consumers are often distracted or processes for time when consuming products or making product decisions (Friese, Hofman & Wanke, 2009). For example, cell phone images can be replaced with cars in order to develop the experiment using a second product category. As with phones, vehicles were chose , due to their wide appeal, user involvement and variety of models for potential testing.

In these experimental studies, the consumption psychologists selected products from two categories (phone models and car models) with the intention of measuring significant differences in approach bias among product stimuli. These consumption psychologists aim to test that of the method could be defined to measure attitudes with sufficient sensitivity, variants of particular designs could also be used as stimuli, offering feedback on the viability of different design directions. The consumption psychologists feel it will be helpful to add multiple questions to the self-report stage . Instead of a single attractiveness rating, who might as about " liking" or "employing additional methods". Comparison with real would measure , such as willingness to pay, prior ownership or observed consumption behavior may also be instructive. It may also be worthwhile test a version of the task where the correct response is determined by a feature, such as class membership (product color), shape, brand etc. instead of image ,location or rotation. It seems survey method can be used to predict whether how to design environment protection product to attract many consumer choices. In the economic view point, instead of consumer will compare different similar product price, who also compare product color, shape, size of design factor to decide to make final consumption decision.

● Reference

Ajzen, I (1991). The theory of planned behavior. Organizational behavior and human decision processes, 50(2), 179-211. doi: 10.1016/0749.5978 (91) 90020-7.

Alba, Joseph W. and J. Wesley Hutchinson (1987). " Dimensions Of Consumer Expertise", Journal of consumer research, 13 March, 411-454.

Bailey, L., Mokhtarian, P.L. Little, A. (2008). The broader Connection Between Public Transportation, Energy Conservation And Greenhouse Gas Reduction, Report Prepared As Part Of TCRP Project J-11/Tasks Transit Cooperative Research Program, Transportation Research Board Submitted To American Public Transportation Association in http://www.apta.com/research/into/online/land_use.cfmi, accessed 17 April 2008.

Baucer, R,"Consumer Bhavior As Risk Taking , In Risk Taking And Information handling In Consumer Behavior", D. Coxceds Harvard University Press, Cambridge, Mass 1976.

Bogers, R. P., Brug, J. Van Assema, P., & Dagnetie, P.C. (2004) , Explaining fruit and vegetable consumption: The theory of planned behavior and misconception of personal intake level. Appetite, 42,157-166.

Bolton, Ruth N. (1998), " A Dynamic Model Of The Duration Of The Customer's Relationship With A Continuous Service Provider: The Role Of Satisfaction", Marketing Science, 17 (1), 45-65.

B.Shiv and A. Fedorikhin, " Heart And Min In Conflict: The Interplay Of affect And Cognition In Consumer Decision Making", J. Consumer Res., vol. 26, pp. 278-292, Dec. 1999.

Brown, K.W., Ryan, R.M. Reswell , J.D. (2007). Mindfulness: Theoretical Foundatins And Evidence For Its Salutary Effects. Psychological Inquiry, 18, 211-237.

Burke, R.R. : Behavioral effects of digital signage, J. Advertising Res. 49(2), 180-185 (2009).

Conner, M. & Abraham, C. (2001). Conscientiousness and the theory of planned behavior: Toward a more complete model of the antecedents of intention and behavior. Social psychology bulletin, 27, 1547-1561.

Cooper C. Mallon, K, Leadbetter S, Pollack L, Peipins (2005) , cancer internet search activity on a major search engine, United States 2001 to 2003, J Med Internet Res. 7(3): e36.

Cope, R. R. Cope and H. Davis (2008). Disney's virtual Queues: A strategic opportunity to co-brand services ? Journal of Business & economics research, vol. 6 no10, 13-20.

Cornelia, B.F. (1999) Rural development news, the North Central Regional Center For Rural Development vol. no 24 , IOWA.

David J. Nowak & Gordon M. Melsler (2016) " Air quality effects of urban trees and parks." National recreation and park association, USA.

De Hollander, A. E. M., J.M. Melse, Elebret & P. G.N. Kramers (1999), " An Aggregate public health indicator to represent the impact of multiple environmental exposures" Epidemiology: 606-617.

De Visser, R.O., & McDonnell, E.J. (2013). " Man points": Masculine capital and young men's health. Health psychology, 32(1), 5-14. doi:10. 1037/a0029045.

Dunn, J & A Neumsister (2002). Knowledge management in the Information age. E. business review, Fall , 37-45. Jounral of service, spring 2011, vol. 4, no1, De Grovte (2009).

Eysenbach G (2006) Infodemiology: Tracking flu- related searches on the web for syndromic surveillance. American Medical Informatics Associaion

Annual Symposium Proceedings , Curran Associates, Red Hook, NY, pp. 244-248.

Ettredge M, Gerdes, J. Karuga , G (2005) Using web- based search data to predict macro-economic statistics. Commun ACM 48: 87-92.

Felce, D. and Perry, J. (1995). Quality of life: A contribution to its definition and measurement, vol. 16, no.1 pp: 51-74.

Feldman, Jack M. And John G. Lynch Jr. (1988), "Self-
Generated Validity And Other Effects Of Measurement On Belife, Attitude, Intention And Behavior", Journal of applied psychology, 73(3),421-35.

Fiese, M, Hofmann, W., & Wanke, M (2009). The impulsive consumer. Predicting consumer behavior with implicit reaction time measurement. In M. Wanke (ed.) Social psychology of consumer behavior (pp.335-364). New York, NY: Psychology press.

Fitzsimons, Gavan, J. And Vicki G. Morwitz (1996), " The Effect Of Measuring Intent On Brand-Level
Purchase Behavior", Journal of consumer research, 23 (1), 1-11.

Hallerman , D. (2008) video Advertising Online: Spending And Pricing , New York. E-Marketer.

Harriet Griffey. (2010) The art of concentration, enhance focus, Reduce, stress and achieve move. Macmillan publishers ltd,Basinastoke and Oxford, London UK.

Helleman, D. (2008) Video Advertising Online: Spending And Pricing , New York, E-Marketer.

Huang, H.I. (2012). An empirical analysis of the strategic Management of competitive advantage: a case study of higher technical and vocational education in Taiwan (Doctoral dissertation, Victoria University).

Jamieson, Linda F. And Frank M. Bass (1989), " Adjusting Stated Intention Measures To Predict Trial Purchase Of New Products: A Comparison Of Models And Methods," Journal of marketing research, 26 (August), 336-45.

Kremers, S.P. J., De Bruijn, G.J., droomers, M., Van Lenthe, F. J., & Brug, J. (2005). Environmental interventions for selected dietary behaviors in adults. In J. Brug & F. J. Van Lenthe (eds.) , Environmental determinants and interventions for physical activity, nutrition and smoking: A review pp. 282-315. Rotterdam: Erasmus Medical Center.

Los Angeles Country Department Of public Health (2016), Country Health Ranking Model, Retrieved From www.countryhealthrankgings.org/our-approach. USA.

McGregor, S.L. T., & Goldsmith, E.B. (1998). Expanding our understanding of quality of life, standard of living and well-being. Journal of family and consumer science, 90(2), 2-6, 22.

McMichael, A.J. M. Mckee, J. Shkolnikov and T. Valkanen (2004), " Morality trends and setbacks, global convergence or divergence?", Lancet 363, 1155-1159.

Melse, J.M. & A.E. M. De Hollander (2001). " Human Health And The Environment", background document for the OECD Environmental Outlook, OECD, Paris.

Moschis, George p. & Roy, L. Moore (1979), " Decision making among the young. A socialization perspective " Journal of consumer research , 6 (September).

Mulligan, M. Banerjee, T & Thomas, N. (2008) ,European Paid Content And Activity Forecast, (2008 to 2013), Jupiter Research.

Peter, J., Ryan, M, M, " An Investigation Of Perceived Risk At The Brand Level, " Journal of marketing research, 13 May 1976, pp. 184-188.

Pieters, R., & Wedel, M. (2007). Goal Control Of Visual Attention To Advertising: The Yarbus Implication. Journal Of Consumer Research, 34, 224-233 (August).

Parasuaman, and Leonard L. Berry (1985), " Problems And Strategies In Sevices Marketing", Journal of marketing, 49 (Spring), 33-46.

R.C. Oliver, " When is consumer loyalty?" J.Marketing vol. 63, pp.33-44.1999.

Shostack, G. Lynn (1984), " Designing Services That Deliver", Harvard Business Review, 62 (January-February), 133-9.

Shostack, G. Lynn (1985), " Planning The Service Encounter ,in the service encounter" , John A. Czepiel, Michael R. Solomon, and Carol F. Suprenant, eds. New York: Lexington Books, 243-54.

Shostack, G. Lynn (1987), " Service Positioning Through, Structural Change", Journal of marketing, 51 (Janurary), 34-43.

Soloman, Michael R. (1985), "Packaging The Service Provider", Service Industries Journal , 5(1), 64-71.

Stevens, C.W. (1980), "K-MartStores Try New Look To Invite More Spending" The Wall Street Journal, Nov. 26, 29-35.

T. Ambler, A. Ioannides, And S. Rose, " Brand s On The Brain : Neuroimages Of Advertising ", Business Strategy rev., vol. 11, 3. pp. 17-30. 2000.

Westbrook, Robert A. (1980), " Intrapersonal affective influences on consumer satisfaction with products, " Journal of consumer research , 7 (June) 49-54.

Wiig, k.(1993). Knowledge management foundations: Thinking About thinking. How people and organizations create, represent and use knowledge vol.1 , of knowledge management series schema press: Arlington, TX.

World Health Organization (2003). Diet, nutrition and the prevention of Chronic diseases report of a joint WHO/FAO. expert consultation. Geneva: World Health Organization.

Wysocki, B. (1979), " Sight, Smell, Sound: They're all arms in retailer's arsenal" The Wall Street Journal, Nov. 17, 1979. 1-35.

Yale Center For Environmental Law And Policy (2006). Environmental Performance Index. Data available on-line at http://epi.yale.edu

CHAPTER FOUR

Psychological method predicts consumer behavior

What is the standard economic model? It is the standard economic model, the way most economists think about consumer welfare and consumer choice. What is the rationality in the standard economic model? The standard economic model relies heavily on the assumption that consumers are rational. Standard economic model assumes that consumers are fully aware of all the options who have, who can always and consistently , rank whose options in accordance with their preferences, and always choose the option, who like the best option. Thus, what the assumptions of the standard economic model of consumer are? The assumptions include consumers act with full information, consumers have known preferences, consumers choose the best option available.

The standard economic model of consumer behavioral prediction method advantages includes: A logically consistent theory of consumer behavior can be built, that theory can be used to make predictions about consumer behavior and those predictions can be compared with reality and those models often correspond to actual behavior of consumption reasons. What is the inconvenient truth? It includes clear evidence from psychology has shown that the rationality assumptions of standard economic model are wrong. Evidence from psychology has shown that consumers often are irrational and also who are predictably irrational. So these are wrong view point to influence how economists judge what cause consumption of behavior. Thus, it beings this question? What is mean of predictably irrational? It means that of irrational consumers were irrational in random ways, who would cancel each other out, leaving the overall outcomes determined by the behavioral consumption of rational consumers. As that case, economic theories that ignored irrational behavioral consumption would work just fine. But, psychology has shown that consumers are irrational in similar and predictable ways. Therefore, irrationality doesn't cancel out and can't be ignored to judge why the behavioral consumption has been caused.

How can economists judge each behavioral consumption cause? Economists will see evidence that consumers often are unable to make use of what consumers know about whose available options and whose preferences to figure out the best available option. However, although economic theory doesn't always assume self- interested behavior to any consumers, as a practical matter, most applications of economic theory assume that consumers act according to self- interest to decide every behavioral consumption of choice. For example, insurance market competition can make rational consumption. Such as competitive market in auto vehicle accident insurance will charge very high rates to some insurance buyers who might to drive a fast speed, but unsafe motorbike, this one might argue will protect the driving insurance buyers from taking stupid risk. So learning can make rational consumers. Even if consumers are predictably irrational, who can learn from their families and other consumer' or friends behavioral mistakes, therefore, over time irrational consumers will learn to be rational to make the most irrational consumption. As a result, there are few opportunities to learn from consumer individual mistakes of any consumption of decision. Finally, if there are many potential; bad choices and one good consumption of choice, it might take a lot of costly experimentation to figure out the right consumption of choice. Thus, the standard economic model of behavioral consumption of prediction method, which is standard economic theories assume that consumers are rational, strong-willed , and self-interested, but evidence from psychology shows that who are not and that evidence also shows that consumer individual irrationality has predictable features. So, it seems behavioral economic model can make economic predictions more accurate by using the evidence on consumer individual predictable irrational behavioral prediction in any kind of the similar products in competitive market nowadays.

Psychology is the science of human behavior and mental consumption processes. Consumption behavior is any consumption behaviors well as consumer mental consumption process is consumer individual internal experiences, comparison with alternative products, products choice of the best, making decision to consume or not consume for the product. So, advertisers often persuade to influence consumers' behavior to attract them to choose to buy whose products.

Why businessmen need to learn consumer psychology? Because psychology can help businessmen scientifically to evaluate common consumer beliefs and misconceptions about consumption behavior and consumption decision making mental processes. Consumption scientific psychology has four basic goals: To describe , explain, predict and change consumption behavior and consumption decision making mental process. Consumption psychological information is based on evidence, this is information based on direct observation and measurements with consumption behavior with scientific method. How are typical images of psychology? Consumption psychologists need to use scientific method to help businessmen to think what predicts who own, make a list of words would who use to describe a psychological scientist and what use to describe a psychological scientist and what images the businessmen have. However, consumption psychologists have difference ways of looking at the same problem for the businessmen, which is why there are so many sub-fields of consumption psychology. Consumption psychology's roots began in philosophy, but the focus changes to a scientific focus consumer.

Behaviorism is focused on consumer buying behavior that can be measured and observable. This returned the scientific approach to consumption psychology. Consumption behaviorist's believe consumers are controlled by their environment. Consumption behaviorism focuses on consumption observable behavior. However, consumption cognitive psychology believes that consumption behaviors are preformed because of the product ideas and thoughts. The cognitive perspective focuses on such consumer decision making and choice processes, such as perception, memory and thinking to the product.

So, I shall indicate how to apply psychological method to predict when consumer behavior will be changed from external environment factor influence from below different methods.

How to apply online psychological advertising method to predict behavioral consumption?

Online advertising can give relevance information to represent the similarity between advertisement and queries. These existing online advertisement works mainly focused on interpreting advertisements clicks in term of what consumers seek. (i.e. relevance information) and how consumers choose to watch TV or magazine or online advertisement etc. from different promotion media. (historically to know the product is selling on the market through advertising information). However, few of manufacturers or sellers attempted to understand why consumers chose to watch the advertising from TV or magazine or internet etc. different media.

Online Advertisement can be as a commercial search engine for manufacturers or sellers to gather data to concern how behavioral consumption is. The online advertisement's each observations motivate who to systemically model to test what each consumer individual psychological desire in order for a precise prediction on behavioral consumption after online advertisement promotion from internet media.

Today, internet is one kind of effective psychological advertising promotion method. For example, an online advertisement system, sponsored search has been one of the most important business models for commercial web search engines. It generates most of the revenue of search engines by presenting to users sponsored search results, i.e. advertisements (ads), along with organic search results. To deliver the most interesting ads to the users, a sponsored search system consists of technical components, including query-to-ads matching, online click prediction for matched ads, online click probability and auction to determine the ranking, placement, and pricing of the remaining ads. To aim to attempt to predict behavioral consumption for any kinds of product sale from online advertisement media.

In today's industry, generalized second price auction (GSP) is the most widely-used auction mechanism , in which the price that an advertiser has to pay depends on the predicted online click probability of the online buyers, whose own ads as well as the bid price and predicted online click probability of the ads ranked in the next position. The online sponsored search systems typically employ a machine learning model top predict the probability that an online user clicks an advertising from internet.

However, in practical sponsored search system. There are many ads without adequate historical click through data, even after query levels. Then online ads can been click improved prediction accuracy to consumer individual behavioral consumption when each click is occurred to the seller individual website. For example, online ads, such as : free Nike coupons ad. It shows " Go-Get_couptons.com/Nike, Download and print Nike coupons (100% Free)" ; another Nike-sales prices ad. It shows www.calibex.com, clothing, latest fashions and styles on sale. Buy Nike Fast!" ; another

Perfume.com official site ad. It shows "www.perfume.com, 10,000 + brand name perfumes and colognes-up to 80% off retail!" ; another Luxury English Perfume Ad. It shows " www.florislondon.com, shop online for luxury perfumes for men, women and the home". Above of these are example online ads. For two queries, "Nike" and "Perfume" , and two ads under the same query field similar relevance to the query.

Despite the usefulness of the relevance and historical of what users click and how users click. Specially, relevance information can indicate what relevant content users seek to click from online (internet) media. However, as it is well-known that users are not active to search for ads., the search engine, instead has to recommend ads. To users during their generic web search. Therefore, the relevance between query and ad can't perform as the key driver for click. In my opinion, in order for more click prediction, businessmen need to examine why users click.

How to apply psychological research to analyze of online user desire in sponsored search for behavioral consumption of reasons? First, according to literatures on consumer behavioral analyses, many factors will influence the decision making for consumption, including thought based effects and feeling-based effects. Though-based effects are basically win or loss analysis (e.g. trade-off between price and quantity), when feeling-based effects are more subjective (e.g. brand loyalty and luxury seeking). Note users online clicking the ad. Usually are with the intention to purchase something. In this situation, it is natural that the factors mentioned in consumer behavior analyses will influence their online click behaviors. So, advertisers can gather online advertisement data to choose how to design whose online advertisement to follow either is based on win or loss analysis, either focusing on product price and quality features or is based on more subjective analysis , focusing on brand loyalty and luxury seeking features to attract any consumer individual attention to choose to watch whose online advertisements from online advertisement media more easily. So, it seems that online advertisement is a promotional and gathering data channel to persuade consumer individual attention to predict whose behavioral consumption for any manufacturer or seller how to design whose online advertisement to sell whose products more accurate.

The application of consumer psychology, and in particular to branding, has gained popularity over the past decade in academic research and business practice. What neuroscience can bring to advance manufacturers' understanding of the consumer psychology of brands choice of behavioral consumption. The brand preference formation over time has four basic components: (1) representation and attention, (2) predicted value , (3) experienced value and (4) remembers value and learning.

First, on representation and attention component, it means that the amount of information consumers are exposed to is enormous, yet consumer's processing capacity is limited. How consumers represent, attend to, and perceive incoming information may have a profound influence on their behavioral consumption , i.e. brand identification. Representation is the first process in brand decisions , which involves forming the representation of the choice alternatives, that is brand identification. For example, different beer brands provide different options for choice are identified to consumers. At the same time, the consumer needs to integrate information on internal state , (e.g. thirst level) and external states , e.g. (location , social context) that drive attention. For example, when faced with a choice between a consumer's choice is likely to depend on whose own level of thirst (an internal state) and level of thirst chooses to drink (an external state). However, the brand image is a visual system allows for rapid brand and product identification. One of the key questions at this stage is what consumers pay attention to (i.e. focus on) once who are exposed to a number of rapidly identified choice alternatives (i.e. brands).

Attention is the mechanism responsible for selecting the information that gains preferential status above other available information for researching on branding. Thus, if the product brand image is attractive, then it will be probable attract the initial eye movement of consumers and thus may have a profound effect on related consumer behavior. For example, Pieters and Wedel (2007) showed that ensuring that consumers pay attention to the brand displayed in a print ad. It is the most effective way to ensure that who will transfer their attention to other elements of the print ad. So, brand image of attractive visual selection and eye movement can enhance the quality of incoming information to consumer individual behavioral consumption for the product of choice. The suggestion of eye-tracking is as a useful tool for determining the extent to which consumers find different brand extensions plausible. In sum, representation and attention are complex processes that influence all subsequent steps in our brand decisions framework.

Next, the step is predicted value, it is of each brand that is available for choice to represent the consumer's belief about the experienced value of that brand at same time in the future. In other words, the predicted values involves the consumer's evaluation of how much enjoyment who will desire form consuming among of different brands of product choice. For example, clothes are at different retail stores (e.g. H&M vs. Zara), consumer who are loyal to a store as measured by real purchasing behavior. (i.e. amount spent, frequency and recent of purchases based on loyalty card data) show more activation in the compared to consumers who are less loyal. The cloth brand inviting loyalty card holders who will be persuaded by the brand . So, the loyalty card of the brand of cloth seller can be the predicted value to the brand of the cloth to persuade the loyalty card holders to choose to buy.

Next, the step is experienced value , it is based on the pleasure derived from consuming a brand. It is a concept of motivational value to the consumer. Motivational value is a concept that is related to how predicted and experienced values interact is the motivational value or incentive of an option to the consumer. So building good brand image memory us important to influence consumer psychology. For example, the information of channel ,.e.g. ad. can build brand image memory to consumer more easily. Thus, good brand image can build good memory to consumers to prefer to choose to buy the brand of product easily. Otherwise, bad brand image can build bad memory to consumers to not prefer to choose to buy the brand of product easily. Thus, manufacturers or sellers can not neglect how to build good brand image to attract any consumer individual attention by attrative advertising because good brand image has close relationship with psychological consumption for shopping. It seems brand loyalty of famous degree can help businessmen to predict whether consumers are accepting or are not accepting to choose to buy their products or consume their service provision more accurate. For example, if the product brand is very famous long term, it seems consumers are accepting to choose to buy the product. Otherwise, if the product brand is not famous long term, it seems consumers are not ccepting to choose to buy the product.

How can store atmosphere environment influence consumer individual shopping behavior?

On the one hand, some consumption psychologists suggest in-store variable factor can influence consumer emotion to feel either pleasure or displeasure of intended shopping behaviors within the store, thus these consumption psychologists who believe retail store environment can influence consumption behavior. On the other hand, some employment psychologists also suggest work environment can influence employee individual emotion to work, work environment include hospitals, schools and prisons etc. public work environment. It seems consumers and employees whose emotion will be influenced by environment factor. It brings this question. Can store atmosphere environment predict consumers buying decision?

These consumption psychologists feel the component of store image, physical in-store variable , such as aisle width, brightness and crowding, when clearly these physical variables are store environment's major factor which can influence consumption behavior will be changed. Some retailers have claimed large effects from manipulating store atmosphere via layout, lighting, color and music (Wysocki 1979; Stevens 1980).

Some consumption psychologists also show these avoidance behaviors can cause consumer individual shopping emotion. First, physical approach and avoidance, which can be related to store patronage intentions at a basic level. Exploratory approach and avoidance can be related to in-store search and exposure to a broad or narrow range of retail offerings. Second, Communication approach and avoidance can be related to interaction with sales personnel and floor staff. Third, performance and satisfaction approach and avoidance can be related to repeat shopping frequency as well as reinforcement of time and money expenditures in the store.

In consumer psychological view point, pleasure or displeasure refers to the degree to which the consumer feels good, joyful, happy or satisfied in the situation. Then, another degree to which a consumer feels excited, stimulated, alert or active in the situation. Thus, if the consumer feels the shopping environment is comfortable, joyful, happy or satisfied. The shopping environment, it will have more chance to influence the consumer chooses shopping. Otherwise if, the consumer feels the shopping environment is excited, alert, stimulated or active. The shopping environment will have less chance to influence the consumer chooses shopping. It seems each consumer individual emotion will influence whose consumption behavior as well as store atmosphere environment has close relationship to influence each consumer individual emotion also.

Thus, retailers need to concern how to design whose store environment, e.g. what kind of furniture color, style and size; how much area of the store. For example, the store area is either large or middle or small area to let many or small number of consumers to stay in the store at the same time. How to let consumers to enter or leave the store? For example, how to let consumers to feel to leave the store easily when the fire is happening in store, it can make the consumers feel more safe, so who will have more probable to stay in the store to consume. How to display whose products to let consumers feel to touch or see to find any products on the shelves more easily. Choosing what kind of music to let consumers to listen during who are staying to shopping in store, e.g. soft music or none any music (quiet environment). These different store external feeling factors will influence each consumer individual emotion to feel more comfortable or uncomfortable feeling to decide to spend more long time or short time to stay in the store. Thus, it seems store atmosphere environment can influence consumer individual shopping behavior, so retailers can not neglect how to design store atmosphere environment to let whose customers feel more comfortable and safe to stay in stores.

Can model for understanding service encounter evaluation that can synthesize consumer satisfaction, services marketing, and attribution to influence consumption behavior to the retailer? These factors concern on the service industries how to influence consumption behavior, which focus on service encounter satisfaction and service quality to both the importance and the complexity of the issues. First and foremost, customer satisfaction depends directly and most immediately on the management and monitoring of individual service encounters (Parasuraman, Zeithaml, and Berry 1985; Shostack 1984, 1987; Sollmon et al. 1985).

What is the conceptual definition of service encounter? The model of service encounter evaluation relies on Shostack's (1985, p.243) definition of the term" service encounter" as " a period of time during which a consumer directly interacts with a service." The author identified all aspects of the service firm with which the consumer may interact, including its personnel, its physical facilities and other tangible elements, during a given period of time. I give this hypothesis, such as when an employee offers to compensate the customer for service failure, the offer may influence attributions. The employee performance will lead the customer to have negative beliefs about the firm, when the bad employee offer leads the customer to think bad image to the firm. So, the employee's bad service attitude can influence the offer is made to compensate for service failure to build bad service image to the company. Moreover, physical surroundings also are hypothesized to influence customer emotion in service failure situations. For example, if a customer experiences service failure in an organized , professional environment, e.g. lawyer, doctor, accountant professional services. The customer may not have more confidence to find the firm to serve to him again. In contrast, in a disorganized environment, the physical cues may suggest incompetence, inefficiency and poor service. In such an environment, the customer may attribute greater responsibility to the firm and be more likely to expect the same type of problem to occur in the future. Thus, any professional service firms, whose employees' service performance can influence customers' confidence to decide to find whose professionals to give any professional service opinions again. Thus, any professional service firm, whose employees' service performance can influence customers' confidence to the service firm likely.

How can the impact of personality and emotion on post-purchase service processes influence consumption behavior? Will consumption behavior be influenced to the retailer by consumer satisfaction or dissatisfaction and post-purchase service behaviors? Such as complaints, recommendations, and repeat purchase intentions, toward loyalty and word of mouth. Developing a new customer is expensive. Particularly in mature markets, competition is strong, product differentiation is low, and promotional costs have skyrocketed. So, understanding who these customers are, why who are dissatisfied, and how or even whether to market to them is an increasingly important issue.

That a customer's level of satisfaction affects much post-purchase behaviors, such as complaining and negative word of mouth is well documented. Satisfaction itself is influenced by comparing actual product performance to expectation. So, some consumption actual product performance will be needed to expectations by the product manufacuter or seller. So, some consumption psychologists began to research that the role of consumption based emotion in consumer satisfaction formation how to make recent personality research particularly concerning. It seems post-purchase processed can be a response to influence consumption- based emotions and consumption behavior to any retailers. The degree of satisfaction is a specific consumption experience, it has a direct impact on such post-purchase processes as repeat purchase intentions and complaining. So, any retailers need to concern on how predicting post-purchase consumer behavior will be.

Because personality should be an important predictor of consumption experiences, and thereby of post-purchase processes. Post-purchase processes can include either on positive consumption-based emotions or on negative consumption-based emotions. When the consumer satisfies to use the product, the useful of product expectation will be increased. Otherwise, when the consumer dissatisfies to use the product, the useful of product expectation will be decreased and the consumer complaint behavior will be increased. So, it seems post-purchase processes can influence consumers to decide to continue to choose to buy the products from the retailer again as well as how to reduce consumers have negative emotions to the products which is an important factor to influence any consumption behavior changing to the retailer.

How can constructive consumer choice processes influence consumption behavior?

Consumer decision making has been an interest in consumption behavior research, e.g. how technological changes, an information explosion factor can influence consumer individual choice decision to buy any products. Due to limited processing capacity, consumers often don't have well-defined existing preferences, but construct them using a variety of strategies contingent on task demands. Rapid technological changes for instance, has led to multitudes of new products and decreased product lifetimes. In addition, new communications media, such as the world wide web have made amounts of information on options potentially available (Alba et al. 1987). It seems time pressure, such as fast product lifetimes and new communications, media, internet advertisement can influence consumers how to make decision to buy any thing which is the best to them, e.g. choice of gathering products of advertisement information to buy products from internet (electronic shopping) instead of traditional visiting shops consumption behavior. So, new information advertisement media, e.g. internet advertisement consumer information media will influence consumer individual decision tasks. For example, a consumer may be fairly certain about the values of some of the attributes to choose to buy which kind of mobile phone from electronic shopping easily at home. However, the consumer may not have information for all of the mobile phone options on some attributes (e.g. reliability information would not be available for a new mobile model) from internet advertisement. In addition, some attributes, such as safety may be difficult for consumer to trade off; making trade off requires possibly accepting a loss on such an attribute with potentially threatening consequences.

What is characteristics of consumer decision strategy in product choice process? It includes the total amount of information processed, the selectivity in information processing, the pattern of process, (whether by alternative brand or by attribute). First, the amount of information processed is very a great deal. For example, a mobile phone choice may involve detailed consideration of much of the information available about each of the available mobile phone, as implied by more rational choice models, or it may have a consideration of a limited set of information (e.g. repeating what are choices last time). Second, different amounts of information can be processed for each attribute or alternative (selective processing), or the same amount of information can be processed for each attribute or alternative (consistent processing). For example, suppose a consumer considers the mobile phones to decide that life time is the most important attribute, processed only that attribute and chooses which mobile brand, with the famous brand value on that mobile phone attribute. Third, choice process would involves on that attribute. This choice process would involve highly selective processing of attribute information (since the amount of information examined differs across attributes), but consistent processing of alternative mobile phone brand information, since one piece of information is considered for each mobile phone. The fact that working memory capacity is limited effectively requires selective attention to information, e.g. internet advertisement media.

In general, the more selective consumers are in processing information, the more susceptible their decisions may be to factors that influence the salience of information, some of which may be irrelevant, such as different mobile phone brands of product life time comparing information. Information may be processed primarily by alternative, in which multiple attributes of a single option are processed before another option is considered, or by attribute, in which the values of several alternatives on a single attribute are examined before information on another attribute is considered. For example, a consumer might engage in attribute processing by examining the price of each of the mobiles, concluding that mobile brand (A) was the most expensive, another mobile brand (B) was the least expensive, and the another mobile brand (C) had a very good price . However, the consumer could process in an alternative-based fashion or is design by examining the reliability, price, safety of mobile phone brand (A) in order to form an overall valuation of that mobile phone brand (A).

Finally, an important distinction among strategies in the degree to which are compensatory. A compensatory strategy is one in which a good value on one attribute can compensate for a poor value on another. A compensatory strategy thus requires explicit trade off among attributes. Deciding how much more one is willing to pay for very good rather than average reliability or long useful life time in a mobile phone involves making an explicit trade -off between reliability long useful life time and price for examples. Thus, in general, constructive consumer choice processes attribute , such as the product's price, quality, life of time , reliability, design , brand information of media sources as well as electronic internet shopping or visiting shopping buying channels of these factors will influence the consumer to do the final decision to choose to buy which kind of product in the consumption market. Also, any retailers need to concern whether which is the major influence of attribute to the product. Because wrong evaluation of the major attribute of the product will influence the consumer to make final buying decision when who compares the retailer's product to other retailers whose similar products in the consumer's choice process.

How can be survey research measured that is applicable to intentions, attitude or satisfaction data to predict consumer behavior? Whether surveyed consumers will be predicted how consumers behavior are more easier than non surveyed consumers. Most academic studies of satisfaction use consumers' intention to repurchase as the criterion variable (for an exception, see Bolton 1998), and most companies rely on consumers' purchase intentions to forecast their adoption of new products or the repeat purchase of existing ones (Jamieson and Bass 1989).

In practice, some consumer psychologists' studies adjust the intention scores by analyzing that actual purchase behavior of consumers whose purchase intentions have been measured previously. For example, the popular ACNIELSEN BASES model forecasts aggregate purchase rates by applying conversion rates to measured purchase intentions (e.g. it seems that 75% of consumers who checked the top purchase-intentions box will actually purchase the product). To obtain these conversion rates, BASES uses previous studies that measured the purchase intentions of consumers and then tracked their actual purchases. However, investigating whether survey research is useful to measure consumer behavior. It has a weak point, a limitation of these studies is that companies (businessmen) focus on the internal rather than the external accuracy of purchase-intention measures. That is, the company studies measure the improvement in the ability to forecast the behavior of consumers whose intentions who previously measured for survey research experiments, not the behavior of consumers whose intentions who did not measure. Therefore, the studies assume that the companies can predict the intention-behavior relationship of non-surveyed consumers on the basis of the relationship that surveyed consumer exhibit.

It would suggest that studies measure the strength of the association between intentions and behavior on the same sample of consumers overstate that external predictive accuracy of purchase intentions by survey method. This would explain why so many new products fail even after which are performed well in purchase-intention tests by survey method. I shall suggest survey framework distinguished between two sources of measurement reactivity. The first is self-generated validity effects, it is as a strengthened relationship between latent intentions and behavior, due to the measurement of intentions from post-survey research. The second source includes all measurement effects that are independent of latent intentions, such as those that social norms or post-survey intention modifications create.

I also suggest a two stage procedure to detect whether the act of measurement alters the strength of the relationship between a latent construct that is measured through surveys, experiments or observations and its consequence (e.g. intentions-behavior, attitudes-intentions, attitudes-behavior, satisfaction behavior) and to determine the time relationship in the absence of the difference between non-survey and survey consumers behavior measurement. For example, prediction of consumer behavior purchase intention to achieve more profitability. Survey method can measure to these products , such as groceries, mobiles and personal computers etc. Companies can show the strength of the relationship between latent intentions and behavior is stronger for surveyed consumers than for similar non surveyed consumers.

I also suggest the survey questions can concern to compare with other inputs for purchase decisions. e.g. tastes, mood, competitive environment may make subsequent purchase behavior more consistent with prior intentions. For example, Feldman and Lynch's (1988) survey method predictions, Fitzsimons and Morwitz (1996) found that measurement of general intentions to purchase automobiles increase the likelihood that buyers will repurchase the automobile brand that they also previously consume and that first time buyers will purchase brands will large market shares. Under the assumption, if the survey's result showed the automobiles brand-specific purchase intentions. Thus, Fitzsimons and Morwitz's results suggest that the measurement of general intentions increases the association between latent, brand-specific intent and brand choice. So, brand is a factor which can influence consumers to choose to buy which automobiles. In conclusion, it seems companies can attempt to use survey method to investigate consumer behavior to predict what kind of factor is the most influential to attract consumers to choose buy whose product or consume whose service.

What is consumer neuroscientific research method to predict consumer behavior?

The key motivation has not been possible to directly observe the mental processes when subjects perceive marketing stimuli, such as advertisement or when who make purchasing decisions. Despite the long history of consumer research, little is known about the neural representation of how marketing stimuli affects consumers' perceptions, their decision-making processes and their consumption experience.

In the past, consumer researchers had to rely on varying the stimuli , e.g. prices or packaging and context factors, e.g. putting subjects in a good or bad mood in order to measure participants' reactions , e.g. choice behavior or brand preference. However, same researchers suggest scientific tools can observe brain activity to predict consumers behavior (Ambler et al., 2000 and Shiv and Fedorikhin, 1999 et al).

However, some consumer psychologists showed advertising research studies have often pointed out the important role of emotions for advertisement memorization (Ambler, 2000). In advertising research, who suggest that emotion and ratio are represented in different hemispheres of the brain. Research on the neural representation of stimuli-induced emotions, however, could show that emotions are not only processed in the left brain hemisphere, but are also processed bilaterally (e.g. in the left and right hemispheres of such cortical structure.

Customer loyalty is as an example, which can be defined as " a deeply held commitment to rebuy or a preferred product/service consistently in the future (Oliver, 1999). Consumer loyalty is a popular predictable consumer behavior topic for marketing researches, early research tried to establish whether customer loyalty has impact on aspects of business performance (such as profit margin and sales).

Loyalty is a psychological construct that develops over-time during a learning process of the consumer. Thus, loyalty research can benefit from insights in neuroscience and neuro-economics about how learning processes are represented in the brain. Some brain psychologists also explained how people learn to be loyal. They showed the following three processes in order to learn to be loyal.

(1) The brain should be able to memorize and retrieve positive and negative outcomes of former decisions, such as positive experiences after choosing brand A over brand B.

(2) The brain should be able to predict several outcomes of choosing between alternatives (buying A or B).

(3) The brain needs to integrate the information from processes 1 and 2 into the decision process.

Thus, it seems retailers need to concern how to develop loyalty and advertment promotion method and commitment to let consumers to have more confidence to choose to buy whose products or consume whose services more easily.

I shall indicate brain image and psychological feeling can influence consumer behavior. Such as digital signage is a new technology, where people broadcasting displays adapt their content to the audience demographic and features. In some shopping centers, retailers like to use machine learning methods on real-world digital signage viewer data to predict consumer behavior in a retail environment. Digital signage systems are nowadays primarily used as public information interfaces. They display general information, advertise content or serve as media for enhanced customer experience.

Interaction design studies show that the interaction level of users with digital signage systems will increase, including also the mobility of users around the display. Since digital signage systems can have a significant effect on commerce, which are also rapidly shopping centers ad retail stores. Retail generalization studies reveal that in-store digital signage increases customer traffic and sales (Burke, 2009).

Some consumer psychologists believe purchase decision processes can be described with five stages. The first stage is problem recognition, where consumer recognizes a problem is a need. The second stage is search for information via heightened attention of consumer towards information about a certain product, which can even resolve in actual proactive search for information. The third stage represents the evaluation of alternatives , which usually involves a comparison between various options and features based in the models of the expected value and beliefs. In the fourth stage of the purchase decision process, a provider, place, time, value , type and quality of the selected product or service and determined. The fifth stage are the final stage describes the post purchase use, behavior and actions.

Why will digital signage influence consumers choose to buy the product? It is possible that some consumers who like to use visa card to go to shopping as well as who like to use digital signage to confirm who are the visa card holders to let the businessmen to feel who are rich to let bank give trust to issue visa card to them to use. So, who do not need to bring much money to leave home to prepare to buy anything and who only bring one visa card to leave home safely. Thus, the digital signage systems are a new approach to automatic modelling of in-store consumer behavior based on audience measurement data. It is a unique machine payment method, which can also be used to predict more distinctive characteristics, such as an consumer individual's role in the purchase decision process. So, I believe digital signage audience measurement data can be used to model various user behavior for one kind of in-store consumer behavior prediction of method.

Can food consumption for trust cooperation influence food consumption choice?

Whether has it relationship between food consumption for trust and cooperation to influence eating similar vs dissimilar food consumption? Some consumption psychologists have attempted to do research to prove that food consumption with strangers who are assigned to eat similar food cooperating more in a labor negotiation and therefore earning more money. I image meeting for coffee with a colleges that just met. Is it possible that eating the same snack could increase your trust in that person? Similarly, could eating the same snack as a salesperson increasing your trust information about the similar food.

In general, people prefer to gather to share in a meal with others rather than eat alone, cultures define themselves partially through shared tastes and cooking traditions, and religious improve food regulations and restrictions meant to increase bonding among in-group members. Some psychologists had examined the relationship between food consumption and social connection. Development research finds that attraction increases similarly in food preference and also that similarity, in food preference increase attraction. Whereas, past research focused on the outcome of goods for food choice and consumption behavior is possible that group's food consumption results in social connection as increases liking and smoother interactions, presumably leading to interpersonal closeness. If the psychologists' research of social group similar food consumption is proved which can influence the people like to consume more than one person alone eats dissimilar food consumption, then restaurant businessmen only need to arrange what kind of similar food can attract group customers to eat as well as what kind of dissimilar food can attract one person customer to eat alone by their design food product advertising information.

We define incidental similar food consumption as group people choose to consume similar good more than dissimilar food with one restaurant table that is assigned and unrevealing of either preferences or prosocial intentions. Such that people eating together could become closer and more similar, with benefits for work performance. Eating may thus serve as a strong cue for signaling liking and closeness and more importantly trust and cooperation.

Our main focus is on understanding how food can be used as a connecting device that increases consumers' cooperation and trust. To the extent that similar food consumption promotes closeness and liking, it follows that it would increase trust and cooperation, and this would be particularly true for strangers who can't rely on past behavior to establish trust. Unlike preference , such as taste in music or political beliefs, some food consumption psychologists feel that the role of food consumption on trust and cooperation is influenced by food product information. Thus, consumers can be strategic in food who consume, utilizing food when eating dinner on adapt or when out for lunch with a colleague . Similarly, marketers can use incidental similar food consumption to increase trust in product information when advertising a non-food product. Some food psychologists believe that similar food consumption lead to increase in cooperative behavior, such that those who consume similarly will be better at resolving a negotiation conflict than those consuming dissimilarly. Additionally, who also believe consequences of similar consumption for trust in product information. So, some food psychologists predict group close friend or family relationship consumers assigned to eat similar food as a product advertiser will like the advertiser more, which will translate into increased trust in the information presented about the similar food product.

Summarize incidental similar food consumption should increase closeness and liking, when group people are absence of dissimilar food choice, when people are influenced to consume similar food by food product information. Thus, the increase in closeness and liking should subsequently lead to an increase in trust and cooperation for the group of consumers who consume similarly. So, some food psychologists predict similarity in food consumption serves as a storage cue of trust compared with other incidental similarity and is therefore an important domain for examining implications of similar food consumption. These food psychologists suppose to consumers who eat the same food as product advertiser will trust information about the similar food product is more consumption as well as consuming similar food can increase cooperation resulting in a faster resolution of a labor conflict and more beneficial outcomes to both parties. Finally, who indicate similar food taste includes, sweet food ,e.g. sweet bread or ice cream or cookie as well as salty food , e.g. potato or chip etc. So, restaurant food shall divide sweet or salty taste similar food. If one person chooses to eat the restaurant food, the restaurant can advertise dissimilar sweet and salty taste food both product information to let the person to choose. Otherwise if one group people chooses to eat the restaurant food, the restaurant can advertise either all sweet taste food or all salty taste food product information to let the person to choose.

Does habit strength moderate the intention behavior to consumption?

Scientific evidence provides a sufficiently strong basis to justify the systematic development of intervention programs to increase healthy nutrition behaviors (World Health Organization, 2003). Such as an adequate consumption of fruit, a high consumption of fruit is associated with lower risk of cancer (Kremers et al., 2005, World Health Organization, 2003).

Will the concept of habit influence consumption behavior? Such as, fruit is a kind of health food. If the consumer has habit to choose to buy different kinds of fruit to eat everyday. Is habit as a factor to influence the consumer to choose to buy fruit to eat? Otherwise, if the consumer has no habit to choose to buy different kinds of fruit to eat everyday. Is non-habit as a factor to influence the consumer individual consumption behavior to choose any kinds of fruit to eat everyday.

Traditionally, habit has been measured by the number of times that behavior has already been performed in the past by an individual. Evidence to date indicates direct effects of past behavior on current behavior (Conner & Abraham, 2001). Some consumption psychologists had done experiment to research whether habit factor can influence fruit consumption. Their showed fruit consumption was assessed with a five item questionnaire, which was validated against seven day dietary records and biomarker for fruit intake (Bogers et. al 2004).

According to this consumption questionnaire result, it showed that intention is hypothesized to be the most immediate determinant of consumption behavior, yet several recent lines of research suggest that intentional control of behavior may be difficult to change, due to habit behavior consumption is caused to the individual consumer. Thus, it is difficult to change the consumer's behavior, when who have habit to choose to consume different kinds of fruit every week. However, results showed that the influence of intention on fruit consumption was weak and non-significant for those who had a strong habit toward fruit consumption. In constant, for those with a low or medium habit strength towards fruit. For those with low/medium habit strength, path analyses confirmed the reasoned, intentional process is for fruit consumption. In contrast, for those with high habit strength, it had the strongest influence on behavior. Thus, perceived control ability of fruit consumption seems to overrule the planned and intentional processes of fruit consumption for those with a strong habit. The environment behavior link also relates to the origins of habit, which are thought to originate from repeated performance of a given behavior in a stable situation. Thus, it seems environment can be one factor to influence strong habit consumers to buy fruit to eat every week as well as strong habit fruit consumer will buy much fruit to eat more than weak habit fruit consumer per week.

Nowadays, in UK suggests that consumer buying behavior has changed significantly. Consumers can buying different things, at different times and through different channels. As a result, forecast accuracy is very poor and many companies feel automated forecasting systems can not predict buying behavior more accuracy and relying on analysts to predict buying behavior by psychological methods. Automated forecasting systems weaknesses are such as: Historical data alone can't be used to predict feature sales in times and drawing together a wider range of internal and external data would help improve forecast accuracy. The impact on revenue manager varies widely. When sales forecasts are important, adjustments to revenue management system outputs are needed to retain credibility. When customers' behavior are poor to understand, there may be a need to sell from auctions or online experimentation to predict the market response. So, these automated forecasting system have these weaknesses to cause companies feel technological method can not be better than psychological method to predict further consumption behavior for whose products.

In psychological consumption of prediction view point, learning how to predict changes in consumers' attitudes and behaviors which is important to any companies. For example, in part behavior has changes as a result a recent major disruptive events, such as recession and exchange rate changes etc. economic factor, but there are other non economic factors to change consumers' attitudes and behaviors. For example, consumers are becoming smarter in their use of the internet to research products based on previous customers' view, seek out the best, deals and offers and then buy online, with a corresponding increase in the number of price comparison sites. So , companies are percentage seeing the rise of the strategic consumer who observes the dynamic of supplier pricing and adapts their buying strategy in response. However, some observers suggest that these changes to consumers' attitudes and behaviors are fundamental long, lasting and likely to continue to be disruptive.

Some consumption psychologists feel sales have become less predictable. In general, sales forecasts based on historical patterns in time series have become less accurate and hence less useful in the past year in many industries, not just these traditionally served by revenue management. Does forecast accuracy easily? For some revenue managers may be not too much, in some businesses prices are set by reference to the main competitors and forecasts have limited impact on operating and decisions about capacity. Marketing forecasting is aim to setting prices, maximizing revenue and managing operations.

However, forecast accuracy is very important to find why changing consumer attitudes and the implications for customer segmentation and forecasting of buying behaviors are not just relevant to revenue management. They are also fundamental to sales, marketing , brand management, customer loyalty, product design and beyond. Perhaps it has an opportunity for revenue managers to take a lead in influencing thinking of their colleagues in these areas. Some consumption psychologists forecast the future, who concern the historical data of companies collection before the recession, it can no longer be applied to forecast consumer behavior during the recession or after. At the opposite extreme, companies can simply continue to between auto prediction system to predict when the market stability will return soon and how to influence consumer behavior.

Sales are likely to depend on the economic situation, the competition and consumer behavior. However, these are external environmental factor to influence consumption of behavior. If it is possible to separate out these effects, then the forecasting model can take account of them by either building the economy/market into the model or segmenting consumers in an economy/market invariant way. External data, for example on the economic situation can also provide a good indicator of future sales. For example, internet (online) web site research technology is one possibility for combining and processing data from different sources on the web using automated tools. If buying behavior is changing and every consumer demand is becoming elastic, not only to increase revenue, but also to improve knowledge of the customers. For example, online auctions are mainly used in the travel and hospitality industries for offloading surplus capacity have been shown when facing only uncertain consumer demand. However, analyzing external economy environment factor is not effective to minimize risk to the sellers. Because sale forecasts are never going to be completely accurate and there is an argument for moving the focus away from being smarter with existing data towards making the business less dependent on sale forecasts. For example, taking close look at increasing flexibility in the supply chain or operations or re-examine the strategy for setting price.

What the current situation really emphasizes however is that there is certainly a need for forecast accuracy to be taken seriously by revenue managers and reported on by revenue management system. Thus, revenue managers need to concern how to predict whose consumers' psychological emotions to find why the reasons can influence whose consumption attitudes and behaviors changing to cause their product sale numbers had been falling. So, it seems that consumers' emotions can be influenced whose buying behavior by online auctions factor.

How can economical environment factor predict consumers consumption?
   The dominant approach to industrial economics is
the one which is usually described as the structure-conduct-performance approach. So, predicting the performance of an industry in terms of profitability and advertising growth can predict consumer consumption in possible. The structure of an industry covers factors like the relative and size of firms, involved the ease of entry into the industry and the elasticity of demand for the output of that industry. The conduct of firms covers the objectives of the firms, price setting behavior, and attitudes to competitors (actual and potential), and from that the performance of that industry predicted, particularly in respect of profitability.

What are the main features of the structure of an industry? Many consumption psychologists discuss on the structure-conduct-performance topic, the number and relative size of the firms and the extent of barriers to entry into the industry to influence the product suppliers to consumption choices in the market. The number and relative size of firms is usually placed under either the size distribution of firms or individual concentration. Most industries don't fit into the category of a large number of small firms or of one firm.

Barriers to entry into an industry comprise all the factors which lead to new entrants into the industry being at a disadvantage to the existing firms because consumers have more choices to buy the similar products from the competitors . The first factor is the existence of economies of scale which means that a new entrant would have to produce on a relatively large scale increasingly. The second factor, the brand of products are supplied by a significant amount and thereby depressing price a significant amount , differentiation and advertising, so that a new entrant has to incur costs to overcome the loyalty of consumers to existing products. A third factor is the ability of existing firms to produce and distribute at lower costs than new entrants. Although, for example, access to cheaper new materials, accumulated knowledge of the industry etc. So, these external marketing environment factor will influence consumption behavior choices. For example, if the industrial structure determines or influences performance, the governments concerned with aspect of industrial performance (particularly aspects like price changes, technological progress and employment levels).

Consumption psychologists have often been assigned that the level of concentration in an industry is largely technological determined and that increases in concentration reflect impact of technological advance with increase the desired size of factory or firm. For example, mobile phone manufacturing industry, if the brand of mobile phone manufacturer had technological advance to manufacture any new model to attract consumers have more buying choices from their mobile products. Then, technological factor will influence consumers have more choices to buy the brand of mobile phone products. Other some psychologists believe the way in which unit costs change with the scale of production (cost conditions and economies of scale) factor which can influence consumers choice behaviors. When public policy favor active industrial intervention to change industrial structures, some indication is required as to whether the minimum efficient scale is small or large relative to the total market to supply their product numbers to influence consumers' behaviors. In the former case a policy favoring small units would be indicated, whereas, in the latter case large units may be favored.

Increasing returns to scale and economies of scales are usually defined as a situation when all inputs into the productive process are increased in the same proportion the volume of output increases in a greater proportion . How can economies of scale influence products supplying numbers? For example, that is the scale of output increases the degree of capital intensity rises. But within that change the type of the capital equipment is likely to be varied. Further, the balance between skilled and unskilled or between manual and non-manual labor may change. Thus , it is necessary to adopt a view of both increasing and decreasing returns.

The definition of unit costs of output declining with increased output. This must refer to all costs(including capital costs, and can only relate to a particular set of relative prices for inputs from which the unit costs are calculated. It would include any change in the price of input usage, such as mobile phone products which need to use different materials to manufacture any mobile phone products Thus, if a mobile phone firm had to pay more wages as its use of labor increased, that would have to be included. It is generally assumed that, for any scale of output, the firm is combining the impacts in an efficient manner. This efficiency includes economies efficiency (choosing the least cost combinations of inputs) and technical efficiency (producing the maximum feasible output from given inputs). The measurement of returns to scale under this definition may be only relevant to a particular economy, as it depends upon the particular relevance prices used.

Such as, each mobile phone product price will influence consumer individual behavior of choice to buy only one among the different brands of model mobile phones. So, mobile phone manufacturers need to concern how to reduce cost to gain economies of scale input to raise mobile phone output. For example, from a reduction in the effective price of an input to the model of mobile phone, as the volume of the styles of mobile phones purchases increased arising from an increase in monopsony power. For example, three mobile phone plants, A, B, C are assumes to have a fixed mobile phones output, and initially produce with unit costs A1, B1, and C1. Respectively. Supposing plants A and C would make subnormal profits and plant B super-normal profits, when capital costs are based on the historical cost of the mobile phone plant. Now the capital values of plants A and C are, it is argued, unlikely to fall and that of plant B to rise , for the amount which another mobile phone firm could be prepared to pay for a plant will reflect its profit prospects. If the decline in capital value fully reflects the initial deviations for normal profits, unit costs shift to A2, B2 and C2 respectively. Thus, there is a tendency at work towards mobile phone constant unit costs being observed. How far this tendency operates depends upon the based on which mobile phone firms value their assets. When the value is based on historic cost, the tendency does not operate. But the tendency does operate when the value is based in some way on the assets' profit prospects. Thus product manufacturers need to concern how to earn economic of scale to cost to avoid each product price will be changed often to influence consumer choices to other competitors more easily.

Some consumption psychologists had investigated several psychological variables which have been suggested as causes or effects of debts. Economic and demographic factors can predict debt category well to support this influence of factor. How can consumer manage money skills to pay debt which can influence when who plan to consume? Debtors were more likely to buy cigarettes and Christmas presents for children than non-debtors. Conclusions must be qualified because of low return rates, but the results suggest that a complex of psychological and behavioral variables affect debt and are affected by it. It is argued that these variables are linked to the psychology.

In general, economical environment is poor, it will cause many unemployed people, even some people will loan debt to pay daily essential expenditure from banks. If those debtors can't manage whose debt to be better to spend. Whose behavior will cause who do not have more spending desires often. Because these debtors will feel themselves as being in a community where debt was more common and more tolerated than non-debtors. The whole question of the classification of products a necessities or luxuries and its consequences for purchasing behavior is of current interest in economic psychology. Since debt is associated with poverty and poor people tend to give external reasons for economic phenomena, such as poverty and unemployment, causality may run the other way. In either case, however, there should be a positive correlation between external control and debt. There have different variables offer explanations of debts at different levels. One factor may be a consequence of another, or the mechanism by which it takes effect (for example, different patterns of economic socialization might generate different attitudes towards debt).

Some debtors need to borrow debt (loan) for house purchasing need. So, if the house loan debtors who need to pay back whose house loan to bank for long time. It is possible that their house loan will influence to reduce to spend much of daily consumption behavior to buy non luxury and daily essential products for long time. Thus, the result is these house loan debtors will reduce every day essential expenditure, such as food and soft drink, entertainment etc. to consume too much to compare to non house loan debtors for long time. It seems that retailers can attempt to apply debt management behavior to predict consumer shopping of desires.

Can firm's conduct and behavior factor influence consumer consumption ?

The usual assumption about the objectives of firms made by economists is that firms seek to maximize profit. The means that firms feel that who are protected against the possibility of new entrants, and proceed to maximize short-run profits. Firms feel that the barriers against new entrants ensure that their profits won't induce new firms to enter the industry and to reduce competitors enter to industry to raise consumers' choices to buy any similar products.

A major challenges to the profit maximization objective has come from proponents of the view that modern larger corporation are under a managerial control, which it is argued leads to the pursuit of other objectives, such as growth. The pursuit of non-profit objective is not unique to managerial-controlled firms, although the growth of such firms and of theories about than have emphasized these types of objectives.

Another view has focused on the controllers of the firm, whether owners or managers, having a wider range of objectives and that the achievement of profit maximization and the cost minimization requires considerable time and effort by the controllers. Thus, the controllers have incentives to forge profit maximization, unless who are forced to do so. Under oligopoly, firms can earn profits above the normal level, e.g. one country has only two electricity power companies are existing in the country's energy supply market. They may change a profit maximizing price, but actual reported profits may be less than potential profit.

This could raise from technical inefficiency or from higher than necessary payments to the factors of production. The technical inefficiency can arise since it takes effort by the controllers to reach full efficiency and which may be willing to make necessary effort. The higher payments can involve higher salaries to the controllers of the firm. For either reasons, company needs to concern how to report profit fall below true profit of the firm, with the difference used to finance inefficiency and higher factor payments in fair business conduct behavior. Particularly, company also need to concern how to carrying on fair business conduct behavior, e.g. none mislead advertising information, correct profit differentiation financial information, product reputations of the existing products presentation, none mislead consumption motives performance (which favor the established over the unestablished) and lower trade-in values of second –hand products of entrants (particularly in the car market). So, it seems that any one firm none mislead conduct behavior factor can influence consumer choices to increase or decrease to buy the firm's products in fair buying and selling transaction.

Another view point, for same products differentiation none mislead conduct factor is also important to influence each consumer behavior. For example, cars don't have a common prototype and each manufacturer must design its particular model. In constant , for a product like sugar , there is a common prototype, and differentiation through branding is within the discretion of the firm involved. This for some good product differentiation may be benefit whereas, for other products differentiation depends upon the activities of the firms involved, although the costs and benefits to the existing firms varies between profits. However, the height of the barrier to entry by product differentiation is likely to be influenced by the conduct and behavior of the firms involved, and thus in the case , there is an element of firm's behavior and conduct can influence any consumer buying behavior of choice to its products.

Advertising is one kind of promotion method to any firms. Advertising is a subject on which people tend to hold strong and often opposing views, and economists are not expectations to this. Some economists regard advertising as one means by which firms concentrate on promoting whose tastes and opinions in the direction of their products and also more generally in favor of private consumption (consumer behavior). Other economists see advertising as an efficient way by which firms supply information to potential consumers. Otherwise, some economists see advertising as a barrier inhibiting new entrants into an industry thereby enabling the established firms to reap high profits, when others see advertising as evidence of competition and an aid to new entrants in establishing themselves. So, it seems advertising can influence consumer choices possibly.

Advertising relatives to sales varies considerably between industries. For example, the ratio of advertising in 1968 year varied from over 15% in the toilet preparations industry to over 10% in the soap and detergents industry to near is in a number of toilet preparation producer industries. A distinction is frequently made between information an persuasive advertising , and it is often suggested that some forms of advertising (such as classified ads.) are likely to have more informative content than other forms (such as television advertising).

What is the sale of advertising in the demand function? One response is that a firm can sell more of its products because consumers have more information on that product. The information may relate to its existence, price, quality etc. Thus advertising is seen as essentially supplying information to consumers how to choose the similar kinds of products to decide which is the suitable product to buy. The other response is that advertising seeks to persuade consumers to purchase with favored people or situations, repetition of the same message. This advertising seeks to promote tastes rather than to inform. One firms' advertising may not be successful through false judgement by that firm and its advertisers or because of the impact of the advertising of other firms. The difference between the two responses can be put in terms of the conventional; utility maximization approach top consumer demand theory. The first response regards consumers' taste (i.e. the utility function) as fixed and advertising informs the consumer about availability, price etc. So, that utility maximizing process can take place more effectively . The second response regards advertising and seeking to promote consumers' tastes and change the consumers' utility function in a manner favorable to the advertiser. So, different types of advertising have been as containing information and persuasion in varying proportions and varying in the degree of desirability. But for the firm, the intention is to sell its products, and it will present any information in a way which seeks to influence the consumer to purchase its products.

Some consumption psychologists believe utility maximization by well-informed individuals plays a central role in conventional micro-economies. However, advertising can be a part of the conduct of firms in that firms use advertising amongst many other things to seek to increase profits or whatever their objectives it. Finally, advertising can be a part of performance, influenced by industrial structure. Some consumption psychologists also believe the highly differentiated products are more suitable for advertising than undifferentiated ones. They suppose existing firms benefit from their past investment in advertising and new entrants have to overcome those advantage.

If advertising is a profitable activity for firms to undertake, then the question arises as to why other firms don't follow suit. If other firms possibly including new entrants did follow suit, then the returns to advertising are likely to be reduced. It is useful to discuss the returns to advertising in terms of the returns in increased sales per advertising message and the cost of delivering an advertising message. Increasing return would occur form a message of repeated showing of a particular advertisement led to the product demand increasing at an increasing rate. Thus, of the product demand per unit of time is same to the number of advertising message per unit of time, then increasing sale returns would be raised possibly. The implications of any increasing sale returns to advertising may depend upon whether the increasing returns operate for advertising of a single product or for advertising of a number of products. Thus, it seems advertising promotion behavior can create barriers to entry to reduce consumers have more choices from other competitors' similar products sale.

In general, under short –run profit maximization,
the price was seen as a mark –up marginal cost with the marketing determined by the elasticity of demand. However, economists have used these methods to determination of how prices change behavior. The first is the indicated prices are determined relative to costs by firms in the pursuit of objectives. In the view point, the first is firms are price-makers and let prices in a way which think will achieve these objectives. Subject to constraints arising from demand and cost conditions. The second is theory of perfect competition, firms are effectively price-takers and the interaction between demand and supply in the market set price. So, firms are regarded as price-takers, and hence not in position to set prices, such as price-adjuster . The third is the idea of observing the process of price decision-making and seeking observation is on the prices of price determination. Their view is expressed as price is based on full average cost , including a conventional allowance for profits and full average cost . Is determined as follows? price or direct cost per unit is taken as the base, a percentage addition is made to cover overhead or on cost or indirect cost, and a further conventional addition of percentage is made for profit. This, it seems price

change behavior can influence consumer individual consumption behavior to any products.

Can scientific research be predicted consumer behavior by experts?

Using scientific research methods to predict consumption behavior phenomena in this field, some experts had attempted to do research in predictive validity to evaluate whether a measure of scientific achievement to consumer behavior. There are three groups thought to have varying knowledge of and ability to predict consumer behavior are academics, marketing practitioners and consumers in general. Academic groups use their scientific knowledge of consumer behavior as a basic for such activities as teaching, consulting for corporations, and testifying in legal and regulatory proceedings. In contrast, marketing practitioners are likely to be as familiar with this scientific literature. However, practitioners gain expertise through their experience. This expertise might help them to make accurate predictions of consumer behavior. Finally, when few studies on consumer behavior reach the general public, consumer's personal experiences should help them to predict certain aspects of customer behavior. So, it seems that how to predict consumer behavior, personal experiences (psychological feeling) method is more accurate than to scientific method.

In this discussion, I shall imply two hypotheses about how experts measure consumer behavior predictions. The first hypothesis, experts can make more accurate predictions than novices as well as the second hypothesis, academics can make more accurate predictions them practitioners. Thus, these hypotheses bring the questions and asked the subjects to predict whether each hypothesis tended to be true or false. For example, whether the more frequently an adolescent interacts with peers about consumption matters is the greater the tendency to use peer preferences in evaluating products? (Moschis & Moore, 1979). Will a person be more satisfied with their recently purchased car if the car met or exceeded whose expectations? (Westbrook 1980).

Their consumer research result indicated that for the practitioner group, who worked with marketing problems, but who were unlikely to be familiar with scientific research on consumer behavior. For example, systematic sampling was used to select 100 practitioners from the 1984 year American Marketing Association Membership Directory (academic addresses were excluded), a self addresses envelope was enclosed in the original mailings, and two postcard reminders were sent. Replies were received from 20 academics and 13 practitioners.

Subjects were asked whether who had previously read each of the studies. Two academic had read most of the studies because few of their predictions were usable (three or fewer), all responses from these subjects were excluded. Two academic respondents said that who did not understand all of the hypotheses, so who were also excluded. This left 16 academics. Other practitioner was excluded because who said that who did not understand the instructions, which reduced the number of practitioners to 12. Six academics and one practitioner reported reading one or more studies and their responses for these studies were excluded. Finally, the predictions by expects and native subjects showed that the prediction of consumer research percentage is larger than academics experts. For example, by assuming that researchers typically found what who were looking for and as a result, predicting
" true" for all hypotheses a subject would have been correct for 74.2% of the predictions, subjects who gave a higher percentage of these answers would be expected to achieve higher level of accuracy.

I shall indicate web site (internet) example, to judge whether which can be used to predict consumer behavior. Recent work has demonstrated that web search volume can "predict the present", meaning that can be used to accurately track outcomes, such as unemployment levels, auto and home sales and disease prevalence in near real time. Consumers are searching what for online can also predict their collective future behavior days or even weeks in advance. For example, specifically businessmen can use search query volume to forecast the opening weekend box-office revenue for feature films, first month sales of video games and the rank of songs, finding in all case that search counts are highly predictive of future outcomes from online google research. Finally, businessmen can reexamine previous work on tracking trends and show that, perhaps surprisingly, the utility of search data relative to a simple auto regressive model is modest.

Nowadays, people increasingly use the internet for news, information and research purposes. From this perspective, it is a short step to conclude that what people are researching for today is predictive of what who will do in the near future. For example, consumers may search to prepare to buy a new camera, moviegoers may search to determine the opening date of a new film, or to locate cinemas showing it and individuals planning a vacation may search from a places of interest, to find airline tickets, or to price hotel rooms. So online can aggregately count of search queries related to retail activity. Movie going or travel might be able to predict collective behavior of economic, cultural, or political interest. Determining the nature of behavior that can be predicted using search, the accuracy of such predictions and the time scale over which predictions can be usefully made are therefore all questions of interest.

Researchers have focused on the observation that search " predicts the present". For example, Ettredge et al (2005) found that counts of the top 300 search terms during 2001 to 2003 year were correlated with US Bureau Of Labor statistics Unemployment Figures; Cooper (2005) et al found that search activity for specific cameras during 2001 to 2003 year correlated with their estimated incidence and Eysenbach (2006) found a high correlation between clicks on sponsored search results of flu-related keywords and epidemiolopical data from the 2004 to 2005 year Canadian flu season.

Thus, motivated , I indicate one example how investigates whether search activity is a systematic leading indicator of consumer activity by forecasting. For first example, supposing to opening weekend Box-office revenue for 119 feature films released in the united States between Oct. 2008 year and Sept. 2009. For second example, supposing to first month sales of video games across all gaming platforms, e.g. Xbox, Play station etc.) for 106 games released between Sept. 2008 and Sept. 2009 year. These search data can be collected from yahoo using research rank from the current and previous weeks.

Can online search also predict the near future? A finding that may apply usually to a wide range of consumer behaviors , e.g. airline travel, hotel vacancy rates and auto sales and economic indicators , e.g. real-estate prices, credit card and confidence indicators. It seems all research based predictions simply models to build on publicly available information. For movies, baseline predictions can be used a linear model that includes production budgets, the number of screens on which each movie opened and box office projections from the Hollywood Stock Exchange (HSX) (hsx.com) on online, play money prediction market that is known to generate information prediction. For video games, many of the key indicators of revenue, including production budgets and initial available. Thus, it seems that businessmen can attempt to use internet (online) search technological method to search past information to concern whether what number of customers will be estimated.

In psychology view point, implications tests have been developed in an attempt to overcome and to obtain investigates the adaptation of implicit methods to measure product preference. Two questions are for test. (I) establishing an acceptable methodology for tests using product images . (ii) determining whether response to products can produce significant effects in affective experiments.

How can design researchers predict how to design product to be more attractive? Understanding how consumers experience designed products have important implications for design research and design practice. These questions are often investigated experimentally by presenting consumers with a range of products or design variants and measuring subjective response for future design development. Measuring consumer response to design product testing, e.g. survey methods, questionnaires, interviews and focus groups. Questionnaire methods are especially popular, and often feature attitude response, such as choice questions. Although, those explicit measures can provide helpful feedback to product designers, who are also subject to a number of limitations. Consumer survey responses to a product or predict future behavior, such as purchasing decisions in the marketplace.

In some cases, participants might be motivated to answer a questionnaire dishonestly, or in a way that seems most socially acceptable. However, the survey may not be targeting the same thought processes that a consumer faces in the product use scenario or in the marketplace. There is evidence that actual product-related behavior is affected by more spontaneous or processes, as consumers are often distracted or pressed for time when consuming products or making purchasing decisions. Other methods include psychophysiological techniques, such as eye tracking, brain imaging, heart rate measurement, and voice pitch analysis for an overview of these methods applied to design product measuring to consumer responses.

Can implicit design questionnaire (survey) or /and interview methods test product preference for measuring consumer response?

Some design researchers often use interviews and/or questionnaires to measure consumer response to products. In psychology, " implicit" tests have been developed in an attempt to overcome self-report biases and to obtain a more automatic measure of attitudes. Two exploratory studies have conducted to (i) establishing an acceptable methodology for implicit tests using product images, and (ii) determining whether response to products can produce significant effects in affection.

How to contribute design-research methodological developments for measuring consumer response. For example, product design research and conventional methods need to be gathered consumer feedback. How can consumer research in product design? Understanding how consumer experience designed products has important implications for design research and design practice. Thus, product manufacturers need to attempt to develop knowledge about the relationship between product designs and the responses who elicit from consumers, e.g. borrowing which product features can contribute to consumer preference by presenting consumers with a range of products or design variants and measuring subjective responses to them. This process can offer guidance for what products or design variants might be most preferred and can give useful clues for further design development.

Consumer response can be measured by questionnaires(surveys), interviews and focus groups. Questionnaire methods are especially popular and often feature attitude response. However, consumer survey responses may not fully capture reactions to a product or predict future behavior, such as purchasing decisions in the marketplace. This is evidence that actual product-related behavior is affected any more spontaneous or impulse processes , as consumers are often distracted or processes for time when consuming products or making product decisions (Friese, Hofman & Wanke, 2009). For example, cell phone images can be replaced with cars in order to develop the experiment using a second product category. As with phones, vehicles were chose , due to their wide appeal, user involvement and variety of models for potential testing.

In these experimental studies, the consumption psychologists selected products from two categories (phone models and car models) with the intention of measuring significant differences in approach bias among product stimuli. These consumption psychologists aim to test that of the method could be defined to measure attitudes with sufficient sensitivity, variants of particular designs could also be used as stimuli, offering feedback on the viability of different design directions. The consumption psychologists feel it will be helpful to add multiple questions to the self-report stage . Instead of a single attractiveness rating, who might as about " liking" or "employing additional methods". Comparison with real would measure , such as willingness to pay, prior ownership or observed consumption behavior may also be instructive. It may also be worthwhile test a version of the task where the correct response is determined by a feature, such as class membership (product color), shape, brand etc. instead of image ,location or rotation. It seems survey method can be used to predict consumer behavior.

In economic view point, demand is a model of consumer behavior. It attempts to identify the factors that influence the choices that are made by consumers. In microeconomics, the objective of the consumer is to maximize the utility that can be derive given their preferences, income, the prices relates products and services for which the demand function in derived.

Utility is the capacity of a product or service to satisfy a want. It can explain the phenomenon of value. Since utility is subjective and can't be observed and measured directly. The objective in microeconomics is to maximize the satisfaction or utility of individuals given their preferences, incomes and the prices of products or services who buy or consume. Thus, total utility of more or less satisfaction degree be caused by consumer behavior. It is consumption psychological result (effect) and it has close relationship.

Are internet delivered electronic services being made available to consumers about how who are evaluated for potential adoption to predict consumer behavior? Some psychologists' past researches had focused primary on the positive utility gains attributable to information technology adoption. However, their results indicate that e-service is adversely affect primary be performance-based risk perceptions, when perceived ease of use of the e-service reduces risk perceptions. E-services are interactive software based information systems received via internet. E-services are important in business to consumer (B2C) e-commerce because which represent ways to provide on demand solutions and improving customer satisfaction. So, it brings this question shows that whether businessmen can predict consumer adoption of e-services.

It is important to distinguish the different between conducting basic purchase transactions and adopting e-service. The e-service adoption decision is essentially different from most typical e-commerce purchases as which create a longer-term relationship between the consumer and service provider. Hence, even, if e-services are an e-commerce application to which some adoption models exists. It requires a distinct conceptualization to businessmen and businessmen need focuses on the role of perceived risk on influencing on adopting intentions of e-services. When e-services are convenient and create efficiencies for businessmen users. Little is understand about how consumers evaluate them for adoption. So, e-service performance quality and the potential utility of the service usefulness is a difficult task for consumers, especially given the newness of the online environment. If the consumer feels e-transaction is not suitable to him/her to use for shopping, then it is possible that it will reduce the chance to the consumer to choose to use the kind of e-transaction service to buy the brand of products. So, this e-service transaction will include both risks (potential negotiations utility) and perceived usefulness (potential positive utility) to let every customer to feel either of high utility or low utility after who choose to use e-service to shopping.

How important are risk perceptions to the overall e-services adoption decision? What types of risk are influenced and therefore important to the customer of e-service? Perceived risk is commonly thought of as an uncertainty regarding possible negative consequences of using a product or service. It has formally been defined as " a combination of uncertainty plus service of outcome involved" (Bauer 1960, 1967) and " the expectation of losses associates with purchase and acts as an inhibitor to purchase behavior" (Peter & Ryam 1976). Their research's pilot test result have indicated some electronic service shoppers concern for the theft of their private information, or simply its misuse by the businessmen collecting it. Members of a focus group drawn from the population studied to concern for the loss of privacy of personal financial information as an identify-theft. So, privacy risk was gathered and modeled as a deterrent to utility evaluations and the adoption choice to influence consumers choices to buy the product from this e-service sale channel.

Overall, some consumers will feel those perceived risks to influence who decide to buy the product from e-service sale channel. Such as performance risk, it means the possibility of the product manufacturing and not performing as it was designed and advertised and failing to deliver the desired benefits, financial risk, it means the potential monetary outlet associated with the initial purchase price as well as the subsequent maintenance cost of the product (ibid). The current financial services include potential for financial loss , due to fraud, time with means consumers may lose time when making a bad purchasing decision by wasting time researching and making the purchased, learning ow to use a product or service only to have to replace if it does not perform to expectations, psychological risk means potential loss of self oneself. Consumers feel unwise if they experience a non-performing products and may experience their feelings of harm to their self-image from the frustration of not achieve their buying goals, social risk means potential loss of status in one's social group as a result of adopting a product or service, looking foolish, privacy risk means potential loss of control over personal information, such as when information about purchase used without the customer's knowledge or permission. A consumer is carrying a criminal use whose identity to perform fraudulent transactions. Overall , when any one consumer feels one of those perceived risk will occur, then any one of these risks will influence who to choose to use e-service transactions method to buy product from internet. So, internet shopping seems have bad image to influence consumer shopping choice of channel as well as consumer demand of the product will be reduced if who feel e-service transaction channel is not safe to whom.

Is online video and television service is to be affective in predicting technology adoption to influence consumption behavior choice? Nowadays, online video and television services have become one of the most promising activities in terms of advertising revenue. E-Marketer has estimated that online video or television advertising will soar at 56% to 70% in the next five years (Halleman, 2008). To predict user acceptance of online video and television services. Despite a digital growth in online video and television to service over the span of a few years.

What factors can influence consumers to choose to buy the product after who watch online video and television advertising? Some psychological experiments shows a greater influence of perceived behavioral control on intention to use this type of services. The effects of attitude toward use and subjective norm were positive, but more moderate. The lesser effect of attitude towards use may be explained by the evidence benefits of watching videos online. However, search recent consumer studies have confirmed that watching online videos and televisions has become one of the favorite online activities for internet users (Hallerman 2008. Mulligan et al. 2008).

In the past, if somebody wanted to buy a book, on little learned about from whose friends or relatives, first who had to go into more bookstores to see of that book exists and after to make some price comparisons in order to decide from where to buy it from one bookstore choice only. These activities were time and money consuming. The situation has changed how the person can learn about launching a book easily from social networks, and by simply accessing an online store, such as Amazon . com , readers who can purchase the book to save time and energy by pressing a button activity only. So, the process of buying a product simplified in terms of time and money spent, but because more difficult in terms of decision making which has become more complex. The main reason is people have too many options to choose from in terms of product or service, price, quality and time.

Can digital internet technological electronic service influence consumers to choose this shopping style when who is habit to spend time to play internet . Is lifestyle a tool for understanding buyer behavior? Consumption psychologists had examined to confirm that it has relationship between the consumers' general life styles and their consumption pattern and the brands of products are used by them. They concluded that consumers often choose products, service and others because who are associated with a certain lifestyle . The products are the building blocks of lifestyle, marketers should therefore, have a complete idea of these changing lifestyles. So, dividing to segment them and position their products successfully.

The lifestyle of individuals has always been of great interest to marketers. They deal with everyday behaviorly oriented facets of people as well as their feelings, attitudes, interests and opinions. A lifestyle marketing perspective recognize that people sort themselves into groups on the basis of the things groups on the basis of the things who like to do, how who like to spend their leisure time and how who choose to spend their disposable income. Lifestyle is an important concept used in segmenting markets and understanding target customers, which is not provided by the study of demographics alone.

Many researchers have focused on identifying the lifestyle of the consumers to have better information about them. This study used the lifestyle analysis to identify market segments. Otherwise, some consumption psychologists believe to apply life style analysis for market segmentation, the developed of product strategy and the developed of the most appropriate communication strategy. They suggested successful retailers based on general application of lifestyle analysis have begun to implement a portfolio management approach which focuses on the needs of the key target markets. So, lifestyle segmentation can provide a valuable insight into the task of creating an effective brand identity. The study of lifestyle often provides fresh insights into the market and gives a more dimensional view of the target consumers. The marketing managers may be able to develop improved multi-dimensional views of key market segments, uncover new product opportunities obtain better product position, develop improved advertising communications based on a richer more life-like portrait of the target consumer and generally improve overall marketing strategy. These consumption psychologists assume that the members of any target client groups are all similar. The first hypothesis is people differ in their lifestyle they can be grouped into segments and the second hypothesis is people belonging to lifestyle segments differ in their demographics.

Thus, in consumption environment, a consumer chooses a product or a brand , which indicates a maximum possibility of the definition of whose lifestyle identity. Alternatively, a person makes a choice in a consumption environment in order to define actualize whose lifestyle identity if through the products or brands chosen. It can be assumed that the individual's consumption behavior can be predicted from an understanding of how who represents whose would be himself/herself of the details of choosing lifestyle system are known. Thus, digital internet is one good channel to research consumer lifestyle to predict whose consumption style.

Research question: Can behavioral economy method and psychological method predict consumer behavior.

Some consumption psychologists had attempt to research whether planned behavior can predict alcohol consumption. This research aims to quantify variables between theory of planned behavior variables and (i) intentions to consume alcohol in habit and (ii) reducing alcohol consumption reasons. They showed some drunken violence alcohol consumers who will reduce to consume much alcohol if who feel driving accident or causing death or violence behavior or alcohol poison causing non-health after who have consumed too much alcohol often. Thus, it is important to understand the psychological determinants of alcohol consumption.

A model of human behavior that has been extensively utilized to predict health-related behaviors, such as alcohol consumption in the theory planned (TPB; Ajzen, 1991). This model proposes that the most important determinant of behavior is a person's intention to perform the behavior. Three variables are identified as determinants intention, attitude, subjective norm and perceived behavioral control . Attitudes are an individual's positive or negative evaluation of performing the behavior. Subjective norms reflect an individual's perceptions of social approach or disapproval for performing the behavior. It represents an individual's perceptions of control over behavioral performance in the face of internal and external barriers. These results suggest the possibility that alcohol consumer behavior that are harmful to health, such as alcohol consumption, may yield different relationships when compared with results for behaviors that are beneficial to health. Specifically, individuals may wish to emphasis a lack of control over health risk behaviors, because these behaviors are not seen as socially , desirable and may need to be explained away be reference to external causes, such as peer pressure (De Visser & Mc Donnell, 2013).

Hence, it seems fear feeling psychological factor can influence alcohol consumers to reduce alcohol consumption in these situations, such as what action is being considered (e.g. heavy episodic drinking and the action is located (e.g. driving car) and what is the time frame for the action(e.g. needs car), the staff is a company driver when needs to drive car every day. Thus, whose action will influence to reduce whose alcohol consumption. Although, who has drinking alcohol in habit, but because who is one company driver, who is fear to cause accident to hurt himself/herself and whose staffs when who sit in whose company car together. So, who will choose to reduce to consume alcohol in possible.

In general, consumer will have choice behavior, when who needs to do decision to buy automobile among of more than one product choice or with the determinants of such consumer behavior as buying life insurance, putting money in a pension plan, using credit cards etc. actions. By comparison, questions about behaviors that involve a choice among less or more options are usually studied at a lower level of generality. Thus, consumption psychologists may be interested to know why consumers buy one second of automobile rather than another, why who choose one type of medical treatment over another, or why who fly one airline rather than another. So, consumption psychologists must clearly define the action, target, context and time elements of the behavioral alternatives to predict whose consumption behavior. For example, the decision to buy tickets on one airlines rather than another can be affected by the destination (target element): A consumer may prefer one airline for overseas flights , but another for domestic flights. Similarly , choice of insurance company may vary depending on whether who buy life insurance, automobile insurance or property insurance.

Why will decisions under uncertainty cause? In consumer choice process, who has chance to encounter decisions under uncertainty. For example, the attributes of each product were assumed to be known with certainty. Thus, the consumers knew the price, picture, quality, reliability and visual appeal of each product type. All consumers need to do was to be importance weights and subjective values to these attributes and then derive a weighted average. In many of choice alternatives are not known with certainty ahead of time. Often, the outcomes are produced by decision depend on the state of the world at the time and the decision is made. For another example, a LCD television can produce a high -definition picture only of the service providers transmit high-definition programs. To take this uncertainty into account, the consumer has to judge not only the value of a high-definition display , but also the likelihood that this attribution will be available.

Perhaps, more readily recognized are the risks and uncertainties inherent in investment decisions. The investment outcomes of a decision to invest in a fixed interest certificate of deposit or a stock market mutual fund depend on future market conditions. Whereas the CD produces a known payoff over a given time period, the amount and probability of possible gains or losses to be expected of the mutual fund can only be estimated.

Thus, advertising can reduce decision uncertainty to consumers' choices. If the product advertising can attract to consumer's consideration , it will persuade the consumer to choose to buy the brand of product. Clearly, information about the decision making process, in general, as well as about decisions of particular relevance to consumer behavior. Thus, it seems advertising information can reduce consumers' choices processes under uncertainty to decide to buy the brand of product preference choice.

Why businessmen need to divide customer segment(s) to decide who is target customer group to predict consumer behavior. Nowadays, consumers are unique in themselves. A comprehensive knowledge of consumers and their consumption behavior is essential for a firm to succeed. In order to understand and predict consumption patterns and behaviors within segment(s), market research becomes essential.

Why businessmen need to concern market research with consumer behavior. Each individual is unique himself/herself and needs and wants vary from person to person. Markets identify segments and target one or few of these segments and target one or few of these segments and thereby fulfil the qualifications of the marketing concept. First, marketers need to identify customer needs and wants and then, deliver product and service offering, so as to satisfy the customers more efficiently and effectively, than the competitors.

In order to understand and predict consumption pattern and behavior within segment(s), market research becomes essential. Market research defines to gather information about market and the customers. The environment of a firm may be grouped as the micro and macro environment both. The micro environment firm comprises forces to close affect the firm directly. For example, the firm's internal environment, the founder/leader and whose vision and mission, clients, competitors, suppliers and channel intermediaries. The macro environment, on the other hand, companies forces in the environment that first affect the micro environment and thought that which affect the firm, in other words, which affect the firm indirectly, including the demographic factors, socio-economic factors, political factors, technological factors, cultural factors, natural factors etc. The micro environment is studied in terms of strength(s) and weakness and when the macro environment is studied in terms of opportunities and threat(s) analysis of both comprises the SWOT analysis.

Thus, market research can help firms to understand the specific marketing situation facing a firm. Identifies the needs and wants of client segment(s), identifies variables target segment(s), serves them better through formulation of appropriate marketing strategies a mix of the 4(p)s. It's goal is to achieve maximum efficiency and effectiveness to meet customer needs and wants and client satisfaction . Thus is obtained through a conscious attempt at understanding " what" the client buy(s), "why" who buys, "when" who buy, from "where" who buys, "how" much who buys and "how" often who buys. Thus, the integration of market research with consumer behavior: marketing research can understand and predict consumer behavior as well as consumer research is a process and tools to be used to study consumer behavior both.

Marketing research objective is to study the marketing environment and the clients who are a part of it, as well as to study consumers as individuals as groups. It focuses to establish trends and identify opportunities and threats in the environment, to study the market and forecast potential and to predict buying patterns based on modeling and , to understand consumption behavior and consumption patterns. Besides, consumer behavior research has tradition approach and current approach has traditional approach and current approach.

Traditional approach divides positivist and interpretivist both approaches. Positivist approach refers to as modernism is the earliest approach to studying consumer behavior and trends the study as an applied science. It lays emphasis on the causes of consumer behavior, these causes are directly related to effects. Thus it treats consumer as "rational" human things, who make purchase decisions after collecting information and weighing all alternatives. The process of consumer decision making, it seems of rationality, rational decision making and problem solving is the key. It is based on certain assumption, consumer actions based on cause and effect relationship can be generalized, who can be objectively measured and tested. If researchers could identify the reasons behind consumption behavior, who would be able to predict it, and if who could predict consumer behavior, who could influence it.

The methods focus on prediction of client behavior, including surveys, observations and experiments. It aims at drawing conclusions a large samples. The positivist consumer actions can be objectively measured and tested. It focuses to predict consumer behavior, e.g. large samples of quantitative methodology. Otherwise, the interpretivist consumer action is a cause and effect relationship can't be generalized , consumption pattern and behaviors are unique, these are unpredictable. Consumer actions are unique and different both between two consumers, and/or within the same consumer at different times and situations. It can't be objectively measured, tested and generalized. It focuses the act of understanding the consumption rather than predicting the act of purchase, e.g. methodology small samples of qualitative methodology.

In consumption psychological view point, the current approach is the term " dialectics" , considers all forms of human behavior, thus the current approach to the study of consumer divided into four approaches: materialism approach implies that consumer behavior is shaped by the material environment, e.g. money, possessions etc. , change approach means consumer behavior is " dynamic" in nature, it is always in a process of continuous motion, transformation and change. Totality means consumption behavior is " interconnected" with other forms of human contradiction means views changes in consumer behavior as arising from their internal contradictions, like moods, emoting etc. The approach studies the consumer as a complex total whole and views consumer purchase as well as consumption processes.

The current approach to studying consumer behavior uses both the quantitative as well as qualitative approaches. There are three broad research perspectives in consumer behavior: they are as follows:

Decision making perspective, the experiment perspective and behavioral influence perspective. According to decision making perspective , the buying process is a sequential in nature, with the consumer perceiving that there exists a problem and that moving across a series of logical and rational steps to solve the problem; stages being problem recognition, information search, evaluation of alternatives , purchase decision and past purchase behavior, it emphasizes rational , logical and cognitive approach to consumer decision making and purchase process.

The experiential perspective believes that not all buying may be rational and logical, in some cases, buying results are from a consumers' desire for fun and fantasy, pleasures, emotions and moods. The perspective emphasizes that consumers are feelers as well as thinkers. The behavioral influence perspective holds that forces in the environment stimulate a consumer to make purchases without developing beliefs and attitudes about the product.

In general, quantitative research is used by the positivists and qualitative research is used by interpretivists. How to use quantitative research in consumer behavior? It comprises (i) research techniques that are used to gather quantitative data over large samples randomly and (ii) statistical tools and techniques, e.g. survey, observation and experiments techniques. Thus type of research is descriptive in nature. It is primarily used by the positivists when studying consumer behavior with a focus on prediction of consumer behavior and techniques are also used by " dialectics" approach.

How to use qualitative research in consumer behavior? It comprises (i) research techniques that are used to gather quantitative data over small samples techniques , e.g. depth interviews, focus group of study is subjective in nature. The focus is on understanding consumption behavior and consumption pattern . the objective is to gain an understanding of consumer behavior and the causes marketing situations are unique, and hence the finding can't be generalized to marketing situations. It is primarily used by the interpretivists when studying consumer behavior. However, the qualitative techniques are also used by " dialectics" approach.

Today, both approaches and are used to study consumer behavior. In some causes, qualitative research may act as an indicator to qualitative research through case studies and other qualitative measures. Qualitative research is very often a prelude to quantitative research are used to prepares scales for surveys and experiments.

Consumer decision making has long been of interest to research. The most prevalent model from this perspective is " utility theory" which proposes that consumers make choices based on the expected outcomes of their decisions. Some consumption psychologists view consumers are as rational decision makers and who are only concerned with self interest. However, utility theory views the consumer as a rational economic man. Consumer behavior considers a wide range of factors how to influence to change the consumer behavior , and acknowledges a board range of consumption activities beyond purchasing.

These activities commonly include need recognition, information search, evaluation of alternatives, the building of purchasing intention, the act of purchasing, consumption and final disposal. Some psychologists regard man and rational and self interested, making decisions based upon the ability to maximize utility when spending the minimum effort.

It concerns economic man theory, in order to behavior rationally in the economic sense, as consumers must aware of all the available consumption options be capable of correctly rating each alternative and be available to select the optimum course of action. Some psychologists view point, behavior is subject to biological influence through instinctive force or drives with act outside of conscious thought. So, the consumption psychological behavior is determined by biological drives, rather than individual cognition, or environmental stimuli thoughts and feelings can be regarded as consumer behaviors.

Some psychologists feel environmental variables influence consumer behaviors. However, an influential role of the environment and social experience is acknowledged with consumers activity seeking and receiving environmental and stimuli is as informational inputs aiding internal decision making . Input variables are the environmental stimuli that consumer is subjected to influence to choose either to buy or not buy the product, e.g. brand, advertisement, price, sale channel, place, salespeople service, quality, loyalty, durability etc. different elements can influence consumer final decision making.

Some investigations indicated about the changes in consumer behavior are caused by external environment influences, e.g. globalization and development of information technologies. It can help to understand the specific factors what should be taken into account in evaluation of consumer behavior.

In macroeconomic environment view point, for example, the global trend of economic liberalization, new political geography, gradual removal of international trade barriers , rapid technological advancement these environmental factors are just a few of the factors that have had major effect on the business management practices nowadays. The most obvious impact on the practical level of doing business has these macroeconomic environmental factors intensified competition. So, these factors can influence micro economical consumer behavior indirectly. Consumer behavior is mix of elements from psychology, sociology, sociopsychology, anthropology and economic. Management process will identifies, anticipates and supplies customer requirement efficiently and profitably.

Consumer decision making has long been of interest to research. The most prevalent model from this perspective is " utility theory" which proposes that consumers make choices based on the expected outcomes of their decisions. Some consumption psychologists view consumers are as rational decision makers and who are only concerned with self interest. However, utility theory views the consumer as a rational economic man. Consumer behavior considers a wide range of factors how to influence to change the consumer behavior , and acknowledges a board range of consumption activities beyond purchasing.

These activities commonly include need recognition, information search, evaluation of alternatives, the building of purchasing intention, the act of purchasing, consumption and final disposal. Some psychologists regard man and rational and self interested, making decisions based upon the ability to maximize utility when spending the minimum effort.

It concerns economic man theory, in order to behavior rationally in the economic sense, as consumers must aware of all the available consumption options be capable of correctly rating each alternative and be available to select the optimum course of action. Some psychologists view point, behavior is subject to biological influence through instinctive force or drives with act outside of conscious thought. So, the consumption psychological behavior is determined by biological drives, rather than individual cognition, or environmental stimuli thoughts and feelings can be regarded as consumer behaviors.

Some psychologists feel environmental variables influence consumer behaviors. However, an influential role of the environment and social experience is acknowledged with consumers activity seeking and receiving environmental and stimuli is as informational inputs aiding internal decision making . Input variables are the environmental stimuli that consumer is subjected to influence to choose either to buy or not buy the product, e.g. brand, advertisement, price, sale channel, place, salespeople service, quality, loyalty, durability etc. different elements can influence consumer final decision making.

Some investigations indicated about the changes in consumer behavior are caused by external environment influences, e.g. globalization and development of information technologies. It can help to understand the specific factors what should be taken into account in evaluation of consumer behavior.

In macroeconomic environment view point, for example, the global trend of economic liberalization, new political geography, gradual removal of international trade barriers , rapid technological advancement these environmental factors are just a few of the factors that have had major effect on the business management practices nowadays. The most obvious impact on the practical level of doing business has these macroeconomic environmental factors intensified competition. So, these factors can influence micro economical consumer behavior indirectly. Consumer behavior is mix of elements from psychology, sociology, sociopsychology, anthropology and economic. Management process will identifies, anticipates and supplies customer requirement efficiently and profitably.

In consumption psychological view point, technical criteria concerns the cost aspects of purchase, durability, reliability, comfort and convenience. Economic criteria concerns the cost aspects of purchase, include price, running costs and residual values, e.g. a trade in value of a car.

In conclusion, economic environmental and consumption psychological factors can influence consumer behavior changing, so businessmen can attempt to do any surveys, experiment etc. research methods to predict how consumer behavior will change to attract them to choose to buy their products more easily.

● Reference

Ajzen, I (1991). The theory of planned behavior. Organizational behavior and human decision processes, 50(2), 179-211. doi: 10.1016/ 0749.5978 (91) 90020-7.

Alba, Joseph W. and J. Wesley Hutchinson (1987). " Dimensions Of Consumer Expertise", Journal of consumer research, 13 March, 411-454.

Baucer, R,"Consumer Bhavior As Risk Taking , In Risk Taking And Information handling In Consumer Behavior", D. Coxceds Harvard University Press, Cambridge, Mass 1976.

Bogers, R. P., Brug, J. Van Assema, P., & Dagnetie, P.C.
(2004) , Explaining fruit and vegetable consumption: The theory of planned behavior and misconception of personal intake level. Appetite, 42,157-166.

Bolton, Ruth N. (1998), " A Dynamic Model Of The Duration Of The Customer's Relationship With A Continuous Service Provider: The Role Of Satisfaction", Marketing Science, 17 (1), 45-65.

B.Shiv and A. Fedorikhin, " Heart And Min In Conflict: The Interplay Of affect And Cognition In Consumer Decision Making", J. Consumer Res., vol. 26, pp. 278-292, Dec. 1999.

Brown, K.W., Ryan, R.M. Reswell , J.D. (2007). Mindfulness: Theoretical Foundatins And Evidence For Its Salutary Effects. Psychological Inquiry, 18, 211-237.

Burke, R.R. : Behavioral effects of digital signage, J. Advertising Res. 49(2), 180-185 (2009).

Conner, M. & Abraham, C. (2001). Conscientiousness and the theory of planned behavior: Toward a more complete model of the antecedents of intention and behavior. Social psychology bulletin, 27, 1547-1561.

Cooper C. Mallon, K, Leadbetter S, Pollack L, Peipins (2005) , cancer internet search activity on a major search engine, United States 2001 to 2003, J Med Internet Res. 7(3): e36.

De Visser, R.O., & McDonnell, E.J. (2013). " Man points": Masculine capital and young men's health. Health psychology, 32(1), 5-14. doi:10. 1037/a0029045.

Eysenbach G (2006) Infodemiology: Tracking flu- related searches on the web for syndromic surveillance. American Medical Informatics Associaion Annual Symposium Proceedings , Curran Associates, Red Hook, NY, pp. 244-248.

Ettredge M, Gerdes, J. Karuga , G (2005) Using web- based search data to predict macro-economic statistics. Commun ACM 48: 87-92.

Feldman, Jack M. And John G. Lynch Jr. (1988), "Self-
Generated Validity And Other Effects Of Measurement On Belife, Attitude, Intention And Behavior", Journal of applied psychology, 73(3),421-35.

Fitzsimons, Gavan, J. And Vicki G. Morwitz (1996), " The Effect Of Measuring Intent On Brand-Level
Purchase Behavior", Journal of consumer research, 23 (1), 1-11.

Fiese, M, Hofmann, W., & Wanke, M (2009). The impulsive consumer. Predicting consumer behavior with implicit reaction time measurement. In M. Wanke (ed.) Social psychology of consumer behavior (pp.335-364). New York, NY: Psychology press.

Hallerman , D. (2008) video Advertising Online: Spending And Pricing , New York. E-Marketer.

Helleman, D. (2008) Video Advertising Online: Spending And Pricing , New York, E-Marketer.

Kremers, S.P. J., De Bruijn, G.J., droomers, M., Van Lenthe, F. J., & Brug, J. (2005). Environmental interventions for selected dietary behaviors in adults. In J. Brug & F. J. Van Lenthe (eds.) , Environmental determinants and interventions for physical activity, nutrition and smoking: A review pp. 282-315. Rotterdam: Erasmus Medical Center.

Mulligan, M. Banerjee, T & Thomas, N. (2008) , European Paid Content And Activity Forecast, (2008 to 2013), Jupiter Research.

Peter, J., Ryan, M, M, " An Investigation Of Perceived Risk At The Brand Level, " Journal of marketing research, 13 May 1976, pp. 184-188.

Pieters, R., & Wedel, M. (2007). Goal Control Of Visual Attention To Advertising: The Yarbus Implication. Journal Of Consumer Research, 34, 224-233 (August).

Parasuaman, and Leonard L. Berry (1985), " Problems And Strategies In Sevices Marketing", Journal of marketing, 49 (Spring), 33-46.

Jamieson, Linda F. And Frank M. Bass (1989), " Adjusting Stated Intention Measures To Predict Trial Purchase Of New Products: A Comparison Of Models And Methods," Journal of marketing research, 26 (August), 336-45.

Moschis, George p. & Roy, L. Moore (1979), " Decision making among the young. A socialization perspective " Journal of consumer research , 6 (September).

R.C. Oliver, " When is consumer loyalty?" J.Marketing. vol. 63, pp.33-44.1999.

Shostack, G. Lynn (1984), " Designing Services That Deliver", Harvard Business Review, 62 (January-February), 133-9.

Shostack, G. Lynn (1985), " Planning The Service Encounter ,in the service encounter" , John A. Czepiel, Michael R. Solomon, and Carol F. Suprenant, eds. New York: Lexington Books, 243-54.

Shostack, G. Lynn (1987), " Service Positioning Through, Structural Change", Journal of marketing, 51 (Janurary), 34-43.

Soloman, Michael R. (1985), "Packaging The Service Provider", Service Industries Journal , 5(1), 64-71.

Stevens, C.W. (1980), "K-MartStores Try New Look To Invite More Spending" The Wall Street Journal, Nov. 26, 29-35.

T. Ambler, A. Ioannides, And S. Rose, " Brand s On The Brain : Neuroimages Of Advertising ", Business Strategy rev., vol. 11, 3. pp. 17-30. 2000.

Westbrook, Robert A. (1980), " Intrapersonal affective influences on consumer satisfaction with products, " Journal of consumer research , 7 (June) 49-54.

World Health Organization (2003). Diet, nutrition and the prevention of Chronic diseases report of a joint WHO/FAO. expert consultation. Geneva: World Health Organization.

Wysocki, B. (1979), " Sight, Smell, Sound: They're all arms in retailer's arsenal" The Wall Street Journal, Nov. 17, 1979. 1-35.